Bread to Eat and Clothes to Wear

Bread to Eat and Clothes to Wear

LETTERS FROM JEWISH MIGRANTS IN THE EARLY TWENTIETH CENTURY

Gur Alroey

Wayne State University Press
Detroit

Manufactured in the United States of America.
15 14 13 12 11 5 4 3 2 1

Library of Congress Cataloging-in-Publication Data

Alroey, Gur.
Bread to eat and clothes to wear : letters from Jewish migrants in the early twentieth century / Gur Alroey.
p. cm.
Includes bibliographical references and index.
ISBN 978-0-8143-3519-2 (pbk. : alk. paper)
1. Jews, East European—Migrations—History—19th century. 2. Jews, East European—Migrations—History—20th century. 3. Jews, East European—United States—Correspondence. 4. Jews, East European—Palestine—Correspondence. 5. Immigrants—United States—Correspondence. 6. Immigrants—Palestine—Correspondence. 7. Europe, Eastern—Emigration and immigration—History—19th century. 8. Europe, Eastern—Emigration and immigration—History—20th century. 9. Jews, East European—Migrations—History—20th century—Sources. 10. Europe, Eastern—Emigration and immigration—History—20th century—Sources. I. Title.
DS135.E83A46 2011
305.9'0691089924047—dc22

2010039465

∞

Designed and typeset by Anna Oler
Composed in Adobe Garamond

Letter translation supported by a research grant from the German-Israeli Foundation's Young Scientists' Program.

To the thirty-four Jewish immigrants in the Illowo station on the Polish-German border (letter 3) and to Mashe Zilazne (letter 20)

As a bird that wandereth from her nest, so is a man that wandereth from his place.

PROVERBS 28:8

Contents

Acknowledgments

THIS BOOK, *Bread to Eat and Clothes to Wear: Letters from Jewish Migrants in the Early Twentieth Century*, is the result of the research I completed for my last two books, which were published in Hebrew and which dealt with the mass Jewish migration in the late nineteenth century and early twentieth century. During the writing of these books, I discovered letters in the Central Zionist Archives and in the American Jewish Historical Society written by Eastern European Jews to information bureaus asking for information to help them decide whether to migrate and begin a new life in one of the countries of destination or to remain behind and continue with their familiar way of life. I found the letters most interesting. They revealed the human aspect of Jewish migration at the initial stage when the family was at a crossroads and its future was unknown. As I read the letters and exposed the dilemmas within them, I concluded that there was great importance in publishing these original letters with notes to explain and clarify the text.

Many important studies have dealt with the characteristics and the implications of the mass Jewish migration from Eastern Europe, its patterns of absorption and the acculturation of the immigrants in the receiving societies. This book aims to bring a different approach to Jewish migration in the early twentieth century. The sixty-six letters published in this book enable the reader to trace the hardships, suffering, and fears of the Jewish immigrant until his arrival at the destination country and to learn how the immigration changed the intimacy of the family cell.

As migration is an individual experience and not a collective one, it is necessary to examine it inductively to reach deductive conclusions and interpretations. The main purpose of this collection of letters is to offer scholars and students contemporary letters that will enable them to hold a comprehensive discussion on Jewish mass migration. As a researcher and lecturer in the Department of Land of Israel Studies at the University of Haifa, I recognized that my students (and also those I taught in New York University) like to read and analyze primary sources. The feedback that I received from my students and the cross-checking we carried out against the research literature strengthens my belief that there is place in the literature for a hybrid book such as this, in which the first half is a comprehensive introduction that explains the letters and puts them within the historical context, and the second half reproduces the original letters.

The letters duplicated here were written in Yiddish and Hebrew. Although I read and understand Yiddish, and Hebrew is my mother tongue, I decided that the translation of the letters should be done by professional translators. Thanks are due to Yankl Salant, who translated the letters from Yiddish into English, and Deborah Stern, who translated them from Hebrew into English. I am also grateful to Batya Leshem and Rachel Rubinstein of the Central Zionist Archives and Susan Malbin of the American Jewish Historical Society, who gave me permission to publish the letters. Special thanks are due to Professor Hasia Diner and Professor Jonathan Sarna, who recognized the importance of the letters and encouraged me to publish them. Part of the final editing of the manuscript was done while I was a visiting scholar in the Taub Center for Israel Studies at New York University. Thanks to Professor Ron Zweig for his invitation and hospitality.

It was an extraordinary experience for me to work with Wayne State University Press. Thanks especially to Kathryn Wildfong, the editor in chief, for her patience, goodwill, and good advice; Carrie Downes Teefey, the production editor; Mary Tederstrom, for her professional copyediting; Maya Rhodes, the assistant design and production manager; and to the rest of the team at Wayne State University Press.

Introduction

BETWEEN 1875 AND 1924, more than 2.7 million Jews from Eastern Europe immigrated to countries overseas. The departure of millions of men, women, and children effected a radical change in the entire aspect of the Jewish people in modern times, and in many ways its consequences are recognizable to this day. This was the Exodus from Egypt in modern form, the exodus of a people who wished to free themselves from economic subjection and from the persecution they suffered in their lands of origin and to create new lives in countries across the ocean. Historians refer to this time as the "period of the great migration" and have discussed it extensively and intensively. For nearly every destination country in which the Jewish migrants settled, scholars have written studies on their absorption into the surrounding society and their impact on it. These studies have addressed absorption patterns, working conditions, relationships between old-timers and newcomers, similarities and differences between Jewish immigrants and immigrants from other ethnic groups who moved to the same place, and many other issues. But very little has been written on the actual process of migration, on the dramatic moment when a family came to the decision that there was no longer any hope for them in Eastern Europe and that they would have to move to a new land—despite all the difficulties—and build a new, safer life.

The collection of letters published in this volume is intended to divert historiographical discussion from the absorption process to that of the actual move to a new country. Tracing the decision to migrate is one of the most difficult and complex projects that a scholar can undertake. Historians of the migration—both Jewish and non-Jewish—who have tried to examine this angle have noted how problematic it is, first and foremost because of the lack of primary sources. This lack has forced scholars to use secondary sources—memoirs and oral testimony—that were recorded many years after the immigrants settled in their new land.[1] These sources did not reflect the dynamics involved in making the decision to migrate and did not trace the path taken by the migrants from the moment they left their old homes until they arrived at their destinations. In his monumental book *World of Our Fathers,* the historian Irving Howe notes that it is doubtful that the memoir literature contains even a reliable echo of the drama of being uprooted: "The statements one finds in the memoir literature are persuasive through their repetition. We came because we were hungry; we came because we were persecuted; we came because life in Russia or Poland had grown insufferable. These are the answers one gets over and over again, and there is not the slightest reason to doubt them. But what they do not, perhaps cannot, explain is why some Jews acted on these urgent motives and others did not."[2]

Haim Avni writes that "this subjective drama multiplied by hundreds of thousands merits a fascinating study in itself."[3] The initial process of doubts and vacillations within the premigration family circle has not yet been researched or documented. The "drama of migration" for the ordinary migrant family is therefore absent from the scholarly literature, and the stories of millions of migrants have been lost among the quantitative statistics.

Historians who have studied non-Jewish immigration to America have pointed out a similar difficulty in trying to understand how the decision was made to migrate and what hardships the migrants faced before reaching safe haven in another land. This difficulty led these historians to the realization that if they wanted to understand the motives for migration they would have to focus on the towns and villages from which the migrants had come. Philip Taylor, in *The Distant Magnet,* notes, "It is never enough to think of migration continent by continent, or nation by nation. Emigrants were not Europeans or even Germans and Swedes: they were dwellers in a Norwegian valley, or in the Black Forest district of Württemberg; they were

Slovaks from the northern hills of the Kingdom of Hungary, Bulgarians from Macedonia, or Ashkenazite Jews from Western provinces of Czarist Russia. No scholar, of course, will ever be able to comprehend all this local detail."[4]

In *Immigrants in the Lands of Promise,* the scholar of Italian migration Samuel Baily emphasizes the importance of the "local level" in understanding the causes and characteristics of migration. If we wish to know how the decision to migrate was made, Baily maintains, we have to focus on the village, which is where all the macro factors accumulated that led to westward migration.[5] For this reason, he studied the village of Agnone as the exemplar of many towns in southern Italy from which emigrants left for the United States.

Dudley Baines, in *Emigration from Europe, 1815–1930,* also warns against regarding an emigrant's country of origin as a single geographical unit and advises scholars to focus instead on the individual provinces and villages.[6] This classic work by Baines does not relate the story of the migration of Eastern Europeans and Central Europeans to America; rather, it raises a series of problems and methodological difficulties involved in migration research and offers solutions. For example, Baines recommends emphasizing issues that have been heretofore perceived as self-evident and thus relegated to the sidelines of research, such as the decision-making process regarding whether to emigrate and where to go, the selective process in migration, and the difficulties involved in reaching the new country. The stages of settling in and adapting to the new country receive less attention in his book. In order to cope with the challenging questions that he raises, Baines points out sources and research methods that could advance migration research. For example, he suggests emphasizing personal data sources that by their very nature are more specific and contain more extensive, richer information than aggregate data.[7] Letters from migrants are also, in his opinion, an excellent source for understanding the dynamics of migration and the motivations of the migrants. One of the main problems in migration research, claims Baines, is that "we cannot know what actually passed through the minds of potential emigrants."[8] For this reason, the letters of ordinary migrants that were written during the process of migration allow us to trace in real time the migrants' doubts and vacillations before they set out on their way.[9]

Publication of the migrants' letters as a means of understanding migration, its causes, and all the different aspects that constitute it is not something new in historiography. The first to do it were William I. Thomas and Florian Znaniecki in their five-volume work *The Polish Peasant in Europe and America,* published between 1918 and 1920. The importance of this study is that it includes letters to relatives from Polish peasants who had immigrated to America as well as letters to the migrants from their family members in Poland. It is also innovative in terms of its methodology that places the individual migrant at the center of the migration research. In fact, migration is primarily the story of individuals, and the key to a thorough understanding of the migration process is to focus on the individual "and not class determinants, codes and structures, statistical quantities, or other abstracted 'objective factors.'"[10] David Fitzpatrick, in the introduction to his book *Oceans of Consolation,* also notes, "Human movement was pictured as a flow, subject to 'push' and 'pull' factors governing its dynamics. The individual human mover was invisible, except in the shape of an identikit figure, conforming to some general model of motivation."[11]

Withold Kula, Nina Assorodobraj-Kula, and Marcin Kula's book, *Writing Home: Immigrants in Brazil and the United States, 1890–1891,* is another example that emphasizes the importance of letters for understanding immigration to the Americas. The letters reproduced in their book were sent by immigrants (Jews and non-Jews) to their relatives in Eastern Europe a short time after their arrival and during the process of their adaptation into the host society. Scrutinized reading reveals to the reader the immigration process in all its levels and layers: the relationships between those who left and began a new life in new lands and those who stayed behind in the old countries, the immigrants' attempts to preserve family unity and solidarity, their yearnings for home, and their complicated encounter with a new society. A touching fact that emerges from the volume is that the letters did not reach their destination. They were confiscated by the czarist censor and were found years later by the economic historian Withold Kula.[12]

The use of migrants' letters to understand the migration experience was not neglected in studies of Jewish migration. In 1971, Isaac Metzker published *A Bintel Brief,* a collection of letters, and answers to them, taken from the column of the same name that appeared in the Yiddish newspaper *Forward* starting in 1906. These were letters from immigrants to the editor of the paper, Abraham Cahan, asking his advice on various matters. One immigrant asked whether it was his duty to send money to his parents in Eastern Europe for the approaching Passover festival. A woman asked what to do about her irresponsible son, whom she could not control, and her husband, who did not earn enough money. There was a letter from a Galician woman who had been insulted by a Russian Jew because of her origins, one from a woman whose husband had left her for another woman, and many other letters. Although some of the letters were clearly made up by the editor to encourage the immigrants to cope with their daily problems, others were actually sent by immigrants and can give us information about their lives in the city and the difficulties and hardships they experienced.

Another collection of letters, *Words of the Uprooted,* was published by the historian Robert Rockaway. While working on a study on the Jews of Detroit, he found in an archive of the American Jewish Historical Society some letters from Jewish immigrants to the Industrial Removal Office (IRO). The aim of this organization—to be discussed in greater detail later—was to reduce the number of Jews in New York by dispersing them throughout the United States.[13] Years after completing his study on Detroit, Rockaway published the collection of letters that the immigrants had sent to this office, which revealed another aspect of the lives of Jewish immigrants in the United States since the beginning of the twentieth century. The letters depict the immigrants' living conditions in the American interior, the stages in the process of Americanization, and their success or failure, anxiety and despair, hopes and aspirations.[14]

The present volume, which contains sixty-six letters, adds still another dimension to the scholarship on Jewish migration. These letters allow us to address a series of challenging questions—some of which were raised in Baines's book—that have not yet received the attention they deserve from historians. These letters are a mine of information from the period of the great migration; they were written by people who were considering migration and wanted specific information on economic opportunities in the destination countries.

The scholarly importance of publishing these letters cannot be overestimated: we can learn from them about the complexity of the migration process, including the decision to emigrate and the obstacles that the migrants faced on their way to their destinations. Most of the letters were written in Eastern Europe (Russia and Galicia), and they describe the gestation stage of the migration process—that is, before the decision was made to emigrate and a destination was chosen. From the letters we learn of the migrants' fear of making a decision; their desire for advice and information before they took the fateful step; the gnawing anxiety of women whose husbands had already sailed for America, and who were waiting impatiently for a ticket so that they could join them; women whose husbands had disappeared in America and had broken off contact with their families; pogroms (documented in real time); and the obstacles and hardships on the way to the port of exit, as described by people who had already set out.

The letters, published here for the first time, were written in the early twentieth century by Eastern European Jews to Jewish organizations and information bureaus that had been set up in the countries of origin and in the destination countries to deal with Jewish migration. The main purpose of the organizations was to assist potential migrants in reaching a decision and carrying it out. In order to get good advice, the writers had to describe their hardships and problems in great detail. Through the questions they asked—and sometimes the answers they received—one can better understand the issues that migration historians have so far barely dealt with due to the lack of primary sources. Furthermore, these letters give us a glimpse into the lives of the flesh-and-blood people concealed behind the numbers and statistics of Jewish migration and tell the story of Jewish migration from the viewpoint of the ordinary migrant. The migrants themselves stood at the center of this mass migration, and they, in effect, created this historical episode.

This introduction is divided into four main parts. The first focuses on the extent of Jewish migration between 1875 and 1924. The second describes the unique characteristics of Jewish migration. The third presents the reasons for the establishment of information bureaus during the period of the great migration. The fourth deals with three specific aspects of migration as manifested in the letters: how the decision to emigrate was made, the difficulties involved in carrying out the decision to emigrate, and the impact of migration on family members left behind in the country of origin.

The Extent of Jewish Migration, 1875–1914

If we attempt to calculate how many Jews emigrated overseas from Eastern Europe during the period under study, we will find that there are no exact figures and that there is a real difficulty in estimating the number. Throughout the period of migration, no orderly record of emigrants was kept in the countries of origin. All the statistical information regarding Jewish migration is derived from records in the destination countries. But even there, the records do not always make it possible to calculate the scope of Jewish migration. Until 1899 immigrants entering the United States were not asked about their ethnicity—they were recorded by the immigration officials as Russians, Austro-Hungarians, or Poles—so it is hard to know which of them were Jews. For other destination countries, there are hardly any data on Jewish immigration. This means that any attempt to determine the number of Jewish migrants from the early 1870s until the end of the nineteenth century is based only on estimates.

At the beginning of the twentieth century, there was a significant improvement in immigration records. In nearly all the destination countries, the immigration authorities began to draw up detailed lists of those entering according to the following criteria: age, occupation, country of origin, and, most important for our purposes, ethnicity. On July 1, 1898, the U.S. immigration authorities began to classify immigrants by nationality. Thus only from 1899 do we have complete, detailed statistics on Jewish immigration to the United States.[15] Canada and Australia began recording immigration statistics in 1900–1901; Argentina did so in 1904.[16] In Palestine, records were kept starting in 1905 (by the information bureau of the Odessa Committee—the bureau that handled the registration of emigrants sailing from the port of Odessa).[17] South Africa started keeping these records only in 1912.[18]

However, despite the difficulty in calculating Jewish emigration from Eastern Europe between 1870 and 1898, an attempt has been made to obtain a general picture of the scope of Jewish migration in this period. On the eve of World War I, Samuel Joseph published a book on Jewish immigration to the United States from 1881 to 1910. His main sources for the quantitative immigration data were the statistics collected by Jewish activists on behalf of charitable institutions in New York, Philadelphia, and Baltimore between 1886 and 1898.[19] The information was recorded in the charities' annual reports and formed the basis for understanding the demographic traits of the Jewish immigrants. In order to obtain a similar picture of Jewish immigration to the United States before 1886—a period when no records on the subject were kept—Joseph used the number of Jews who arrived in 1886–98 as a reference for estimating the number of arrivals in 1881–85.

Estimating the number of Jews arriving in the United States in the 1870s is much more complex and problematic. In a 1975 article by Simon Kuznets, "Immigration of Russian Jews to the United States," he estimates the number of Jews entering the United States in 1871–80 at somewhere between fifteen thousand and twenty thousand.[20] Kuznets's calculations were based on immigration statistics from Russia and Poland to the United States during that period, as indicated in the 1890 U.S. census. According to Joseph, about 70 percent of emigrants from Russia to the United States and 43 percent of emigrants from Poland to the United States in the 1880s were Jewish. Kuznets applied these same proportions to the number of Jewish immigrants entering the United States in the 1870s.[21]

Table A.1 in the appendix shows immigration to the United States in 1875–98, which is based on new data that were not available to Kuznets in 1975. In recent years, with the development of genealogy into a full-fledged field of research, the scope of Jewish emigration from Eastern Europe before 1881 can be estimated more precisely. In 1995, the Temple-Balch Center for Immigration Research began to publish books that contained the names, ages, and occupations of immigrants from Russia to the United States in 1875–92.[22] These books were written primarily for the descendants of immigrants who wanted to trace their family history, but they can, of course, also be used for general research purposes.

From Kuznets's calculations and the Temple-Balch Center's lists of immigrants, it appears that immigration to the United States began even before the pogroms of 1881–82; about 10,400 Jewish immigrants entered the United States during the 1870s. Fortified with this information, we cannot regard 1881 as the turning point or watershed in the history of Jewish immigration to the United States, because immigration in the 1880s was therefore merely the continuation of an established trend.[23] In her article "Before the Promised City," Hasia Diner emphasizes the continuity in immigration to the United States rather than focusing on a turning point. She claims that in the 1860s and 1870s Jews were already working in the American garment industry and that there were even Yiddish newspapers for Jews who had recently arrived in America.[24] Later immigration—from the 1880s onward—blended with existing patterns and with the infrastructure that was created in the 1860s and 1870s.

Between 1870 and 1898, slightly more than a half-million Jews immigrated to the United States. Upon arrival, they began to send letters to their families, and information about the new Jewish communities was printed in the newspapers. In this way, a worldwide network of communication developed between the massive Jewish populations in Eastern Europe and the new Jewish communities overseas; this network is discussed elsewhere in this volume. Yet the limited number of migrants in the course of three decades was not sufficient to make a dramatic change in the lives of the Jewish people. Most of the world Jewry still lived within the borders of the Russian Empire, immersed in harsh socioeconomic conditions and discriminated against, and persecuted by, the authorities. The dramatic turning point came only at the beginning of the twentieth century, when a trend started that continued until World War I. During this period—only fourteen years—more than 1.5 million Jews migrated to all corners of the world—three times as many as in the three previous decades, from 1870 to 1900.

The peak years of Jewish migration were 1904–14 (see table A.2 in the appendix). This was the period of the great migration that revolutionized the lives of the Jewish people in modern times. Most of the migrants went to the United States; the others moved in much smaller numbers to Canada, Argentina, Australia, South Africa, and Palestine.[25] An important fact that emerges from table A.2 is that more than 700,000 Jewish immigrants reached the destination countries in 1904–8. In those five years, more than 600,000 Jews entered the United States. Another interesting fact is that the largest number of immigrants arrived in their destination countries in 1914. In just eight months (January to August), about 150,000 Jews migrated, with an average of 21,000 leaving Eastern Europe every month. There is not a shadow of a doubt that had World War I not broken out, Jewish migration would have exceeded 200,000 that year. For this reason, 1914 should be seen as the peak year of Jewish migration, even though the actual number of migrants was less than in 1906.

More than 1.7 million Jews migrated within the space of only fifteen years. If we include those who set out but did not reach their destination, the numbers exceed those shown in the table. If we were granted a bird's-eye view of Jewish migration at its peak, we would see people thronging the roads from the small towns to the big cities, and from there to the border cities and ports. The story of Jewish migration is centered in the years 1904–14—the period that would radically change the image of the Jewish people. For reasons that will be discussed later, most of the letters published in this volume were written during that time.

Characteristics of Jewish Migration

Jewish migration was an integral part of the mass migration of that period, but it also had certain unique features and clear distinguishing marks. First, the proportion of Jews among the migrants was high relative to their share of the population. Of the 60 million emigrants from Europe in 1840–1946, 4 million were Jews. This was more than 6 percent of the total emigration, whereas Jews accounted for just 1.5–2 percent of the general population. At the beginning of the twentieth century, the proportion of Jewish emigrants was even higher. The world Jewish population at that time was about 10.5 million. Between 1900 and 1924, about one-fifth of the Jews in Europe (20.6 percent) moved to other countries. In comparison, only about 11.3 percent of 32 million Italians emigrated—and this was one of the highest emigration rates at the time.

The family character of Jewish migration was a second recognizable trait. Among emigrants from European nations, the husband usually went alone; after he had saved up enough money, he either returned home or brought his family over to the new country. Jewish emigration was different. In most cases, Jewish families emigrated together—sometimes the whole family—husband, wife, and children—and sometimes the husband went alone, and his wife and children joined him afterward. As a result, Jewish emigrants included a high proportion of women and children. Women accounted for 44 percent of Jewish migrants, and children under the age of fourteen accounted for 25 percent.[26] For the sake of comparison, the proportion of

Italian women who immigrated to the United States is estimated at only 23 percent, and among the Poles and Latvians the figure was about 33 percent. Only 9 percent of non-Jewish immigrants to the United States were children. These figures prove that Jewish migration—unlike general migration—was permanent, with the intention to settle in the new land.

A third characteristic of the Jewish migration was the low percentage of returnees to their country of origin—considerably less than among other peoples. Between 1908 and 1924, about 33.6 percent of all foreigners entering the United States returned to their countries of origin, whereas only 5.2 percent of the Jews who migrated at the beginning of the twentieth century returned.[27] The reason for this enormous difference lies in the fact that the Jewish immigrants, unlike other immigrants generally, belonged to a nation without a land to which they could return. Moreover, most migrants wanted to earn money, improve their economic situation, and return home at the earliest opportunity. The Jews, conversely, although they also wanted to improve their economic situation, hoped to settle permanently in the new country and integrate into the surrounding society.

A further characteristic of Jewish migration concerned the migrants' occupations. More than 65 percent of Jewish immigrants to the United States were craftsmen who brought their skills and experience with them. Soon after their arrival, the Jewish immigrants found work in American industry. The demographer Liebman Hersch showed that 60 percent of them worked in the needle industry, 15 percent in the building and furniture industries, 9 percent in the metal and machine industry, 7 percent in the food industry, and the rest in the leather, paper, and printing industries.[28] However, in Eli Lederhendler's latest study of Jewish immigration to the United States, he shows that the immigrants' occupations in the United States did not necessarily match their occupations in their country of origin. Lederhendler found that there were 160,000 tailors in Eastern Europe in the early twentieth century, compared with more than 300,000 in the United States. In other words, many of the Jewish immigrants had not worked as tailors or had even held a needle before arriving in America.[29] This conclusion is consistent with the data from the Jewish Colonization Association (ICA) information bureau. About 50 percent of the applications to the information bureau were from skilled craftsmen, whereas the proportion of skilled craftsmen in the United States was estimated at 65 percent. In addition, 4 percent of the applications to the ICA information bureau were from members of the liberal professions, compared with the estimated 1 percent of the Jewish immigrants in the United States representing these professions. The differences between the ICA statistics and the American statistics stem from differences in the statements made by the immigrants in their countries of origin and those they made in the United States. The new arrivals chose to be recorded by the American immigration clerks as tailors rather than peddlers and storekeepers, or even rather than cantors and teachers (the main liberal professions). Upon arrival in the United States, the immigrants became tailors, even if they had not been tailors before, because this trade was in demand in Manhattan.[30]

These characteristics of Jewish migration were valid for nearly all the destination countries. Even in Palestine, where historians tend to perceive immigration as ideological, the demographic composition of newcomers at the turn of the century was not very different from that of immigrants entering New York. Of those entering Palestine, 60 percent were male and 40 percent were female. One-fourth were children fifteen years old or younger who came with their families to settle permanently. Many of the immigrants were craftsmen who wanted to settle in the cities—mainly Jaffa and Jerusalem—rather than in the small villages or recently established agricultural communities.[31]

As in other countries to which Jews migrated, immigration to Palestine took place in stages. The husband came first, and only after he had established himself (if he did) did he bring over the other members of his family. Only in two parameters did immigration to Palestine differ from immigration to the United States. The first was in the age group of forty-four years and older. Only 6 percent of those arriving in the United States were in that group, whereas in Palestine the proportion was four times as great. This means that half of the immigrants to Palestine were children and older people. The second parameter was the number of people leaving Palestine. As stated earlier, only 5.2 percent of Jewish immigrants returned from the United States to Eastern Europe. But of the number who immigrated to Palestine, the proportion of returnees was similar to that of non-Jewish immigrants to the United States. More than 70 percent left Palestine in the early twentieth century; but with the construction of Tel Aviv in 1909 and the creation of new jobs, the number of returnees dropped to 50 percent.[32]

The letters sent to the information bureaus in Palestine, some of which are published in this collection, are a good reflection of the migrants' profile as derived from statistical analysis. The writers were artisans and small tradesmen who wanted any scrap of information about the possibilities of employment in Palestine. They gave details about their families and their financial status, and they asked about the prospects of absorption and acclimatization in the new country. We do not know whether these letter writers eventually moved to Palestine. The inefficient record keeping by the Ottoman government precludes any examination of this question. However, this does not prevent us from gaining an understanding of the considerations for and against migration and the way the decision to migrate was made.

Immigration Information Bureaus

The family character of Jewish migration and the Jews' desire to make the move permanent and not to return to the countries of origin brought about a new and unfamiliar situation in Eastern Europe. As mentioned earlier, by the end of the nineteenth century about a half-million Jews had left, mainly for the United States. Then, however, the number of emigrants increased to an unprecedented degree. More than 1.1 million Jews moved to the United States in the space of only ten years. The departure of men, women, and children made the migration process a highly complex affair. The emigrants faced innumerable difficulties and obstacles: they had to either obtain the required papers to leave the country legally or sneak across borders and deal with smugglers. They had to sell their businesses and homes, purchase train tickets, travel by train for thousands of kilometers to the port of exit, find their way around, and then purchase tickets for the ship that would take them to their destination. In order to cross the ocean and reach the destination country safely, migrants had to have a considerable ability to improvise and the resourcefulness to overcome unexpected obstacles.

The scholarly literature has paid little attention to this aspect of migration.[33] It treats the transition stage as self-evident and describes the arrival in the destination country as a trivial matter. But if we try to comprehend the whole range of difficulties involved in this change of residence, we find a complex reality that gives us a better understanding of the migration process. Of course, there were many migrants who were unable to cope with the unexpected difficulties on the way, and for various reasons—which I focus on later—did not cross the border and board the ship that would have brought them to the Promised Land. The newspapers of that era are full of stories about migrants who were lost or abandoned. After selling all their property and setting out on their way, these migrants discovered that they were unable to continue their journey.

There were many family tragedies, and heartbreaking stories were frequently published in the press to arouse public opinion and to help ordinary Jewish emigrants reach a place of safety. Thus, in the early twentieth century, information bureaus were opened along the migration routes to help potential emigrants realize their goal. Six such bureaus were established for Jews: one by the ICA; two by the Zionist Organization; one by the Jewish Territorial Organization (ITO); one by the IRO in the United States, which served as an information bureau in addition to its other functions; and one by the Hilfsverein in Berlin.

The Information Bureau of the Jewish Colonization Association

The ICA was the first organization in the Russian Empire to help and advise prospective emigrants at no charge. In the early 1890s, Baron Maurice de Hirsch developed the idea of Jewish agricultural settlements in the Argentinean Pampas. To put his idea into practice, he founded the ICA in August 1891, with the primary goal of bringing out hundreds of thousands of Jews from Russia and turning them into farmers. The plan would prove to the world that the Jews were a productive people. The fortune that Baron de Hirsch invested in establishing the ICA was immense: he bought land for millions of pounds sterling, constructed colonies, built schools, provided the infrastructure, and hired overseers to teach the Jewish settlers how to farm the land. The "mother colony" in Argentina was Moisés-ville, founded with funding from the baron in 1890. This was followed by the colonies of Mauricio (1891), Clara (1892), San Antonio (1892), and many others. In 1894—two years before his death—he approved the inauguration of a migration department under the lawyer M. Bergman, with the aim of solving migration-related problems in general, and not only those pertaining to Argentina. The department appointed agents in a few locations within the colonies and published general information booklets for the immigrants. But Bergman's sudden death soon after the establishment of the migration department, along with a decrease in immigration, shut down the department for a while.[34]

In 1904, after the Kishinev pogrom and in view of the significant increase in the rate of migration and especially the considerable suffering of the migrants, the ICA central committee decided, in consultation with the head office in Paris and the administrative council, to open an information bureau in St. Petersburg. From that year on, the ICA became the most important Jewish philanthropic institution dealing with migration-related matters in the Russian Empire. The chairman of the ICA central committee in St. Petersburg, Baron David Gintsburg, bore overall responsibility for the functioning of the information bureau. The person who actually managed the bureau and supervised its activity was an attorney named Samuel Yanovsky. To enable the bureau to successfully create an information system that would serve hundreds of thousands of prospective emigrants, regional information bureaus were established throughout the Russian Empire. Within a few years, all the larger cities and important emigration centers had authorized ICA information bureaus. By 1906 there were 160 such offices throughout the Pale of Settlement. In 1907 there were 296 offices, in 1910 there were 449 offices, and in 1913 there were 507 offices.[35]

Once work had begun at the central office in St. Petersburg and information was being provided by the local offices, Gintsburg and Yanovsky formulated the policy of the ICA information bureau:

> Not to rely on the recommendation of relatives to go to their places of work and not to be drawn to the big, beautiful cities across the ocean to which the emigrants are streaming, not to be caught in the nets of agents who promise the moon and stars, and not to set out without first consulting the eye doctor, not to get on a train without showing the person in charge all the required documents, not to drag unnecessary clothes and baggage to America, not to apply to any benefactor or committee, whether in the place of departure or in the transit countries, except to the authorized and appointed ICA committees in the city

> of departure, in the transit city, in the border city, and in the destination city.[36]

The directors of the St. Petersburg office divided czarist Russia into three main regions: Congress Poland; White Russia and Latvia; and the southern region, including Volhynia, Podolia, and Bessarabia. Each region was headed by a chief secretary who was familiar with migration matters in general, and with migration arrangements in particular, and was in constant touch with the emigration committees in the cities and towns in the Pale of Settlement. By the outbreak of World War I, the ICA had established about four hundred authorized committees throughout the Pale of Settlement.[37] Many letters reached the central information office in St. Petersburg directly and not through the committees. The job of classifying them was assigned to Zalman Rubashov (later Shazar and the third president of the State of Israel), who at the time worked in the office as Yanovsky's assistant. Rubashov described his work:

> Every day, from eight o'clock in the morning until noon, I would sink up to my neck in the troubles of the Jewish people. I would read, search, reply, catalogue, and send my answers to the secretaries for their signature. . . . Jews who want to emigrate and don't know where to turn; migrants who are deceived by ruthless agents and find no protection; the rabbi of a community who sees the poverty of craftsmen in his town who have been left penniless and without customers and want to leave, but who does not know how to help them; an intellectual from the city whose heart aches for the sorrows of the Jewish people and wants to lend a shoulder to those working to help the nation; an abandoned woman whose husband left her and traveled across the sea, forgetting her and her children and leaving them to suffer unheard. . . . It has not even been a year and I have become familiar with all the different kinds of suffering that carry within them the seeds of an approaching holocaust.[38]

The hierarchical structure of the information bureau allowed the scores of local offices to act energetically: every problem that arose was referred to the local office, and if that office found no solution, it was sent to St.

Petersburg. The large regional offices were run by committees of three to ten people, depending on the number of prospective emigrants in the region, and the local offices in the smaller cities and villages had one agent, or two at the most.[39] Every few months, regional conferences were held in which the local agents discussed common problems and suggested solutions. At these conferences, the heads of the regional offices conveyed messages and requests to the local agents from the central office in St. Petersburg. The agents were asked to keep accurate records of everyone who contacted the local offices, to advertise the aims of the ICA information bureau and its publications, to warn of dishonest agents, and to publish the names of swindlers and the damage they had caused.[40] The purpose of the information bureaus was to answer the questions of prospective emigrants, to help them get passports, and sometimes to give them financial assistance:

> The committees and the correspondents who provide various kinds of useful information to the emigrants have already arrived in all 160 cities in the Pale of Settlement. Every day, these offices receive many diverse questions in writing on various travel-related matters. Hundreds and even thousands of people also come to these committees for information. The latter help the emigrants solve various problems, resolve doubts, and obtain passports to go abroad, and they sometimes even provide financial support to those travelers not going to America.[41]

The Information Bureaus of the Zionist Organization

In the early twentieth century, shortly after the establishment of the ICA information bureau, the Zionist Organization founded two information bureaus to promote immigration to Palestine. The first one was opened in Odessa in January 1905. Its aim was to distribute accurate information about Jewish settlement in Palestine and to collect all available information about laws, conditions for acquiring land, and the possibility of starting a business. In addition,

> the office will provide both oral and written replies to all questions within its purview. It will refer those consulting it to decent, inexpensive hostels in Odessa and to banks where they

> can exchange money at low rates. It will negotiate constantly with shipping companies so that it can always provide accurate information concerning the sailing dates of ships to the shores of Palestine and Syria, and will also attempt to obtain reductions on the price of tickets for the voyage for those who contact it.[42]

The bureau in Odessa broadened its activities, and in 1906 it opened information bureaus in Jaffa, Jerusalem, Haifa, Beirut, and Constantinople. The office in Jaffa, headed by Menahem Sheinkin, was subordinate to the central office in Odessa and maintained close ties and cooperation with it.

In 1908 another information bureau was established in Palestine as part of the Palestine Office, headed by Arthur Ruppin and Jacob Thon. Unlike the bureau in Odessa, which was subordinate to the Hibbat Zion movement, the Palestine Office was directly subordinate to the Zionist Organization.[43] Its main function was to coordinate settlement and land acquisition activity in Palestine with the Zionist Organization, and the information bureau was one of its departments, charged with providing information to potential immigrants about Palestine and their prospects there. Every week Ruppin and Thon received scores of letters from craftsmen, peddlers, tradesmen, and others asking for detailed, up-to-date information on conditions in the country and the chances of succeeding there. At what time of year should they come? What sort of job opportunities were there? How much would the voyage cost? How much could they earn? How much did food cost? These and many other questions show that the issues that concerned potential immigrants to Palestine were similar to those of concern to Jews interested in other destination countries during the same period.

Letters and reports written by the directors of the information bureaus described the immigrants to Palestine. In 1908, Menahem Sheinkin wrote to Otto Warburg, a member of the Inner Actions Committee of the Zionist Organization, with an excellent description of the newcomers:

> As long as you directors do not make an effort to attract certain millionaire capitalists to Palestine, there is nothing we can do. Our position will not be strengthened by the poor people who come to Palestine by themselves. On the contrary, I must say that such immigration diminishes, day after day, the respect

> that the officials and natives have for us. They see before them downtrodden poor people, dispirited and shabby, with parcels containing rags, the miserable poor who are not worthy of bringing blessing to the country and who dishonor us. If no rich, honorable people—respected, well-dressed, and of favorable appearance—begin to disembark on the shores, the name of Jew will be synonymous in the language of the port with weak and poor, with a despicable people, and the concept will then be transferred to other ranks of the people. This is the bare truth of which I must inform you as employees of the information bureau, and I could provide you with this information every week. Everything is at a standstill. Nothing changes, and nothing will change until capitalists come to Palestine.[44]

The Zionist movement's policy about the quality of immigrants needed to settle Palestine was very selective. Back in the early 1880s, the leader of the Hibbat Tsiyyon movement, Moshe Leib Lilienblum, stated, "If we are encouraging [Jews] to settle [Palestine], we have only the rich in mind, those who can buy estates for themselves and prepare all the equipment they need at their own expense. There is no place for the poor in Palestine."[45] When the influx of immigrants to Palestine increased at the beginning of the twentieth century, the leaders of the Yishuv (the organized Jewish community of the prestate of Israel) stepped up their efforts to lure productive immigrants who would be able to support themselves.

The personalities who had the greatest influence on migration to Palestine were Sheinkin and Ruppin. Both agreed that the immigrants who should come to Palestine in the first stage were those with means. Only such immigrants could establish a broad economic infrastructure that would facilitate the absorption of the poor and lower-middle-class immigrants who would follow. This policy was predicated on the realization that Palestine was too poor to absorb destitute immigrants.[46] Palestine, they said, was not a country of refuge for persecuted Jews and could not receive unfit immigrants. Accordingly, the natural destination of Jewish migrants, they claimed, should be not Palestine but the United States.[47]

Analysis of Sheinkin's and Ruppin's replies shows that 61 percent of inquiries were turned down categorically with a recommendation not to come to Palestine. Some 18 percent of correspondents were advised to come, check out the country, and then decide. Only 21 percent were told explicitly that they should come and settle. Examining the correspondence for the inquirer's wealth and the information bureau's reply reveals that the wealthier the inquirers were, the lower the percent of rejections.[48]

The policy of preferring immigrants who could support themselves respectably remained in effect until World War I. In 1913, Sheinkin and Ruppin still adhered to the view that Palestine needed healthy immigrants who could afford to establish themselves. If other types of immigrants were to come, the entire Zionist enterprise would be in jeopardy. All of us, said Sheinkin, have one ambition:

> To build up and improve [the country] by bringing in a larger number of healthy, solid elements who can afford to establish themselves, make a living, and generate life. We also know, by the same token, that the Yishuv and our work in general will be in great danger if undesirable elements, i.e., those who cannot possibly make do here, come here to settle on the basis of our advice and instruction. When they return to their countries of origin, they will be able to destroy in a moment everything that we can build over much time. It is easier, of course, to destroy than to build and rebuild.[49]

The Information Bureaus of the Jewish Territorial Organization and the Industrial Removal Office

The ITO was founded in August 1905 as a result of a quarrel between two factions in the Zionist Organization. The crisis began after the premature death of the unquestioned leader of the Zionist movement, Theodor Herzl. Two years earlier, in August 1903, Herzl had brought the plan for settlement in Uganda to the Sixth Zionist Congress. It was a controversial plan that created a deep rift between his supporters, who wanted to accept the British offer, and his opponents, who claimed that only in Palestine could the Jewish people realize their national aspirations. After a stormy debate, the congress decided to send a delegation to study the country and report on the prospects of settlement in the area. Its conclusions were to be presented to the next congress. But even before the delegation set out, Herzl suddenly died.

In July 1905—a year after Herzl's death—the Zionist Congress convened to decide the matter. This was the first congress held without Herzl, and after a heated debate it concluded that the Zionist idea could only be realized in the land of Israel. This decision not only removed from the agenda all settlement plans for places other than Palestine but also heralded the beginning of a change in the balance of power between the "practical" and "political" Zionists within the organization. The political faction was weakened, and a group of about forty people resigned from the congress. Under the leadership of Israel Zangwill, they declared the establishment of the ITO.

The new organization was motivated by genuine anxiety about the fate of the Jews in Eastern Europe and the danger that threatened them. The pogroms and fears that the United States would close its doors and refuse to admit hundreds of thousands of immigrants led Zangwill to conclude that the Jews could not wait until conditions were right for settling in Palestine. Significant contributions to the development of this idea came, on the one hand, from the heartbreakingly anguished letters sent to him by Jews in Eastern Europe pleading for help, and on the other hand, from the mass movement westward. Zangwill thought that it was possible to change the course of Jewish migration. His was a bold and challenging idea: that persuasion and propaganda could make the Jewish migrants move to a different country that would be given to them to establish a state instead of going to Manhattan or Buenos Aires.

When the ITO was founded, Zangwill began to search for a land that would serve as a life buoy for the suffering Jews in Eastern Europe. For eight years he traveled around the world negotiating with politicians and their aides for British East Africa; Ontario, Canada; northern Australia; and the Benguela Plateau in Angola, which was a Portuguese colony. Of all the attempts by the ITO to settle persecuted Jews in uninhabited regions, only the Galveston plan had any success.[50] This plan was the outcome of a meeting of interests between the president of the ITO, who was at that time conducting diplomatic negotiations with governments for the acquisition of territory, and Jewish philanthropists who were extremely worried about the concentration of Jewish immigrants in New York.

New York, as a port city, attracted a varied population from all corners of the world because of its economic advantages and possibilities. The island of Manhattan, which covers no more than 59.5 square kilometers, was a modern Tower of Babel in which 1 million people of different nationalities intermingled. Jews had first arrived in New York (then New Amsterdam) in the seventeenth century (1654), and there was another influx in the second quarter of the nineteenth century. But in 1881 they began arriving in unprecedented numbers. In 1880 there were about 60,000 Jewish immigrants living in Manhattan. In 1905 the number was 672,000; just before World War I it reached 1.33 million. Most of the immigrants lived on the Lower East Side, and very soon this area became one of poverty, congestion, and crime.

In view of the harsh living conditions in New York, the Jewish banker Jacob Schiff, together with the United Hebrew Charities of New York, B'nai B'rith, and the Baron de Hirsch Fund, founded the IRO on January 24, 1901. Their greatest fear was that the socioeconomic situation in New York would increase anti-Semitism, that calls would be heard to close the gates of the United States to immigrants in general and Jews in particular, and that the status of well-established American Jews who had arrived in the country in the first half of the nineteenth century would be undermined. The main aim of the IRO was to reduce the number of immigrants in New York and other large East Coast cities by sending them to cities in the interior of the country where job prospects were better. By 1905, with the help of the IRO and at its expense, about forty thousand Jews left New York. But suddenly immigrants started streaming into Manhattan from abroad. Nearly 1.5 million Jews arrived in the United States, most of them settling in New York, and all the efforts of the IRO became futile.

As the living conditions of the Jewish immigrants grew even worse, Schiff concluded that immigrants had to be channeled toward cities in the western United States in their country of origin, before they arrived in the port of New York. At this point, he met with the president of the ITO. Both men were aware of the Jews' distress. From the Pale of Settlement came the anguished cries of Jews being persecuted and killed, and in the cities on the East Coast of the United States the poverty and living conditions were unbearable. Zangwill and Schiff entered into a partnership, and they continued to cooperate with each other until the outbreak of World War I.

In order to carry out their plan, three information bureaus were established. The first, the Jüdische Emigrations Gesellschaft in Kiev, was responsible for "recruiting" migrants and sending them to the exit port. The second, in Bremen, Germany—the port of departure for Galveston, Texas—was under the responsibility of the Hilfsverein and the supervision of Dr. Paul Nathan. The third, the Jewish Immigrants' Information Bureau in Galveston, was responsible for dispersing the immigrants.[51] Each bureau was responsible for one stage of the plan. Zangwill, based in London, and Schiff, based in the United States, oversaw the entire process. The migration plan was described by Zangwill as something unprecedented in the history of the Jewish people—"beginning in the lands of persecution, and passing through Germany by the co-operation of the Hilfsverein, it stretches across the Atlantic and reaches by way of Galveston to all the Western States of America."[52]

The only one of these three bureaus that was under the direct supervision of the ITO was the one in Kiev. The others reported directly to those appointed to supervise them—the bureau in Bremen to Nathan, and the bureau in Galveston to Schiff. The Kiev bureau was headed by its president, Max Mandelstamm, and his secretary, David Jochelmann. Their authorized agents—one hundred in 1912—were scattered throughout the Pale of Settlement. Their main function was to advertise the Galveston plan (in both the Yiddish and the Hebrew press), find out who was interested, and send to America only those who were suitable to ensure their absorption. The job of the Kiev bureau—like that of the ICA and the Palestine Office—was to give potential emigrants from Eastern Europe information, in this case about job opportunities in the United States in general, and in western America in particular.

The Central Office of Migration Affairs (Berlin Central Office)

As mentioned earlier, the unprecedented wave of emigration at the beginning of the twentieth century stimulated activity by Jewish philanthropic organizations that wished to help the Jewish emigrants. In October 1904, the Hilfsverein, the Alliance Israélite Universelle, ICA, and other organizations that wanted to draw public attention to Jewish emigration and the problems it entailed held a big conference in Frankfurt, Germany. At the conference it was decided to establish a central information bureau to assist the Jewish migrants. This bureau, called the Central Office of Migration Affairs, was established in Berlin, a major crossroads for migration at the time: "Through Germany passes the largest portion of the migrants, those going down to the ships in Hamburg or Bremen and those making their way by sea from Rotterdam, Antwerp, and Amsterdam."[53]

Like the other information bureaus established during this period, the central office in Berlin and its branch offices scattered along the migration routes did not try to prevent or limit emigration. Its job was to supply the most accurate and relevant information to prospective emigrants, including information about the cheapest and shortest route to the port, ticket purchases, inexpensive hostels in the port city for accommodation before the ship sailed, and adjustment and employment in the destination country. The office also had to "take care of the emigrants, obtain the necessary documents for them, negotiate with the ship owners so that they would know that a watchful eye was overseeing what they did and would not let them abuse the emigrants as often happened."[54] The office also answered more than 6,500 letters asking about employment options in the destination countries, travel and the cost of travel, entry restrictions in the various countries, and so on. Of the 1,858 letters received in 1906 (1,184 were received in 1905), 73 percent contained requests for information about the United States, 19 percent about Canada, 14 percent about Argentina, 8 percent about England, and only 6 percent about Palestine.[55] Because a significant proportion of the emigrants passed through Germany on their way to the port, this office played a prominent role in organizing migration.[56]

The information bureaus for Jews in the countries of origin and the destination countries were of enormous importance in making the migration process successful. This network of local offices subordinate to central bureaus supplied information to prospective emigrants so that they could make an informed decision. But the good of the emigrant was not always the dominant interest of the information bureaus, and local agents often treated their clients in a patronizing manner. Nevertheless, the information bureaus did play a key role in the success of the journey and the arrival in the destination country, thereby increasing the scope of migration. Dudley Baines notes that "the key to emigration may have been availability of information. Information was important because it reduced uncertainty."[57] The economist and historian Arcadius Kahan also writes about the importance of information: "Another precondition for voluntary migrations is knowledge about imagined information that would provide a rational justification for migration. The information might be first- or second-hand based upon some recognizable authority, but it has a critical influence on the actual decision to migrate."[58]

The work of the information bureaus in disseminating information to potential and actual migrants—in Yiddish and Russian—was wide ranging and invaluable.[59] The booklet with the largest circulation, distributed by the ICA information bureau to anyone interested for a token price (6 kopecks), was *Algemeyne yedies far di vos viln forn in fremde lender* (General information for those wanting to migrate to foreign countries). The booklet contained a concise explanation in simple language of what emigrants should know before setting out, practical advice, and a brief description of the destination countries. The booklet advised readers not to leave without a certain amount of money, informed them of exchange rates and the locations of border crossings, and warned them against unscrupulous agents. It described seasickness and how to deal with it; explained where to buy tickets for the ship, how to obtain a passport, and what baggage to take; and summarized the rules of courtesy in the destination lands: the United States, Canada, South Africa, South America, Australia, and Palestine.

The ICA published the booklet—the first of its kind—in 1906, and ten thousand copies of it were printed every year.[60] Prospective migrants could obtain detailed, up-to-date information on the destination countries in special booklets devoted to each destination: Argentina, Australia, Canada, South Africa, Chile, and the United States. Each booklet came out in several editions and was updated with each new edition. In these booklets, readers found a map and a description of the geography of the destination country, as well as information about the climate and the animals in the region, the local population, the exchange rate of the local currency, farming and other means of livelihood, the cost of food, and the fare for the sea voyage to the destination country. The most comprehensive booklet was the one on the United States; it contained information about each state and the prospects of employment there. The policy of the information bureau was to prevent a concentration of immigrants in the larger cities and to encourage their dispersal in the interior. The United States booklet had a circulation of six thousand copies a year and was updated annually.

In 1907 the ICA began publishing a newspaper—*Der yidisher emigrant*—devoted entirely to migration. It appeared twice a month and contained updates and information for prospective emigrants about destination countries. Baron Gintsburg was the editor of the newspaper until his death in 1910; from then on the editor was Yanovsky, the general secretary of the information bureau. In 1911, the ITO began publishing a newspaper on migration matters titled *Vohin* (Where to?). Almost every issue had an article or two dealing with an aspect of migration ("Trade and Industry in Argentina," "Trachoma," "The Economic Crisis in the United States," "The Port of Bremen," "Emigration from Bessarabia," etc.), information from the regional and local offices, announcements by the central office in St. Petersburg, questions and answers by the editorial board, information about rogue agents, lists of fares for the voyage, names of ships, sailing schedules, and ports of call (if any) on the way. The paper's circulation was very high for those times: five thousand in 1906, fifty thousand in 1907, seventy thousand in 1908 (the peak year), and fifty thousand to sixty thousand in subsequent years.[61] Assuming that several people read each copy, the readership was much larger. In addition, the information bureau published dictionaries—English-Yiddish and Spanish-Yiddish—to help immigrants adapt to their new countries.

In 1912, the ICA issued a booklet about swindlers. Titled *Emigrantn un agentn: Nit keyn oysgetrakhte mayses* (Emigrants and agents: Not figments of the imagination), it provided prospective migrants with stories about a variety of swindlers.[62] Spread over twenty pages is a description of methods used by swindlers that the bureau had uncovered while helping emigrants. This booklet had a double purpose: first, to inform prospective emigrants of the dangers facing them and to warn them against swindlers who would try to cheat them, and second, to frighten the prospective emigrants into asking the bureau, and not potential charlatans, for assistance:

> Jewish emigrants should know that they cannot make the long journey by themselves. After many years of migration the time has come to realize that one cannot emigrate without assistance.

> There we [the ICA information bureau] provide explanations and advice on how to get a passport, what route to take, where to go, what conditions are like in the destination country, and so on. This is why we are present in every important city in the Pale of Settlement to give emigrants the appropriate information without charge. This is the only way to prevent emigrants from getting into trouble—to accompany them from the moment they consider emigration, through the course of their journey, until they tread on the soil of the new country.[63]

The agents in the information bureaus often traveled the migration routes themselves. They visited border stations and conversed with migrants, negotiated with travel agents, met with local government officials to ease bureaucratic procedures, and even took a train and sailed to America as if they were migrants. Their reports on their experiences were turned into newspaper articles and published in instruction booklets for migrants that were distributed for token prices in Eastern Europe. The excellent information in these reports was invaluable for potential emigrants, as it helped them make their decisions and carry them out. Many of them had never been far from their towns, and the long ocean voyage was regarded as daring and dangerous. The information they received from relatives who had already emigrated and the extensive instructive material allayed their fears somewhat.

In early 1909, *Der yidisher emigrant* printed an article by S. Bloch, an ICA agent whom the information bureau had sent on a round trip between Bremen and Argentina in order to describe conditions and to let prospective emigrants know what to expect. In the article, Bloch drew his readers' attention to the problem of the distribution of sweet water during the voyage: "Frequently, quarrels would break out over the use of sweet water."[64] Steerage passengers were not given enough water, and Bloch recommended that they be adamant and insist on the amount due them. But what is interesting about Bloch's story is not the struggle over the distribution of water but the need to explain to the prospective emigrants what sweet water is: "Seawater is salty and unfit for drinking. Therefore the ship has to be supplied with drinking water on land. This is called sweet water."[65] Merely from the explanation, we can get an idea of how little general knowledge the Jewish emigrants had; many of them had

Map 1. Distribution of ICA Information Bureaus in the Pale of Settlement, 1909
Sources: Der yidisher emigrant, January 15, 1909, 16; January 31, 1909, 15; March 2, 1909, 12; March 16, 1909, 5; April 3, 1909, 4; April 15, 1909, 12; August 14, 1909, 13; September 1, 1909, 13; November 15, 1909, 17; May 1, 1910, 14; May 30, 1910, 22.

never seen the ocean and didn't know that the sea is salty. They had limited understanding of time and space, and, for many of them, emigration was beyond their capabilities.

The information bureaus made information accessible and available, thereby substantially alleviating prospective emigrants' fears and enabling them to make a good decision with a minimum of risk. The more people knew, the less distant their desired destination seemed.

Map 1 shows the distribution of information bureaus in the Pale of Settlement and Poland in 1909. The most interesting and most important fact that can be discerned from the map is that offices were located in almost all the provinces from which Jews emigrated. Potential emigrants who wanted to know about the complexity of the emigration process and the living conditions that they could expect in the destination country could obtain this information near their homes without any difficulty. The

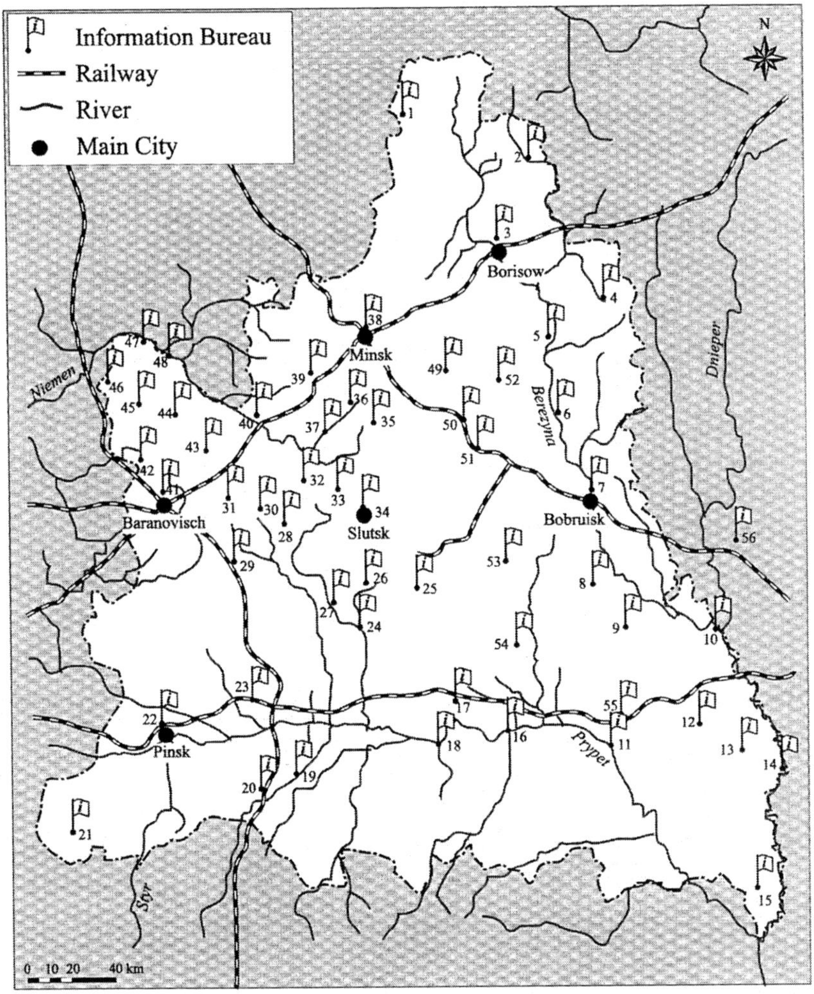

Map 2. Distribution of ICA Information Bureaus in the Province of Minsk, 1909

information bureaus varied in size and composition. In small towns and places with relatively few emigrants, there was no physical office. In the town of Neswizsch (no. 31 on map 2), in the province of Minsk, the local official (B. L. Eisenbud) was a dentist who stored the publications sent by the central bureau in St. Petersburg in his private clinic. In places with a large outflux of emigration such as the cities of Minsk, Pinsk, and Kiev, there were regular offices with paid local officials. As stated earlier, there

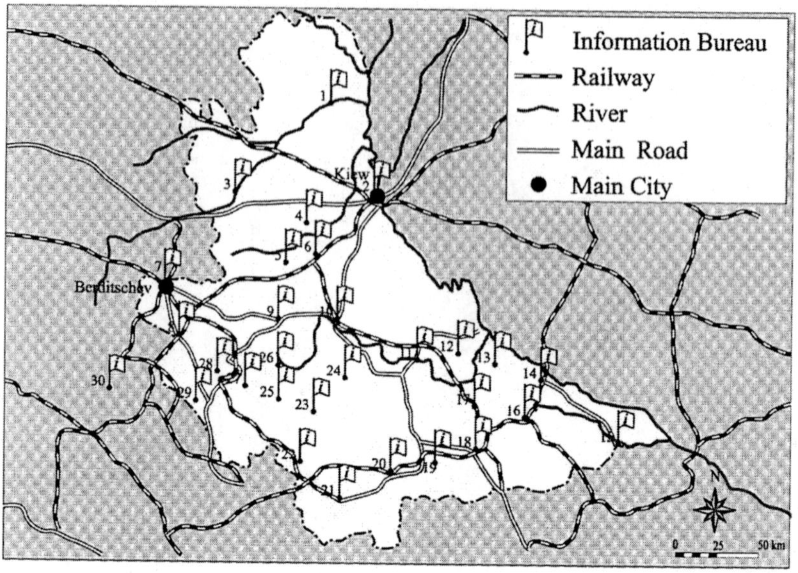

Map 3. Distribution of ICA Information Bureaus in the Province of Kiev, 1909

were information bureaus in remote towns on the periphery as well, so no area was left unserved. The network of information bureaus in the Pale of Settlement enabled every prospective emigrant to obtain information about the emigration process and the preferred destination country without any geographical or financial difficulty. Another fact that emerges from map 1 is the especially high number of information bureaus in the province of Minsk. Map 2 shows, with higher resolution, the distribution of fifty-six of the sixty-one offices in the province (the other five towns that had offices have not been identified).

As the map indicates, the offices were located from Dokschitzei in northern Minsk (no. 1 on map 2) to Ljubischow in the south (no. 21), in places that had a large Jewish population and a high emigration rate, respectively. It seems that there is a correlation between the availability of information and the extent of migration. However, our data do not tell us which led to which. Were the information bureaus established due to large-scale emigration, or did the existence on the information bureaus increase the flow of emigration? Presumably, the two factors were interdependent, and the dynamic that developed made the move to a new land easier.

Table 1. Jewish Emigration from Regions of the Russian Empire, 1905–14, and the Distribution of Information Bureaus[a]

Region	Jewish population in the Russian Empire (%)	Jewish emigration (%)	No. of information bureaus
Northwest	29	32	146
Southwest	29	28	136
South	15	16	41
Poland	27	24	37
Total	**100**	**100**	**360**

Sources: Isaac M. Rubinow, "Economic Condition of the Jews in Russia," *Bulletin of the Bureau of Labor* 72 (September 1907): 487–583 (reprinted as a book, New York, 1970, 491). The data on Jewish emigration are in the Central Archives for the History of the Jewish People (CAHJP), ICA Division.

[a] Northwestern portion of the Pale of Settlement: Minsk, Grodno, Mogilev, Vitebsk, Vilna, and Kovno; southwestern portion of the Pale of Settlement: Kiev, Volhynia, Podolia, Poltava, and Chernigov; southern portion of the Pale of Settlement: Bessarabia, Kherson, Taurida, and Jekaterinoslaw.

Another possible explanation for the relationship between the information bureaus and the scope of emigration is the location of the offices near railways and rivers. Map 2 shows that railroads passed through or near twenty-two of the fifty-six towns and cities marked. In the province of Kiev (map 3), twenty-three out of thirty towns and cities were near main roads or railroads. The combination of available information and access to trains that they could take to the port enabled many emigrants to carry out their decision. Towns that were far from railroads tended to be near rivers; one could take a raft to the nearest railroad and from there travel to a border station and port.

The data from the ICA information bureau, which are based on 150,000 applications to the information bureaus in the Pale of Settlement, paint a similar picture.

If we compare the emigration rates with the number of information bureaus, we find an almost perfect correlation. In regions where emigration rates were high (the southwestern and northwestern Pale of Settlement), the number of information bureaus was also high. Conversely, in southern Russia the emigration rate was the lowest, as was the number of information bureaus. This symbiotic relationship between information availability and rates of migration is a good illustration of how qualitative research (letters from prospective emigrants) combines well with quantitative research (the number of prospective emigrants' applications to information bureaus and the number of bureaus). Not only are the two perspectives not contradictory, but they complement each other.

The letters to the information bureaus in this volume show, first, that the mass Jewish emigration from Eastern Europe was not a flight from imperial Russia or the result of panic. It was a reasoned process, beginning with a limited number of pioneer emigrants in the 1870s. The settlement of a half-million migrants in the destination countries in this period, along with the establishment of information bureaus, laid the groundwork of information that made it possible for 2 million Jews to follow them.

The Letters

What can we learn from the letters about Jewish migration in the early twentieth century, and what do they contribute to our understanding of the migration process and the difficulties it entailed? Three outstanding issues emerge from the sixty-six letters published here. The first involves the decision-making process and the deliberations of the prospective emigrants before they decided whether to leave and where to go. The second involves the difficulties the emigrants faced in carrying out their decision—the hardships they encountered from the moment the decision was made until they reached their destination. The third is the crisis that emigration caused for women and children who were waiting for word from their husband/father, long since gone to America, who had promised to bring them over.

Hesitations, Vacillations, and Decisions

The letters from prospective emigrants to the information bureaus reveal their deliberations at an early stage, even before they reached a decision. The attempt to learn from these letters about the migrants' hesitations before they set out poses a methodological problem that needs to be addressed. Very few prospective emigrants corresponded with the information bureaus. Are the hundreds of letters preserved in the information bureaus enough to understand such a central issue in migration research?[66] The answer to this question is complex. Historians are limited in our access to primary sources and often have no satisfying answers to fascinating research questions due to the paucity of sources. Therefore supplementary sources are required—the population census, lists of migrants, guidance literature, and so on—to support, complement, and sometimes even contradict the conclusions drawn from the letters. Through cross-references we can reach considered insights that can shed new light on how the decisions were made.

Letters 7, 8, 10, 11, 12, 18, 21, 22, 23, 29, 30, 31, 32, 33, 34, 36, 37, 38, 39, 40, 41, 42, 43, 45, 46, 47, 48, 49, 50, 51, 52, 53, 54, 55, 56, 57, 58, 59, 60, 61, 62, 63, and 64 describe the migrants' desire to obtain whatever information they could that would enable them to weigh the advisability of moving to a new country. I do not intend to explain the significance and importance of each letter in this introduction. Readers can gain their own impressions of what factors were considered by the letter writers and how their decisions were made. However, I focus here on a few outstanding letters that attest to a whole range of issues that Eastern European Jews considered when deciding whether to emigrate and where to go.

Letter 55, sent to the directors of the Palestine Office by one of its local agents on behalf of several families, is a good illustration of the families' desire to obtain precise information and to prepare properly for the move to a new country. "Two families want to go to our ancestral land to start a bread bakery in Jaffa," writes the local deputy to Arthur Ruppin, the director of the Palestine Office. Therefore they wish to ask "His Honor" a few questions:

1. Is it true that there is no such business there?
2. Even if there is, can such a business support two families that need 100 rubles a month each?
3. Approximately how much money is needed to run such a business?

4. Is it necessary to bring over expert bakers from Russia, or can they be found there? I should mention, too, that the members of these families cannot do the work themselves. Furthermore, the business is completely foreign to them, but they think that it does not require great expertise and that in [illegible] time they will know how to run the business.[67]

Moyshe Zelnik of the town of Dubossary in the Kherson district (letter 7) was interested in moving to the United States. In his letter to the directors of the IRO he wrote,

> Having nowhere else to turn for a satisfactory answer, I have the honor to write to you and I believe that you will not refuse me and will answer my questions below. By my profession I am a liquor distiller, that is I have served in factories that make various sweet liqueurs and spirits, now I have decided to leave for America as a result of the terribly critical situation in our area. But before I commit myself to the journey, I want to know whether there will be something for me to do in America connected to my profession, and therefore, I would need to know the following:
>
> 1. Do people in America drink a lot of liqueurs, or do they mainly drink unsweetened spirits like Gin or Whiskey and liquor distilled from wheat, corn, rye, and such?
> 2. Are there many distilleries in the United States of America and is it possible to quickly obtain a position in such a distillery?
> 3. If you happen to know, how much does the government get for each level of alcohol percentage per one hundred liters of liquor? If this is not practiced there, then I don't need the information.
> 4. Especially this one: How does one go about getting work and what does one need to do to obtain such a position? Is there a reputable bureau or society that can fill such positions or does one have to advertise oneself in a special journal devoted to my line of work?[68]

H. L. Schilenski of Kovno (letter 57) wanted to open a trading house in Palestine, so he asked Ruppin a few questions about the country:

1. Will the authorities in Jaffa let Russian Jews establish a factory, and would this require a permit?
2. Are heating fuels such as coal, oil, and wood available in Jaffa?
3. If a permit is needed, how much does it cost and how long will it take to get?
4. How do I pay the customs fee for materials imported from Russia or some other country, especially chicory?[69]

Israel Nevelstein was also considering migration. To be sure of making the right decision, he sent Ruppin a few questions (letter 56):

1. Can I establish a factory in our country for whatever oil is in great demand in Palestine or abroad? What kind of oil is this?
2. Can I obtain all the machinery and apparatus necessary for the factory there, and will 6,000 rubles be sufficient for establishing such a factory?
3. Can I hope to earn at least 100 rubles a month?
4. What is the name of the place where I can open such a factory?
5. Let me know the name of the flower or seed from which I can make oil. How much will it cost me by weight and volume before it is processed in the factory, and how much profit will I make on the oil produced from that quantity?
6. What would my monthly expenses be in such a factory?[70]

Moyshe Burgin (letter 8), a pharmacist from the town of Kretingen in the Kovno district, wrote to the directors of the IRO explaining that he had decided to move to the United States but did not know where he would have the best chance of finding work. He asked them questions that would help him make the decision:

1. What region or city is more suitable for me, considering my profession?

2. Can a person in this field find work in these kinds of businesses: drugstores, pharmacies, hospitals, drug warehouses, etc.?
3. What are the average earnings of someone working with these kinds of products?
4. What would a person coming from Russia be required to know to attain this goal?[71]

Letter 22 was written by several Jews in their twenties from Plonsk who wanted information before emigrating. Although they were young and unmarried and had no children, they were afraid of taking risks and wanted to minimize the uncertainty inherent in moving to a new country:

1. A single man of eighteen. He is familiar with the textile trade and his capital consists of two hundred fifty rubles (250 rubles). And he is fluent in Russian and Hebrew. Where in America should he go so that he can earn a living and learn the language?
2. A single man of twenty-three (that is, 23), a pattern designer, fluent in three languages: German, Russian, Hebrew, with capital amounting to one hundred fifty rubles (150 rubles). Where in America should he go to be able to earn a living?
3. A single man of twenty, fluent in Russian and Hebrew, with capital amounting to six hundred rubles (600 rubles). Where in America should he go so that he can enroll in a technical school where his capital will last him until he will be able to earn a living in his field?
4. A single man of eighteen, an agricultural worker, fluent in Polish and Hebrew, and his capital amounts to 200 rubles. Where should he go to be able to earn his living in agriculture?[72]

The deliberations and requests for information show that the decision-making process was a rational one. This was no spontaneous decision triggered by despair, but a reasoned one in which the prospective emigrants tried to figure out what would be best for them. Furthermore, we can learn about migration considerations and the way decisions were made not only from what the letters say but also from what they do not say. The letters to the information bureaus, for example, contain very few references to persecutions and attacks on the Jews. There is almost no mention of the surrounding population and their relationship with the letter writers. Economic hardship and a desire to improve one's standard of living were the major concerns in their decision-making process. This assertion is, of course, based on only a few hundred letters, which may not be enough to give us a reliable picture of the impact of the pogroms on emigration considerations. However, by means of supplementary sources and databases containing tens of thousands of applications from prospective emigrants to the information bureaus, we can tell whether the letters reflect the decisions made by the larger group of emigrants.

Letters 27 and 28, from Moshe Rosenblatt to the president of the ITO, tell of a pogrom against the Jewish population of Kiev in October 1905. Rosenblatt described the pogrom in real time, and his vivid depiction gives the reader a sense of being in the writer's house, looking out the window into the streets of Kiev and seeing Jews being slaughtered. The harsh, detailed description is a rare, first-person testimony of a pogrom documented in real time and not based on memory long afterward. According to Rosenblatt,

> So many people are fleeing Kiev and the vicinity that in four days eight thousand received provincial papers from the provincial officer to go abroad, in addition to those sneaking across the borders, who are seven times that number. All the transports are crammed with men and women like herring in a barrel. The tickets for all classes of the train are sold out a week in advance! The panic is so great that emigration on this scale has never before been heard of. It exceeds all waves of emigration in the history of the world![73]

Despite the panic and flight described in Rosenblatt's letters, the quantitative findings show that the rate of emigration from areas that suffered pogroms was lower than from other parts of the Pale of Settlement. The other letters are inconsistent with this one, which was clearly written in a storm of emotion by someone who feared for the fate of the Jews of Kiev. In his pioneering study "The Geographic Background of East European

Jewish Migration," Saul Stampfer shows that the stream of emigrants from places where pogroms occurred was smaller than from places where the Jews suffered economic hardship but no pogroms. Stampfer's data on emigration from the Russian Empire come from the landsmanshafts established by immigrants in New York during the great migration. Since the landsmanshafts were founded on the basis of city of origin, it is possible to calculate the rate of emigration from each region of the Russian Empire. According to Stampfer, 50 percent of the emigrants came from the northwest, 20 percent from the southwest, 24 percent from Poland, and only 6 percent from southern Russia, which suffered from persecution and pogroms.[74]

Table 1 shows that 32 percent of Jewish emigrants came from the northwestern part of the Pale of Settlement. In this region industrialization was proceeding faster than elsewhere, and the Jews were in dire economic straits. According to the data from the information bureau, the highest rates of emigration in the northwest were in the districts of Minsk and Mogilev. About 40 percent of emigrants from the northwest were from Minsk, 17 percent were from Mogilev, 13 percent were from Kovno, and the rest were from the districts of Vitebsk, Vilna, and Grodno.[75] Table 1 also shows that the rate of emigration was 28 percent in the southwest and only 16 percent in the southern area of the Pale of Settlement (both of these areas were affected by pogroms). Within the southwest, 42 percent emigrated from the Kiev district, 33 percent from Volhynia, 20 percent from Podolia, and the rest from Chernigov and Poltava. By contrast, in the southern portion of the Pale of Settlement, about 40 percent emigrated from the district of Kherson, including 22 percent from Odessa and its environs. The reason for the low rate of emigration in the south was mainly that the Jews there were better off financially than in the northwest.

Moreover, a comparison of rates of emigration with the proportion of the Jewish population in the districts of the Pale of Settlement shows barely any significant differences. If the pogroms were the main factor in emigration, we would expect emigration to have been disproportionately high in regions with pogroms, but this was not the case. In the south and southwest, the proportion of emigrants was almost identical to the proportion of Jews living in those regions. In contrast, in the northwest the rate of emigration was disproportionately high—although only slightly. Only in Poland was the rate of emigration disproportionately low: 24 percent of all Jewish emigrants were from Poland, whereas 27 percent of the Jews in the Russian Empire lived there.

Joel Perlmann, in his article "The Local Geographic Origins of Russian-Jewish Immigrants, circa 1900," reaches a conclusion similar to Stampfer's and to those based on the data of the ICA information bureau. In a sample of 8,897 immigrants who entered New York in the early twentieth century, the rate of emigration from the northwest was higher than that from the southern part of the Pale of Settlement.[76] In addition, the Soviet statistician V. V. Obolensky showed in the late 1920s that emigration from southwestern Russia was significantly less than that from the northwestern portion of the Pale of Settlement.[77] Other sources show a high rate of emigration among the Jews of Galicia in the Austro-Hungarian Empire, despite the absence of pogroms.[78] The findings of the analysis of prospective emigrants' letters to the ICA information bureaus throughout the Pale of Settlement are thus consistent with the conclusions reached by Perlman, based on Ellis Island records, and by Stampfer, based on the landsmanshafts in New York—three different sources for understanding the issue, but all reaching a similar conclusion.[79]

The decision to emigrate was made only after the family was convinced by relatives, acquaintances, and other sources of information that its economic prospects in another country were better than in its country of origin. The pogroms, the revolution of 1905, and other persecutions by the regime merely impelled them to make a decision on a matter that they had thought about and investigated previously. It is highly unlikely that mass emigration would have occurred—even in a period of robbery, violence, and destruction—were it not for the emigration information received by the Jews of the Russian Empire at an ever-increasing rate at the beginning of the twentieth century. For many, the fear of living in a strange country whose language and ways of life were unknown to them far outweighed the fears they endured while living in a familiar environment. Uncertainty about what was in store for them would have kept them bound to their old homes and reduced the likelihood of emigration. The more their fears were allayed by the information they received, the more likely they were to emigrate.

The high level of emigration in 1914 before the outbreak of World War

I supports the view that pogroms were not the main reason for emigration. Average monthly Jewish emigration from Eastern Europe from January through July (21,000) was significantly higher than in 1906 (15,000). (See table 2.) It is noteworthy that Jewish emigration from the Russian Empire reached its peak at this time despite the absence of pogroms or other calamities affecting the Jews. This is because by then potential Jewish emigrants had received more reliable information about employment opportunities abroad from relatives, the local press, and information bureaus.

The letters reflect the profile of the Jewish emigrants who went to the destination countries. Many of them were craftsmen who found it difficult to support themselves under the socioeconomic conditions in the Russian Empire and Galicia at the turn of the century. Accelerated industrialization in Russia and the move of thousands of farmers from rural areas to the cities radically altered Russian society. Internal migration from impoverished villages to industrialized cities created harsh conditions in the urban areas. The enormous demand for work contrasted with the limited availability of factory jobs lowered wages and raised the cost of living, which increased poverty and socioeconomic disparities.

These changes did not spare the Jewish population of the Pale of Settlement; in fact, they affected the Jews even more than they affected the Gentiles. The natural increase among the Jewish population accelerated the migration of Jews from small towns and villages to the cities. This internal migration caused major changes in the Jews' way of life and employment structure: about 70 percent of them were engaged in petty trade and various crafts.[80] Peddlers traveled from city to city offering their wares. Competition with impoverished farmers for jobs only exacerbated the Jews' plight, and unlike their brethren in the West, they were unable to find their place in the new economic circumstances. In the competition between Jewish and non-Jewish workers, who sometimes arrived in the city on the same train, the non-Jews were more likely to be hired by the large factories, while the Jews were forced to support themselves meagerly in small, dark, cramped workshops.[81] The difficulties the Jews endured in adapting to the new economic conditions aggravated their distress and led to competition between Jewish shopkeepers and Jewish craftsmen for every job. This competition reduced prices, and many shopkeepers were forced to sell their wares at a loss.

This situation embittered the lives of the Jewish craftsmen and merchants, as reflected in the letters that mention the writer's place of residence. We find that many of the letter writers lived in small or medium-sized towns where the proportion of Jews was high. For example, Neswizsch, in the Minsk district (letter 5), had 8,460 inhabitants at the beginning of the twentieth century, 4,687 of whom (55.4 percent) were Jews; Wengrow, in the district of Seidlce, Poland (letter 6), had 12,102 inhabitants, 8,136 of whom (67.2 percent) were Jews; Brest Litowsk, in the Grodno district (letter 9), had 46,621 inhabitants, 30,527 of whom (64.9 percent) were Jews; Ljubischow, in the Minsk district (letter 11), had 2,739 inhabitants, 1,888 of whom (nearly 70 percent) were Jews; Ponewesch, in the Kovno district (letter 17), had 12,972 inhabitants, half of whom were Jews; Berdichev, in the Kiev district (letter 26), had 53,355 inhabitants, 78 percent of whom were Jews. As 70 percent of the Jews were engaged in petty trade and crafts, the competition was clearly intense.

The worsening economic situation is reflected in letter 33, from the Koheleth family, which gives a concrete example of the hardship suffered by a typical Jewish family that had managed with great difficulty to support itself in the changing economy of the Russian Empire in the early twentieth century. In March 1913, at the height of the mass emigration, the Koheleths' eldest son, David, wrote to the Palestine Office in Jaffa. His letter gives a stark description of the family's bleak situation in a town in the Mogilev district. The young man painstakingly listed the trials and tribulations of the Jewish family. David's ability to describe the family's dilemmas, hardships, economic situation, and relations with the neighboring non-Jewish population allows us to understand the family's considerations in deciding whether to emigrate and where to go. A rare document from the period of the great migration, the Koheleth letter encompasses the whole gamut of factors that led to the emigration of Jews from Eastern Europe. These factors combined mercilessly to destabilize the economic situation of the Koheleths and many other Jewish families in the Pale of Settlement and led them and many like them to consider emigration.

The Koheleths lived in the small village of Zakharino in the district of Mogilev.[82] They were a family of ten: a father and mother, both fifty-three years old, and eight children—six boys and two girls. The eldest son was twenty-seven years old and a teacher in a Jewish charity school. Two sons were shoemakers who could barely support themselves in their trade; they found jobs in the nearby factory of a wood trader for one ruble per day of work. Two sons, aged fifteen and seventeen, stayed at home with their sisters, aged twelve and six, and a boy of eight was in school. The father of the family—he is not named in the letter—was "a shoemaker whose trade—due to the large number of craftsmen engaged in it and the intense competition among them—brings in barely enough for food, and even that with great difficulty." The poverty and privation in the town in which they had previously lived—probably Mstislavl—prompted them to move to Zakharino. There they leased a plot of land and raised some vegetables, which they sold in the market once a week.

Besides the economic hardship and the difficulty of supporting a family of ten, the Koheleths suffered from the hostility of their non-Jewish neighbors: "The family does not feel any solid ground under its feet, and its [members'] lives are in danger. Being completely dependent on the *uryadni,* who could evict them at any moment, they must suffer insult from the village farmers and must flatter them while they bleed at the sight of such cruelty."[83] The situation had totally undermined the Koheleths' sense of economic security and personal safety. Economic hardship, low wages, the constant search for work, the change in residence, and the necessity of abandoning shoemaking work for a job in a local wood factory, combined with local hostility, led the family to conclude that it would gradually lose its ability to survive. David wrote to Ruppin, the director of the Palestine Office in Jaffa,

> In light of all this, the family is thinking about leaving this country and heading for another country that will treat them in a more welcoming fashion. We family members are aware that it will not be easy to attain our goal, but we trust that with hard work we will succeed. We are not aiming for a life of luxury or asking for easy work; we just long for a quiet, satisfying life. We are not idealists, but we are willing to make sacrifices—provided that we are assured that our future will eventually be secure and stable, and that the ground under our feet will not collapse. If we see that there is no way for the entire family to leave the country all at once, then we have decided that the older sons—that is, the second and third sons—will emigrate first, and after a while the rest of the family will go. . . . Sir! If

> possible, express your opinion on this matter. Please help us by sending us your instructions and your advice: Would we be able to move to Palestine and settle on the land or even in some city? Will we find what we are looking for in the Land of Israel? Or would we better off heading for other countries, because the living conditions in Palestine are not suitable for us?
>
> We are afraid that we will fail and ruin our already-precarious position. Please do not delay in replying.
>
> Respectfully, in the name of the entire family, D. Koheleth[84]

David's letter reveals his family's hesitations in choosing a destination country, fear of what the morrow will bring, economic hardship, and strong but modest aspirations for a "quiet, satisfying life," a place where they can feel safe and not threatened. His letter also reveals the family's desire to minimize the risk of making a decision by first sending two sons to Palestine so that they can lay the groundwork for the rest of the family. We do not know whether the Koheleths moved to Palestine or America or if they remained in Zakharino despite their economic hardship and their neighbors' hostility. Although I could not find the information bureau's reply, similar letters were usually answered in the negative. With only 800 rubles, a family could not settle in Palestine in the early twentieth century, and the directors of the Palestine Office were apprehensive about the country's limited absorption capacity.[85] Naturally, the negative recommendation only increased the family's uncertainty, as they had to reconsider whether to emigrate or to try to survive where they were and hope for better times to come.

En Route to the Destination Country: Agents, Swindlers, and Bureaucracy

Another important issue that the letters reveal concerns the difficulties encountered by the emigrants from the moment they made their decision. After considering, hesitating, and coming to a decision, they then had to put the decision into practice. They had to plan their route, consult train timetables, cross the border, travel to the port, and board the ship that would take them to their new country. For the ordinary Eastern European

Jew, this was no easy task. Most had never gone far from their towns before. Crossing borders and traveling hundreds of kilometers by train was a sensational and exciting experience that made a deep impression on them.

Letters 1, 2, 3, 11, 12, 24, 35, and 66 describe the difficulty of moving to a new country and the obstacles they had to surmount on their way to the port of exit and during the sea voyage to the new country. There were two possible ways of crossing the border and reaching the port of exit. The first was the legal route, which involved obtaining a valid passport and relevant documents. This required knowing how to navigate the bureaucratic minefield of czarist Russia in the early twentieth century. The second—which was more frequently used when it was not possible to obtain the necessary documents from the Russian authorities—was to sneak across the border with the help of smugglers.

Legal Emigration with a Passport

One of the salient characteristics of the period of the great migration was the liberal immigration policy in the destination countries. Until World War I, no passport or visa was needed to enter the destination countries, including the United States. The borders of the American continent were open—almost without restriction—to millions of Europeans seeking to escape poverty and hardship. But in order to cross the Russian border legally and safely and sail from Europe, one needed a passport.

Obtaining a passport and exit visa was an extremely difficult and complex bureaucratic task. Not only was Russian law unsuited to handle mass emigration, but it also varied from one region to another. To obtain a passport, a prospective emigrant had to submit the following documents: an identity card, a certificate from the police stating that there was no impediment to the person's leaving the country, and, if the applicant was male and between the ages of eighteen and twenty-one, a document certifying that he had reported to the army recruitment office.[86] Procuring the necessary documents was a problem in itself—many people were not registered in their places of residence and therefore had no identity card. Those who had an identity card found, in many cases, that the card was no longer valid or that not all the family members were listed on it. To obtain a new card, one had to go to the municipality where one was registered, regardless of how far it was from where one actually lived. The law was changed in October 1906, after which residents could obtain a permanent identity card (with no expiration date) and passport for themselves and their family members anywhere in the Pale of Settlement or in Poland, on the condition that they submitted the required documents. But because the amendment was written in Russian and not circulated as it should have been throughout the Pale of Settlement, Jews tended to apply for identity cards in the old way.

A document of integrity could be obtained from the police upon presentation of an identity card, provided that no complaints had been received against anyone in the family. Along with the document of integrity, the prospective emigrant received from the police the rest of the documents needed to obtain a passport. The passport listed all family members irrespective of age: wife, children, other relatives, and even the servant, if there was one. If the whole family was listed on the identity card, this process was simple and did not involve any special difficulties. But if the wife and children were not listed, the prospective emigrant was asked to present the children's birth certificates and to bring witnesses who knew his children and his wife. Since it was the custom in small towns to record marriages and births in the community records only, many people found it difficult to obtain the necessary documents.[87]

Women who wanted to join their husbands in the new country had even more difficulty obtaining a passport. According to Russian law, a married woman could only get a passport with her husband's consent. But because many men emigrated alone to pave the way for their families to follow and did not leave their wives a separate passport or a notarized document certifying that they were married to each other, their wives found themselves in a serious predicament. This difficulty could be resolved in any of three ways. The first and least practical was for the husband to declare in front of a notary in the new country that he wanted his wife and children to join him. The affidavit had to be signed in the presence of the Russian consul in the husband's area of residence and then sent to his wife. The wife would submit the notarized affidavit signed by the consul and would receive a passport without difficulty. The second way was for the wife to declare at the police station that her husband had deserted her and that his whereabouts were unknown. After a brief investigation, the police would issue a document confirming her statement, after which she could obtain a passport from the provincial governor.[88] The third and most common way was to sneak across the border.

The bureaucratic obstacles to obtaining a passport so that one could leave Russia legally were almost insurmountable. The community's separate population registry, the internal migration that took people far from where they were originally registered, and cases in which wives had no authorization from their husbands to obtain a separate passport all made it difficult to get through the maze of Russian bureaucracy and led many migrants to search for an alternative, illegal way of leaving the country. By doing so they became vulnerable to swindlers of various kinds who took advantage of their dependence and dubious circumstances.

In late 1911, the demographer and economist Jacob Lestschinsky visited one of the border crossings between Germany and Russia to study the emigrants' problems and to endeavor to suggest solutions. Of all the difficulties that Lestschinsky described, the biggest was obtaining a passport—hence the need for the assistance of smugglers. "Based on my numerous conversations with many people," he wrote,

> I realized that ninety emigrants out of a hundred could not obtain passports due to the necessary conditions. Here, for example, is a widow and her daughter, who went through so many troubles while crossing the border, more than a person can bear. Why didn't this wretched woman get a passport? It was impossible. Three of her sons had already left Russia, and she would have had to pay a penalty of nine hundred rubles. Here is a young maid of seventeen, who also had a heap of troubles. Why didn't she get a passport? It was impossible. She is an orphan and has no "papers"; . . . and the same is true of most of the emigrants. However, I realized that ten percent of the emigrants, or maybe even more, could have gotten passports, but even they were unfamiliar with this business and got carried away with the stream.[89]

In view of the difficulties in obtaining a passport, the information bureaus helped prospective emigrants deal with the bureaucracy. They translated documents from Russian into Yiddish and told them where to sign and what documents to submit. These efforts were meant first and foremost to reduce the number of emigrants crossing the border illegally and thereby putting their lives in danger and the success of their journey in question.

Правленіе Еврейскаго Эмиграціоннаго Общества въ Кіевѣ.
Кузнечная 34, кв. 5.
Телефонъ 23-05.

Jüdische Emigrations Gesellschaft
KIEW.
Kusneznaja 34, W. 5.
Telephon 23-05.

החברה היהודית לעמיגראציע
יודישע עמיגראציאנס-געזעלשאפט
קיעוו.
קוזנעצנאיא 34 מעון 5
טעלעפאן 23-05

ווי נעמט מען ארויס א פאס אויף צו פאָרען אין אויסלאַנד?

קודם כל דארף מען אנשרייבן א פּראָשעניע צום איספּראַווניק פון אויעזד, אָדער צום פּאָליצמייסטער פון דער שטאָט, וואו מ׳וואוינט, בזה הלשון:

Въ (דער נאמען פון דער שטאָדט) Полицейское Управленіе
мѣщанина (דעם נאמען, דעם פאטערס נאמען און די פאמיליע)
жительствующаго въ (דעם נאמען פון דער שטאָדט)
(און דעם אדרעס)

Прошеніе

Желая выѣхать за-границу, честь имѣю покорнѣйше просить выдать мнѣ свидѣтельство о неимѣніи со стороны полиціи препятствій къ выѣзду моему за-границу.

אויב די פרוי מיט די קינדער פאָרען אויך, דארף מען די פּראָשעניע שרייבן אזוי:

Желая выѣхать за-границу съ женою моей и дѣтьми, покорнѣйше прошу выдать мнѣ свидѣтельство о неимѣніи препятствій со стороны полиціи къ моему выѣзду за-границу и къ выѣзду за-границу жены моей (דעם נאמען פון דער פרוי)
и дѣтей (די נאמען פון די קינדער און וויפיל יאָהר)

(דא שרייבט מען דעם טאג, חודש און יאָהר) (דא שרייבט מען זיך אונטער)

אין דינער פּראָשעניע בעט מען, או פּאָליציי זאל ארויסגעבן א באוראסמאָיערעניע, אז עס איז פון איהר זייט נישא קיין שום מניעה צום ארויספאָהרען קיין אויסלאנד.

אויף די פּראָשעניע דארף מען אנקלעבן 2 גערבאָווע מארקעס צו 75 קאָפּיקעס.

כדי צו בעקומען די אודאָסטאָווערעניע וואס גיכער, דארף מען איידער מ׳דערלאנגט די פּראָשעניע דעם איספּראַווניק, אָדער דעם פּאָליצמייסטער, זיך פריהער ווענדען מיט איהר צום אוריאדניק (אָדער אקאָלאָטאָטשני נאדזיראטעל) און דערנאך צום פּריסטאַוו, און בעטען אז זיי זאלען איהר פריהער אונטערשרייבען, — דערנאך ערשט דארף מען די פּראָשעניע דערלאנגען דעם איספּראַווניק אָדער דעם פּאָליצמייסטער.

אויף אזא אופן, ווי מיר האָבען אנגעוויזען, קומט דאס צו פיעל גיכער, ווי מ׳זאל דערלאנגען גלייך צום איספּראַווניק אָדער פּאָליצמייסטער.

אז דער איספּראַווניק, אָדער פּאָליצמייסטער, גיט ארויס די אודאָסטאָווערעניע, טוט מען אזוי:

מ׳צאָהלט אין אין קאַנצעלאַריע פון גובערנאַטאָר [illegible] [illegible] רובל (און פוילן — 20 רובל), — דער, וואס האָט א עטזנאָווע רעמעסלענע סוידע-טעלסטווא, צאָהלט נאָר [illegible] רובל 50 קאָפּ. — און מ׳נעמט ארויס א קוויטאנציע פון קאַנצעלאַריע אויפן געלד. די קוויטאנציע פון קאַנצעלאַריע מיט דער אודאָסטאָווערעניע פון פּאָליציי און דעם געוועהנליכען בעשטאָנדיקען פאס (ווער קען איבערנעמען) דארף מען דערלאנגען פערזענליך, אָדער דורך פאסט, אין דער גובערנאַטאָרסקע קאַנצעלאַריע מיט אזא מין פּראָשעניע:

The two photocopied pages here were printed by the *Jüdische Emigrations Gesellschaft* of the ITO. They explain to prospective emigrants in Yiddish how to fill out the passport application forms, which were written in Russian. They tell them where to sign, what the name of the province is, and where to write one's wife's name, one's surname, the date, one's age, and other particulars. The detailed explanation shows how hard it was for

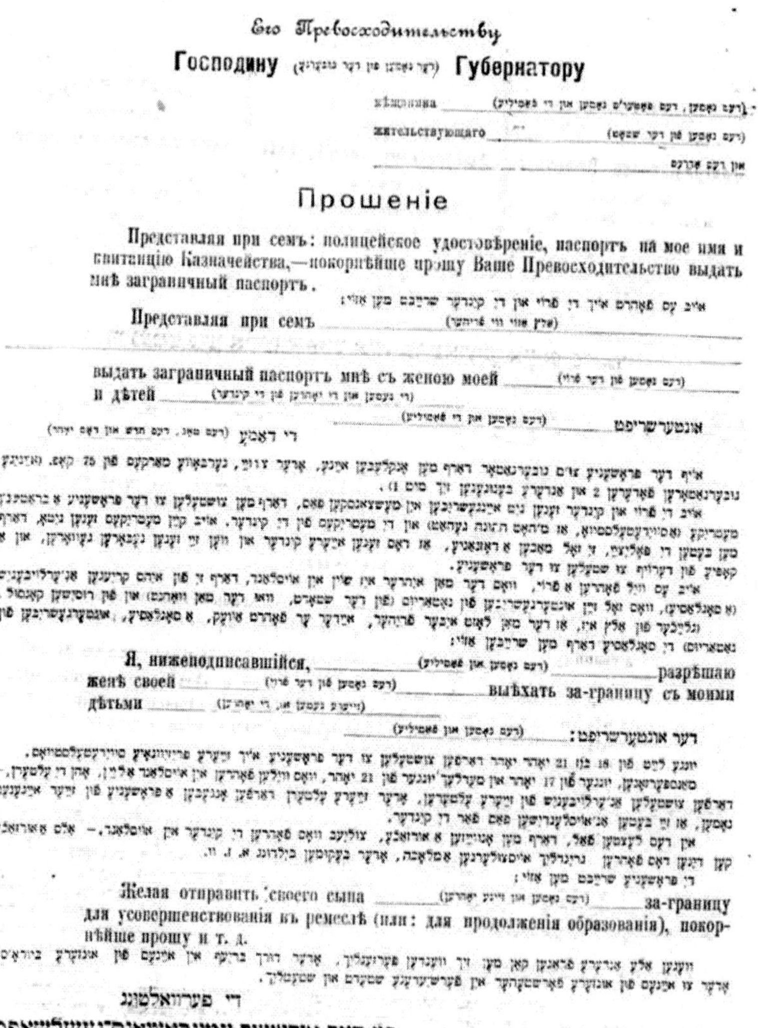
Его Превосходительству

Господину Губернатору

мѣщанина ______

жительствующаго ______

Прошеніе

Представляя при семъ: полицейское удостовѣреніе, паспортъ на мое имя и квитанцію Казначейства,—покорнѣйше прошу Ваше Превосходительство выдать мнѣ заграничный паспортъ.

Представляя при семъ ______

выдать заграничный паспортъ мнѣ съ женою моей ______ и дѣтей ______

אונטערשריפט ______

Я, нижеподписавшійся, ______ разрѣшаю женѣ своей ______ выѣхать за-границу съ моими дѣтьми ______

דער אונטערשריפט: ______

Желая отправить своего сына ______ за-границу для усовершенствованія въ ремеслѣ (или: для продолженія образованія), покорнѣйше прошу и т. д.

די פערוואלטונג

פון דער אידישער עמיגראציאנס־געזעלשאפט

אין קיעוו.

Eastern European Jews to cope with the czarist bureaucracy and how much help and advice they needed if they were to leave legally.

Only after receiving a passport could an emigrant cross the border in an orderly fashion at one of the official crossing points on the Polish-

Map 4. Border Stations

German or Russian–Austro-Hungarian border. The choice of a crossing point was usually based on the ship ticket. Emigrants who sailed from Rotterdam or Antwerp crossed the border between Russia and Galicia at Belzec (Tomaschow), Brody (Radziwilow), Husiatyn (Kamenetz-Podolsk), Nadbrzezie (Sandomir), Nowosielitza (Nowosielitzy), Szcakowa (Granica), Sokal (Wladimir-Wolinsk), or Podwoloczyska (Woloczyska).[90] Those sailing from Hamburg or Bremen crossed the Polish-German border at Eydtkuhnen (Wirballen), Illowo (Mlawa), Prostken (Grajewo), Myslowitz (Sosnowice), or Thorn (Alexandrowo).[91]

The border stations were the bottleneck of Jewish emigration from the Pale of Settlement. In late 1893, at the initiative of the German shipping companies Nord-Deutscher Lloyd and Hamburg Amerikanische Packetfahrt Actien Gesellschaft (HAPAG, or the Hamburg-America Line), border-control stations were set up along the Polish-German border. The impetus was a cholera epidemic that had broken out in Hamburg the previous year, killing 8,600 local residents. Naturally, the emigrants staying in the city were accused of introducing and spreading the disease. These accusations were not necessarily the results of xenophobia and suspicion of the emigrant population; in the spring of 1892, there had been a few cases of cholera in the southern regions of the Russian Empire, and it was commonly believed that the Eastern European emigrants had brought the disease from there. This claim was reinforced when the renowned scientist Robert Koch—who had isolated the cholera-causing bacterium and would later win a Nobel Prize—visited the emigrants' camp in Hamburg and stated that the Russian emigrants had indeed caused the outbreak of the disease. Only much later was it discovered that it had been six French sailors who had carried the lethal germ. But first the Russian emigrants in Hamburg were placed in quarantine, and the Russian-German border was closed to further emigration.

The closing of the border caused the German shipping companies major economic losses and cast a dark shadow over their future. In order to emerge from the crisis, Hamburg-America and Nord-Deutscher Lloyd proposed that the government open inspection stations at the border where emigrants could be given a medical examination before entering German territory. Because the shipping companies financed these inspection stations, they had representatives there, and their agents pressured the emigrants to sail with their firms. Until 1892 many emigrants had chosen to sail to America from the port of Hull, England, and Hamburg and Bremen had been only transit ports, not exit ports. In the early 1890s, the proportion of emigrants who took the indirect route was estimated at about 41 percent. After the inspection stations opened, this figure dropped to only 4 percent. This dramatic reduction indicates the tremendous pressure exerted on the emigrants to sail to America with Hamburg-America or Nord-Deutscher Lloyd.

As a result of the establishment of the inspection stations, huge numbers of emigrants—both Jews and non-Jews—began to gather at these stations on both the Russian side and the German/Austro-Hungarian side. Because the border-crossing stage was the critical one in the emigration process, and the emigrants were being pressured by the shipping company agents, the information bureaus tried very hard to shorten the emigrants' stay in the border towns and help them cross over safely. In 1906 the ICA information bureau sent a representative named Teplitzki to the border stations of Wirballen on the Russian side of the border and Eydtkuhnen on the German side to learn about the difficulties that the emigrants were experiencing in crossing the border.

Teplitzki painted a bleak picture of the situation. Emigrants who chose to cross legally faced numerous difficulties, including a hostile attitude from the soldiers at the border. Crossing the border took a few days. When emigrants arrived at the train station, the police divided them into groups for disinfection and medical examination. After making sure that no emigrants remained on the train, a policeman handed them over to an inspection station official, who led them on foot to a camp far from the train station. Teplitzki described the scene: "men dragging their luggage, women carrying small children in their arms."[92] The heavy baggage usually remained in the train station; in many cases, it disappeared and the emigrants could not recover it. Teplitzki wrote about the inspection station:

> It is separated from the outside world. At the gate of the inspection station, which is always closed, stands a policeman. After passing through the gate, one enters a long, narrow corridor between very high fences; only then does one arrive at the station yard. The inspection station building is small, old, and made of planks. It consists of three equal parts, with waiting rooms for the emigrants in the two outer parts: one of them for new emigrants who have not undergone the medical examination, and the other for those who have undergone the medical examination and have been found healthy. Emigrants who are found to be ill are sent back or taken to a detention camp in the same yard. The inner part of the building is also divided into three sections: at the two ends are bathrooms for men and women, and in the middle section there is a device for disinfecting luggage. . . . The waiting rooms contain long benches and tables, and the walls are full of advertisements for German shipping companies and excerpts from the emigration regulations.[93]

The inspection station staff comprised seven people: a physician, four washing inspectors (two men in charge of the men's washing and two women in charge of the women's washing), a person in charge of disinfecting the emigrants and their belongings, and a guard. In 1905 the washing and disinfection were eliminated, and the station became mainly a place to undergo a medical exam and to purchase tickets for the ship. Medical exams were conducted in Wirballen every afternoon at three o'clock. The purpose was not to safeguard the emigrants' health and well-being, but to identify illnesses that would cause them to be rejected at Ellis Island and thus sent back to Europe at the shipping company's expense. Usually the physician looked for trachoma and favus (a skin disease).[94] Emigrants who stayed longer in Eydtkuhnen had to have a medical exam every day. The exam was usually quick; only seldom were emigrants barred from crossing the border and sent back (a stricter medical exam was carried out in the port prior to boarding the ship). According to Teplitzki, the main reason for rejection was trachoma. Each emigrant was charged 2.25 marks (1 ruble) for the exam.

From the moment the exam was over, the emigrants were not allowed to leave the inspection station. Conditions there were dreadful. "The border station is a cramped place even when there are few emigrants; all the more so in times of pressure," another information bureau representative wrote in *Der yidisher emigrant.* "Most of the emigrants in the station wait a whole day with their luggage, while no one pays attention to them. About 150, or sometimes 200, people are concentrated in two small rooms. It is so crowded and dense that there is not even room to sit down."[95] As Teplitzki described it, "The emigrants' quarters in Eydtkuhnen are unsatisfactory. The apartments are cramped and dirty. A small room has seven or eight beds. When there are many emigrants, they have to sleep two or three to a bed or they can choose to use wooden crates as beds. Linens are clearly visible, but the emigrants are not allowed to use them."[96] The other representative wrote, "Sometimes emigrants had to stay in the border station for about a week, and then food became a problem. Although there was a small shop in the camp that sold hot food, due to their great poverty and the requirements of kashrut many made do with herring and potatoes that they had brought from home or bought on the way."[97]

But the biggest problem at the border stations was the incessant pressure from shipping company agents who tried to sell the emigrants tickets for excessively high prices. Those who already had tickets were urged to upgrade them or exchange them for tickets with a better, faster shipping company. Many emigrants overpaid for their passage, and some of those who paid agents never received their tickets. "It must be stated clearly," the information bureau representative wrote. "The German shipping companies actually own the border stations."[98]

The emigrants who suffered the most from the pressure of the agents were those who held tickets of non-German shipping companies. In 1904, the German interior minister issued an order barring migrants from entering Germany and passing through the country on their way to the port unless they had tickets from a German shipping company.[99] For people from the northern part of the Pale of Settlement who wanted to travel with non-German shipping companies, this was a real problem that lengthened the trip and increased its cost. They had to travel south by train, cross the Russian–Austro-Hungarian border, and take a train from there to the Netherlands or Belgium. The order, which followed the surge in migration at the start of the twentieth century, was in fact the renewal of a similar order issued in the early 1880s. Thus the German shipping companies—Hamburg-America and Nord-Deutscher Lloyd—forced the emigrants to buy tickets from them.[100] Alexander Harkavy, a representative of the Hebrew Immigrant Aid Society (HIAS) who toured European ports and checked on the emigrants' hardships there, wrote in his diary that emigrants in Rotterdam were complaining about their long trip to the port because Germany had prevented them from entering its territory. "They must in consequence make a long route," Harkavy wrote. "They have to go by way of Austria to Basel, Switzerland; from there to Antwerp and then to Rotterdam. . . . For this reason, only the 'prepaid' arrive at this port."[101]

The articles written about hardships at the border stations led to visits by German government officials from Berlin. But these were not frequent enough. During the inspections the emigrants were treated humanely, but afterward the situation reverted to what it had been before. It should be noted, however, that the non-Jewish emigrants were treated no differently. The border stations in the early twentieth century were crowded with emigrants of all backgrounds. According to information bureau data, more than ten thousand people might pass through the Wirballen-Eydtkuhnen border station in a month. Because most of these people, Jews and non-Jews alike, were poor, they did not elicit sympathy. The individual disappeared in this mass examination and classification process. Consequently, many emigrants were hurt by the inflexibility and arbitrariness of the clerks and soldiers.

In her memoirs, Mary Antin describes the trauma of the Wirballen border station, even though her mother had a passport and they had not slipped across the border in the darkness:

> On a gray wet morning in early April we set out for the frontier. . . . The passport was supposed to pass us over the frontier without any trouble. . . . At Versbolovo, the last station on the Russian side, we met the first of our troubles. A German physician and several gendarmes boarded the train and put us through a searching examination as to our health, destination, and financial resources. As a result of the inquisition we were informed that we would not be allowed to cross the frontier unless we exchanged our third-class steamer ticket for second-class, which would require two hundred rubles more than we possessed. Our passport was taken from us, and we were to be turned back on our journey.[102]

From the moment the passport was taken, the family was seized with dread, and the continuation of their journey was in doubt. At first, Mary's mother begged the soldiers to allow her to cross the border. Unable to convince them, she began to argue with them, and then to shout at them. Finally she burst into tears over their hard hearts. It seemed as though all the family's efforts would be in vain. Antin writes, "We were homeless, houseless, and friendless in a strange place. We had hardly money enough to last us through the voyage for which we had hoped and waited for three long years."[103] Eventually they returned to the Russian side of the border, where a kind person helped them overcome the obstacles and cross the border toward the port of Hamburg.

Thus a valid passport was no guarantee of an easy, safe passage. The crowding, the waiting, the medical examinations, the disinfection (until 1905), and the shipping agents turned the border stations into pressure cookers in which the emigrants were vulnerable to coercion by the shipping companies and the soldiers at the borders. This situation led a group of thirty-four Jewish emigrants at the Illowo station on the Polish border to write an open letter to Albert Ballin, a German-Jewish shipping tycoon who was the director general of the Hamburg-America Line (letter 3).

As emigration to the American continent surged, the shipping companies discovered the economic profit inherent in transporting human cargo—thousands of people who wanted to leave Europe for the New World. Whereas older vessels could hold only a few score emigrants, their cargo ships were modified to take in hundreds of passengers. Ballin instigated this process. He dismantled partitions between passenger cabins and created large dormitories (steerage) on both the upper and lower decks to accommodate hundreds of emigrants. By making maximum use of the ship's space to accommodate passengers, Hamburg-America was able to lower the ticket price significantly.[104] Ballin came up with the slogan *Mein Feld ist die Welt* ("The world is my playground"). He began by competing for the emigrants' money, and this competition further reduced ticket costs and led to the introduction of new, direct routes to the main ports on the other side of the Atlantic Ocean. The number of emigrants increased from year to year. The official records of the Hamburg-America Line indicate that in 1897 the company transported about 73,000 emigrants. Two years later its ships carried more than 211,000 emigrants, and in 1906, 432,000 people used the company's services.[105] The money that flowed into Germany made Ballin a highly influential person and led to his close friendship with the kaiser. He controlled a fleet of ten steamships that reached every corner of the world and was a prominent figure during the period of the great migration.

Letter 3 was written by emigrants who wanted to cross the Polish-German border at Illowo. Their letter depicts the difficulty of crossing the border and the suffering that they were experiencing at one of the inspection stations for which Ballin was responsible. The writers addressed six caustic, rhetorical questions to the German-Jewish shipping tycoon:

> In light of the role that you play in the German port, we are addressing the following questions to you, Mr. Ballin:
>
> 1. Do you know, Mr. Ballin, how the Jewish emigrants in the holding camps are being abused and harassed?
> 2. Do you know that the German shipping companies support

the holding camps along with their agents in Russia both morally and financially and that they are responsible for all the crimes and acts of shame that this band of thieves and robbers has committed?

3. Do you know, Mr. Ballin, that the holding camps [and] a wide network of agents in Russia support the trafficking of emigrants over the border with all the associated dangers to their lives?[106] They compel them and do everything within their power to get this defenseless mass of illegal emigrants over the border in order to get at them to blackmail and fleece them while they are in this condition, without rights, under the threat of being handed over to the Russian border patrol.
4. Do you know, Mr. Ballin, that this year at the holding camp Illowo there were two suicides: Mr. Vaznyansky advised a desperate Jewish man to hang himself and the man did hang himself in the synagogue of the holding camp; out of desperation another Jewish man attacked the officials with a knife, wounded several, was captured and brought to a [military] prison where he hanged himself?
5. Do you know, Mr. Ballin, that Jewish men, women, and children who were waiting to go to France were held in the holding camp for a long time living in filth until the children got lice, scabies, and scurvy?
6. Have you ever, Mr. Ballin, seen a holding camp? Do you know what one looks like? Don't they call Castle Garden in New York "the island of tears"? So must one call your holding camps "the islands of the devil." No other name is right for this place. As was Dreyfus on Devil's Island, immigrants are tormented there, women abused, and people hear only disparaging insults and are very often slapped around.[107]

The emigrants' letter to Ballin is interesting not only because it describes the suffering at the inspection stations but also because of their expectation that, as a Jew, he would come to their aid. The emigrants seem to have been well aware of the circumstances that led to the establishment of the inspection stations, and they knew who headed and supported them. Their direct petition to Ballin and their appeal to his Jewish origins show not only their naiveté but also their despair and suffering due to the difficulties they faced at the inspection station. In their letter to Ballin, they wrote, "Other people are treated no better than the Jews, but their governments can stick up for them. We Jews are an orphaned people. Who will stick up for us? But you, Mr. Ballin, even though a Jew, must answer for the troubles of a Jewish immigrant at the holding camp."[108] The letter was signed by thirty-four emigrants. Among them were Moyshe Leyzerovitsh, who had been held up for fifteen days at the inspection station, together with his eight children, and was being threatened by the station workers with being sent back to Russia; Motl Lemelzohn, who had missed the ship to Argentina at the port of Bremen due to unnecessary delays at the inspection station and had no money left; and Ezriel Shirer, who said he had been maltreated for eleven weeks at the inspection station.

It is highly doubtful that Ballin received the letter and replied to the emigrants' charges. The inspection station was primarily a business venture of the shipping company, whose chief aim was to take as many emigrants as possible overseas at maximum speed. The emigrants who needed the company's services paid the price of this aim.

Illegal Emigration

The second—and more frequently chosen—option available to emigrants was to sneak across the border with the help of local smugglers. Those who chose to cross the border secretly and illegally faced severe difficulties and even danger.

Most of the Jewish emigrants crossed the border illegally because they could not obtain the documents required to do it legally. In 1908, for example, 14,000–16,000 Jews crossed at Wirballen—half of them illegally.[109] The ICA information bureau's data on total Jewish emigration until the outbreak of World War I indicate that more than 80 percent of the emigrants crossed the border under cover of darkness.[110]

Crossing the border with the help of smugglers was hazardous and therefore usually done at night. Often emigrants lost their way or lost their luggage while crossing a river. Sometimes they were caught by border patrols, or the local guides disappeared and left them helpless and bewildered. The large number of emigrants in the border towns attracted swindlers who lay in wait for them as they got off the trains. One of the busiest border towns was Sosnowice, where "the most dishonest and dangerous agents" could be found.[111] One of the most professional and dangerous of these was Fischel, who was described as "a master of his craft." Posing as a rabbi, Fischel would join a group of emigrants shortly before they reached the border town. During the journey he would make friends with the emigrants and extract money from them by promising to help them at the border station. But as soon as they arrived in town, Fischel would disappear with their money.[112]

Crossing the border in the dark was the most sensitive and most dangerous stage for the emigrants. Partway across, when they no longer knew exactly where they were, the smuggler would demand extra money for his services, in addition to the amount he had been paid before they set out. The emigrants, afraid of being abandoned in the middle of the forest or caught by the soldiers patrolling the border, had no choice but to pay up so that they could reach their destination:

> When a Jew manages to reach the border village, the agent's cronies come and take more money from him for various services. The emigrant pays against his will, because he is trapped and is anxious about the money he has already spent. Then comes the "border-crossing" process. After midnight drunken farmers, in whose company none of the emigrants would have dared to be even in the streets of a bustling city, come and take the terrified wretches "under their protection," and they go with them to what seems to them a horrible place. They are afraid of what is ahead of them and what is behind them. They are afraid of the escorts and afraid of the border guards. And the drunkards take advantage of the emigrants' mood to abuse them and suck their blood and the rest of their money. Some have everything taken from them and manage to reach the desired "shore" empty-handed; others remain on their original side of the border with their money.[113]

As stated earlier, one of the aims of the ICA information bureau was to prevent emigrants from crossing the border in the company of criminals and smugglers. To warn them of the dangers, the ICA published many stories in *Der yidisher emigrant* about emigrants who had been cheated while sneaking across the border. The case of Liebe Kirzner, a mother of five who wanted to join her husband in America, is one of many examples that demonstrate the dangers awaiting emigrants on their way to a new land.

Like many other women in czarist Russia, Mrs. Kirzner was unable to get a passport to leave Russia legally, so she had to pay 46 rubles to a Jewish smuggler to take her and her five children across the border. The smuggler took them to join a group of emigrants, and they began to cross the border after dark. Unfortunately, they were discovered by a border patrol; in the confusion several shots were fired and one of the emigrants lost her life.[114] Although Mrs. Kirzner and her children came out of the encounter safely, it left a traumatic impression on her and her children and made her question whether she could safely bring her children to their father, who was waiting for them in America.

Another case ended in the death of a Jewish woman attempting to emigrate. A group of emigrants reached the border town of Nowosielitzy and wanted to cross the border. In the group was nineteen-year-old A. Warshavsky from the town of Stepanski in the Podolia district, on her way to join her fiancé in America. In Nowosielitzy the group met three Jewish smugglers. Alik and Fischel were responsible for bringing the group to the meeting point on the Russian-Austrian border, and Moshe Stein was supposed to pick them up and take them to a nearby Austrian village. The time for crossing the border was set for midnight. The group set out, but the smugglers said that the emigrants were making too much noise and decided to turn back and try again the following night. For the next four nights the emigrants kept returning to their starting point, leaving their baggage in the forest as they fled patrols. After a fifth unsuccessful attempt at crossing the border, they asked the smugglers to give them their money back. After a great deal of argument, the emigrants were given 9 of the 17.50 rubles they had paid the smugglers; their belongings remained in the forest. The group now sought other smugglers to take them across, and in the nearby border town of Husiatyn they met the smugglers Anshel Winogradski, Valka Kushnir, and Valka Steinberg. This time they made it across with the help of local farmers from the village of Raschkow who were familiar with the crossing points. The main difficulty in crossing the border was the river:

> Here, near the village of Raschkow, near the Dniester River behind the forest, the farmers and emigrants began to cross the river in small fishing boats called *doshgobkes.* First they took the four young men across, and then they started taking the women. A half-drunken farmer and the women—A. Warshavsky, Frieda Zelniker, and R. C., a fifty-four-year-old woman from Mogilev-Podolsk—sat in the small boat. When they reached the middle of the river, the wind began to blow. The drunken farmer was unable to balance the boat on the waves and it overturned.[115]

Only R. C. of Mogilev-Podolsk managed to reach the shore in the boat; the others fell out into the water. In the morning, Warshavsky's body was found—her head had apparently struck something when the boat overturned and she had drowned.

The difficulties facing the emigrants are described in the letters published in this collection. Letter 35, written by Fieschel Kaufman in March 1914 and sent to Arthur Ruppin, describes the tragedy that overtook a group of emigrants trying to sneak across the border in a small town near Kamenetz-Podolsk. Kaufman wrote that, in his town, "Our shtetl is located close to the border of Austria! Where our poor emigrants cross the border—naturally not with government passes, but through the corrupt 'agents.'"[116] Day by day he saw Jewish smugglers robbing and exploiting the Jewish emigrants. He referred Ruppin to an article printed in the newspaper *Ha-tsefira* that describes what happened to twelve families that crossed the border and got into trouble: "The town of Zvenich stands on the borders of Russia and Austria, not far from Kamenetz-Podolosk. Through this town many migrants passed on their way abroad, and it is no wonder that a large group of agents collected there to transfer people across the border without passports. The lives of the migrants and their property were in the hands of these agents who sucked their blood, robbed them, and sometimes even killed them and took their money."[117] The leader of the group of smugglers was Valka Steinberg, who would take Russian revolutionaries from Austria to Russia and then betray them to the Russians. When it was found that he was a double agent, he was arrested. Jewish houses in the town were searched, and "members of a group for the protection of emigrants" were arrested without due process and were sent with him to Siberia. Kaufman asked Ruppin for help in solving this problem and took the opportunity to find out about immigration to Palestine and his chances of acclimatizing there.

In most cases, however, attempts to cross the border did not end with the deaths of Jewish migrants or exile to Siberia. But even if most of the emigrants managed to slip over the border and reach their destination country safely, the repeated attempts by men, women, and children to cross the border night after night indicate the difficulty and stress experienced by tens of thousands of Jews who left each year for overseas destinations.[118] Despite the difficulties and the danger, they overcame their fears and took the risk. This shows how strong the motivations for emigration were in the Pale of Settlement and in Poland: hundreds of thousands of Jews were undaunted in carrying out their decision to emigrate.

After crossing the border, the emigrants reached the exit ports. The delay until they boarded the ships could be nerve-wracking. They were forced to undergo medical examinations that would determine whether they would be permitted to sail. For those who had crossed the border legally, this was the second medical exam and a much stricter one than they had experienced at the inspection station. In 1897 the U.S. immigration authorities had ruled that trachoma (an eye disease) was contagious and a menace to society, and since that time sick immigrants had been sent back to the port of exit at the expense of the shipping company that had brought them. Since this resulted in major losses for the shipping companies, it was decided that strict medical exams would be conducted before passengers boarded the ship. Emigrants found to be ill were not permitted to sail, and they remained in the port until they recovered. Needless to say, those who were told they could not sail were devastated. After having sold all their property, saved ruble by ruble to finance the transatlantic voyage, crossed the border, and coped successfully with the agents, they felt that their whole world was in ruins and that they were powerless.

Letter 1 gives a stark, unvarnished description of the helplessness experienced by Alter Perling when he was told at the port of Bremen that he had trachoma and could not board the ship. This is an unusual letter from the period of the great migration that lets us feel intimately the difficulties that emigrants faced before reaching their destination. As a last-ditch attempt to solve his problem, Alter Perling wrote to Israel Zangwill, the president of the ITO, describing his troubles. His letter begins,

> The writer of this letter is a "Jewish emigrant," that is, a homeless wanderer, a true wandering Jew. For a year I have been far from my home—the Jewish ghetto in Russia—and have been roaming through Germany. I have been thrown out of Berlin and Köenigsburg many times, and finally, with great difficulty, I obtained a ship ticket from one of my cousins in New York, but in Bremen I was stopped with a mild case of trachoma. In short, I had to stay in Bremen to have my eyes treated, and now they are healed and I should be able to go to America, but the doctor told me that he could not guarantee that I won't be sent back because in America they are very strict right now.[119]

Even after Perling's eyes had healed, the shipping company doctor refused to let him go to America. The scars left in his eyes after the illness lessened his chances of passing the medical exam on Ellis Island, and Nord-Deutscher Lloyd did not want to take the risk because the company would then have to pay the cost of bringing him back to Germany. Being prevented from sailing was a real tragedy for the migrants. It meant a life of uncertainty, because, unlike members of other ethnic groups, the Jews had nowhere to return to: as soon as they decided to leave their place of birth, they became—as Perling says—homeless. But not only "unqualified migrants" were left homeless; hundreds of thousands of Jews on their way westward found themselves unable to say where they belonged. The Jewish travelers were in a state of limbo—no longer part of Lithuania, Poland, or Galicia, but not yet part of the United States, Canada, South Africa, or Argentina. This sense of not knowing who one is and where one belongs is clearly evident in Perling's letter. He wrote to Zangwill,

> I can never go back to Russia and it is impossible for me to remain in Germany. Then the only option left for me would be to jump off a bridge. I myself am a healthy, young man of twenty-one—robust, full of courage and energy. I'm missing only one thing: "a home," a country, a place on this great planet where I can focus my strengths on making a living for myself. I'm not seeking any fortunes, I'm not chasing after luxuries—only what the patriarch Jacob prayed for: "bread to eat and clothes to wear."[120]

The young man's modest request—"bread to eat and clothes to wear"—sums up the story of Jewish migration at the turn of the century. The quest for sufficient food and tranquility were the main factors behind Jewish migration and behind the quiet revolution that took place among the Jewish people in those years.

A Family in Crisis

One of the outstanding features of Jewish migration was its family character. Unlike men from other ethnic groups, who usually emigrated alone and planned to return eventually to their native land, Jews brought their entire families overseas with the intention of never returning to Eastern Europe. The participation of women and children made the story of Jewish migration complicated and difficult to accomplish. It seems that the average Jewish family could not afford to emigrate together. For this reason, the husband usually emigrated alone, and only after having saved up enough money did he bring his family over.

The cost of migration for a single person was about 179 rubles until 1908, and about 232 rubles thereafter. Beginning in that year, immigrants entering the United States had to prove to the immigration officials on Ellis Island that they had at least 100 rubles ($50), and not 50 rubles ($25) as before. Since Jewish migration was a family affair, the cost of the whole journey was very expensive. Often the expenses of the journey were doubled. In many cases, the wife had to take out a passport for herself, and if she was unable to do so, she paid smugglers only a little less than the cost of a passport to take her across the border. Ship tickets for children up to the age of twelve were half price. If a woman and children told the U.S. immigration officials that they were joining their husband/father, they were exempt from showing the minimum amount of money to enter the country.

Thus, until 1908, the cost of migration to the United States for a family of ten (parents and eight children, four over the age of twelve and four under twelve years of age) was approximately 600 rubles for the ship tickets, 15 rubles for a passport or for being smuggled across the border, 256 rubles for the train fare in Europe (the price varied depending on the destination and distance traveled), and 10 rubles for lodging and food. All together, the cost of the journey for the family was approximately 871 rubles ($435).

Table 2. Average Cost of Emigration from the Pale of Settlement to the United States for a Single Emigrant

Item	**Cost (rubles)**
Passport or smuggler	12–15
Medical exam	1
Train fare to border	15 (adult), 7.5 (child)
Train fare from border to port	17 (adult), 8.5 (child)
Passage on the ship	75 (adult), 37.5 (child)
Food	4
Accommodations in the exit port	5
Money to show U.S. authorities	100/($50)
Total	**179–232**

Sources: Since most emigrants went to the United States, the figures in the table are for emigration to that country. On the fare for the ship from Hamburg to New York, see Der yidisher emigrant, April 14, 1908, 30. Passage on a ship to Boston cost 75 rubles; to Philadelphia and Baltimore, 79 rubles; to Galveston, 110 rubles; to Canada, 70 rubles; to Buenos Aires, 81 rubles; to Australia, 190 rubles; to South Africa, 150 rubles; and to Palestine, only 12.5 rubles (ibid., 30). On train fares in the Pale of Settlement, see Korrespondenzblatt des Centralbureaus für jüdische Auswanderungsangelegenheiten, September 1909, 9. Since the train fare depended on the distance traveled, an average price is shown here. On the train fare from the border stations to the port, see Central Zionist Archives, A36, file 95b. On the cost of the medical exam, see J. Teplitzki, "Reisebericht," January 1907, CAHJP, ICA/34c, 6. See also Alexander Harkavy, Etses far emigrantn velkhe forn keyn amerika (fareynigte shtatn) (Minsk, 1905), 16–17.

For an average Jewish family with an annual income of 500–600 rubles ($250–$300), this was a fortune. The difficulty of scraping together this much money was enormous; sometimes a family had to wait years until the husband/father managed to save up the full amount and bring over his dear ones.

In order to understand the real financial cost entailed by migration and the risk taken by Jewish and non-Jewish migrants alike, it is worth translating the value of a dollar in the early twentieth century into its value today. The fare for a direct voyage from Hamburg to New York on the Hamburg-America Line was $37 in 1908, which translates to $755 today.[121] The cost of migration for one person (according to table 2) was $107 in the early twentieth century; in today's terms this would be $2,200. The cost for the entire family, $435, is equivalent to $8,878 today. These figures strengthen the assertion that the poorest Jews could not afford to emigrate. The emigrants were those whose lives were indeed hard, and sometimes even unbearable, but who could at least afford the cost of the journey for the husband.

Being on two separate continents led to a breakdown of the family unit, as expressed very emotionally in letters 4, 5, 6, 13, 14, 19, 25, and 53. In these cases, after their husbands had left for the destination country, the wives remained alone in Eastern Europe and bore the sole responsibility of raising and feeding the children—at least until the money began to arrive from America. Historians who have studied the sociogender aspects of migration in general, and Jewish migration in particular, have focused on the difficulties of absorption and adjustment to the new country. Very little has been written about the family left behind in the country of origin, those waiting for a sign of life from the husband/father, for money, and especially for ship tickets. Because contact between emigrant men and their families tended to be sporadic, the information bureaus served as a link between them. The letters by women in the files of the information bureaus disclose an interesting but little-known aspect of Jewish migration.

Letter 6 illustrates the distress and uncertainty of a person left behind. It was sent to Sam Rosenberg from his wife, Libe, who had remained with her children in Eastern Europe. The letter describes their hardship during the protracted absence of the father of the family. In most cases, testimonies of this kind are not available because they were sent to private individuals rather than institutions or organizations. Rosenberg's wife's letters are in the possession of the American Jewish Historical Society, so it may be assumed that Sam Rosenberg never received them. The letters do not contain any dramatic descriptions of pogroms and persecution; they merely reflect the daily lives of Libe and her two sons, Shloyme-Velvele and Khayiml, trying to survive while their husband/father was in Montgomery, Alabama. The first letter indicates that Sam Rosenberg had sent his wife some money, but for some reason she could not get it until her father came to town. Her strong desire to know what was happening to him in America, the poignancy of the children's taking his picture to bed with them, and her need for money cry out from her letter:

> Dear and Loyal Husband Sam Rosenberg, first I owe you news of my health and our dear, lovely, clever, perfect children's health, and I pray to God that we'll always hear the same news of you. And second, I just wanted to tell you, dear husband, that I haven't yet picked up your dear letter from Montgomery, Alabama with the 50 rubles. The reason is because my father is not at home. . . . So, I'm writing you this letter so that you know, because I'm thinking that the money will be returned to you. I don't want you to get scared. It's only because my father is not at home. So just imagine, dear husband, how good it is for me now. Believe me, before I was destined to lay my eyes on the money, I was going out of my mind with anxiety because from one sum of money to the next it took two months, calculated to cover just what I need with two small children. . . . I beg you most urgently, my dear husband, that the minute you get this letter from me, you answer me right away and send me double the amount of money care of Shaye Kaytelgiser, for God's sake, be sure to send it to no other address than to Shaye Kaytelgiser. You shouldn't think anything of it that I'm writing to you from this address. I'm sure he is a fine person, my money is as good as your money and your money is as good as mine. He is a very fine person, a wealthy man and a Hasid. . . . Shloyme-Velvele sends you loving regards, and Khayiml sends you heartfelt regards. He has no peace without you—he has to hold your tender letters while eating and sleeping. I just bought him a hat for 50 kopeks and a pair of shoes for 5 gilden.[122]

The second letter indicates that Libe had received the money but was still suffering financially and emotionally because of her husband's absence. For example, she did not know whether to rent an apartment for the next year or wait for the ship tickets that her husband was supposed to send her. His absence and the need to take care of her two small children were a heavy burden, and she did not have enough money to live on. The second letter shows her strong desire to know about her husband's life in America in as much detail as possible. But her husband wrote very little—just "half a yellow page" as we learn from her letter:

> Dear and Loyal Husband Sam Rosenberg, at the beginning of my letter I bring you news of my health and our dear, lovely children's health: that we are all—thank God—completely well, and I pray to God that we'll always hear the same news of you. And second, you should know, dear husband, that I happily received your dear letter from Mongomre [Montgomery] with the 50 rubles, and I'm answering you the same day, and I can't read your letter. . . . I beg you to be patient and take the time to write me a real letter. You have nothing more to write than a half a yellow page, and you write me that when you receive a letter from me, you'll write me news. I think you should keep your word. You should have written news in your letter to me precisely because you wanted to receive a letter from me. Dear husband, you should write me whether you think you will send me the ship ticket before Passover, because I need to know if I should rent an apartment. Now, I'm staying in my father's apartment and the apartment goes for 60 rubles without firewood. That is very expensive for me since my father is just a melamed. I give half and he gives the other half. You should know this because I wrote you that the other Hebrew teachers betrayed my father, and no one wants to give him a license. In short, he's actually in Ljublin today trying very hard [to find work]. May you earn in a week what it has cost him so far. Believe me, dear husband, if I were with my father, I swear on my life that I would just live out my years with him and not go to America. But I see that God wills me to go to America. It wouldn't be so bad for me if I had a home. If you write me a real letter right now saying yes or no, I will rent an apartment here for a year in that one's building. And this year is now ending after Passover and I'll have to move out of the apartment eight days after Passover. . . . That's all the news I have to write. Stay healthy and strong, from me, your true wife, Libe Rosenberg. Shloyme-Velvele sends you loving regards, and Khayiml sends you heartfelt regards.[123]

We do not have Sam Rosenberg's letters to his wife, Libe; most probably they were not preserved. Clearly, however, they corresponded during his stay in Montgomery, Alabama. The husband seldom wrote, and when he did his letters were brief and uninformative, whereas his wife did not withhold any details. Yet despite the intercontinental distance, they managed to keep in touch and tell each other about their doings in their countries of origin and destination.

Not all women were fortunate enough to receive even a shred of information from their husbands. Letters 5, 20, 26, and 44 are from *agunot* (deserted wives) who were asking the information bureaus for help in tracing their husbands. These were not isolated instances or historical anecdotes about women left behind while their husbands enjoyed a modern life in the new land. It was a fairly widespread social phenomenon that resulted from the demography of Jewish migration.

In April 1909, Mina Malka Polyakov asked the daily *Der fraynd* to print the following notice:

> My husband deserted me and our six children eighteen months ago, and I am lonely, sick, and in trouble. . . . My husband is from Vitebsk, his name is Meta Polyakov, and he is a painter by trade. He went to America. Anyone who knows him or has seen him would be doing a great act of kindness by writing to me immediately. In the meantime, compassionate Jews, please help me in my time of need, for my children are dying of cold and starvation.[124]

Another notice printed in the Eastern European Jewish press reads, "Compassionate Jews, I call upon you for assistance in finding my husband, who deserted me and his three children five years ago without any means of support, and I do not know where to find him. His name is Moshe Aharon Chaimovitz, approximately twenty-nine to thirty years of age, medium build, with curly blond hair, and shortsighted, dark eyes. He is a cobbler, although I was recently told that he is [working as] a craftsman in a toy factory."[125] The stories of Mina Malka Polyakov and Mrs. Chaimovitz were by no means uncommon during the great migration from Eastern Europe. Many of the men who went overseas first to get settled, save money, and bring the rest of their family over instead severed all contact with their families when they arrived in the New World. Desertion of wives had been almost unknown in Eastern European Jewish society prior to the mass emigration. The only previous occurrences that we know of were in the late 1860s and early 1870s, following a severe famine in the northwestern region of the Pale of Settlement.[126] Husbands went off to search for new sources of income and ended up disappearing, cutting off all contact with their families.

The unprecedented mass migration of the early twentieth century resulted in a new upsurge in the incidence of desertions to levels never before encountered in Jewish society. The scattering of 2 million Jews to all corners of the earth put many women in an intolerable situation, as they received no news from their husbands for several years.[127] Although it is not known how many women were deserted by their husbands during the great migration, references in the contemporary press indicate that desertions were a frequent occurrence:

> That Jewish migration affects every walk of life is nothing new. Young and old, men and women, all . . . hope for a better life. It is no easy thing to come [to a new country] and build a new home there. Not everyone finds a bit of bread there, just as they didn't find it in their home countries. [This] movement of population has unleashed a new disease that was scarcely known previously: women whose husbands go to America or some other country, leaving behind several family members, and are not heard from anymore.[128]

As stated earlier, we have no definitive information about the number of women in Eastern Europe whose husbands deserted them. However, we do have data about their number in the United States in the early twentieth century. In the late nineteenth century, Jewish charities in U.S. cities began to assist poor Jewish immigrants who had settled in various parts of the country. At annual conferences, representatives of these organizations discussed the immigrants' problems and tried to come up with solutions and appropriate funding to implement solutions.

One of the subjects brought up for discussion was the problem of *agunot.* Based on the information presented at the conferences, the problem seems to have been fairly widespread. Naturally, the Jewish charities that addressed the issue most thoroughly were in New York. In 1910, at the annual conference in St. Louis, the director of the United Hebrews Charities of New York, Morris Waldman, painted the situation in bleak colors. In 1909, he said, he had received letters from 1,046 women whose husbands had deserted them.[129] Most of the letters were from women from Eastern Europe who had lost contact with their husbands and were asking for help in locating them. These women were all in New York; if we consider how many wives of emigrants were still in Eastern Europe or had moved to other cities and countries, we see that this was a fairly widespread occurrence directly related to mass migration.

The focus of the discussion in this study is the Jewish woman left behind in Eastern Europe and deserted by her migrant husband, not the Jewish woman who was deserted after having joined her husband in the destination country. A long time passed from the time a man set out on his journey until his family received the first correspondence from him. The search for work in the new country, the long hours of labor, the harsh conditions, and sometimes the husband's illiteracy and dependence on someone else to write for him all led to weak contact with his family.

Only after a prolonged period of time with absolutely no contact with her husband did the wife realize that she was in an impossible situation. Her temporary position as the family provider in her husband's absence became a permanent one. Unlike a widow, who could remarry and rebuild her life, the *aguna* was forced to continue living in poverty and, even worse, in uncertainty. She had two options. One was to ask rabbis or charitable organizations for help in locating her husband and obtaining a divorce from him. The other was to save penny by penny and travel to the destination country with her children and try to find her husband there. One letter to a Jewish charity in the United States was from a woman who had arrived in the United States in 1911 after having had no contact with her husband for seven years. In 1904 he had arrived in the United States, found work, and broken off contact with his family. After his wife arrived, the search for him began: he was finally found in Brooklyn. When asked why he had not stayed in touch with his family, he replied that he was still not financially prepared to receive them.[130] In another case, Louis Rosenblum, twenty-eight, went to the United States six weeks after getting married. At first he stayed in touch with his bride, but as time passed his letters became fewer and fewer, until he finally broke off contact completely. Ultimately his wife decided to move to New York and search for him there. When she did not find him, she appealed to the editor of the *Forward,* Abe Cahan, for help. His picture, side by side with those of other deserting husbands, was printed in the *Forward* under the heading "A galerye fun fershvondene mener."[131]

On November 4, 1908, Sore Sherman of the town of Andrashavka in the Volhynia district wrote to the IRO asking for help in locating her husband, who had been living in America for two years (letter 26): "Two years ago my husband went to America in order to earn his keep, [and] left me with a small child. The whole time he has sent me money to live on and good letters saying that he would soon bring me to New York. But now it has been 3 months since I have received any news of him, and I used to receive a letter from him every week. I am strongly convinced that he has had some kind of accident or misfortune, because his attitude towards me was extremely good."[132] Even if Yankev Sherman did not desert his family, and his letters and money were delayed for valid reasons, the letter shows the fear and dread felt by Jewish women in the Russian Empire. The lack of information, irregular mail service, and numerous rumors from emigrants who had returned from abroad or had sent letters home all completely undermined the regular routine of family life.

The letter from Mashe Zilazne of Sjedletz is a typical one from an *aguna* in Eastern Europe to the IRO, asking for help in searching for her husband (letter 20). The simple language in which she describes her problem is an indication of her status and abilities. It appears from the letter that she went to the local letter writer and described her bleak situation. He seems to have written exactly what he heard without emendation, including a few words in English (written in Yiddish orthography) and a lot of repetition. For this reason it may be assumed that the letter is a reliable, unvarnished expression of the poor woman's distress:

> I, wretched, poor Mashe Zilazne, come to beg your pardon many times over, you highly esteemed people who toil on the committee, forgive me my hardship which brings me to this, that I am forced to write to the gentlemen of the committee that they should be so kind as to have compassion and pity

> on me, a wretched woman with my two poor children. I beg you to hear me out, dear people and gentlemen who are on the committee, ever since my husband who goes by the name Moyshe Zilazne left me and my two poor children, one of whom is called Avrom, and the other son Ayzele, and it has already been nine months since he left me and my two poor children, and six months already that he has not sent us one letter. I don't have any way of feeding my children and I'm as miserable as can be. It is terrible for my poor children and me. And the poor children miss their dear father. And I mourn my young years that I should—God forbid—end up an *agune*. . . . My wretched children will always pray for you because I'm a miserable orphan with no parents who is forced [to ask for this] and for my weak, weak pen it is totally impossible to announce in the paper. And if I receive an answer from the committee and a letter from my dear husband, I will be forever grateful to the gentlemen who work so hard on the committee, certainly I am assured that the committee will definitely fulfill my requests. We have no bread to eat. I will end my writing now, from me, miserable woman Mashe Zilazne of Sjedletz.[133]

Several times Mashe Zilazne mentions her small, fatherless children, and four times she mentions being lonely in her letter. The numerous repetitions tell us something about the depth of emotion that this mother of two felt when writing the letter. It seems that her husband left for the United States when she was in her sixth month of pregnancy, since her children, the letter says, are six months old and her husband has been away for nine months. Mrs. Zilazne also mentions her children's names—Avrom and Ayzele—because her husband does not know their names and does not even know that she had twins. Mashe's biggest fears are of being an *aguna* at such a young age (based on the age of the children, she is probably in her twenties) and having to support two small children in the impossible conditions prevailing in czarist Russia in general and Poland in particular.

Miriam Leskes of the town of Vladimir in the Volhynia district was in a similar situation (letter 4). In late December 1908 she wrote to the IRO, asking its people to try to locate her husband in New York. According to her letter, her husband used to write to his parents in Rovno, but nothing had been heard from him for two years:

> Even though I don't know you, I would like to thank you for your kindness in informing me that you didn't know the address of my husband Khayim Kalikovitsh, whose whereabouts we wanted to find out. In my previous communication to you I wished you to do me the favor of finding out once and for all where he was. But since it seems that he used to write often to his parents in Rovne and now it's already been two years since his parents received the last letter, they actually think he might have died. Therefore I ask you to take pity on me and write to Santerdev where he was living two years ago. Perhaps it is written in some record book where all deaths are recorded, so that I can, through your good heart, be released [from my marriage], because I am a young woman in my twenties, and my husband was only with me for somewhat more than two months and he's already been gone for five years and my life is miserable now that I can't establish where he has disappeared to. . . . Please, I beg you, please save me. And if you answer me, please answer in Yiddish because we cannot read English. It was not easy for us to find someone who could read your response in English.[134]

The great fear of Mashe and Miriam was that they would become *agunot* early in life and would be forced to live in a state of uncertainty and under unbearable conditions in the Russian Empire, and in the case of Mashe Zilazne to raise two children as well.

Why did men desert their wives and children in Eastern Europe? Any attempt to answer this question raises methodological difficulties because it requires looking at the subject from the viewpoint of the deserting husband. Because not all of these husbands were located, and not all of those who were found wanted to give their reasons, our information is limited. Nevertheless, in the early twentieth century Jewish charitable organizations attempted to understand the problem in order to tackle it more effectively. Of 561 husbands who were located and questioned, one-third were found to have left their wives to live with another woman whom they had met in the United States or to live licentiously. One-third claimed incompatibility between them and their wives due to a difference of age or character. Most of the rest—mainly husbands who had deserted their wives after the latter were already in the destination country—said that unemployment had forced them to move to other cities in search of work and to break off contact with their families.

Letter 65 gives us the rare evidence of a husband who had deserted his wife and tells the story of his desertion from his point of view. At the beginning of 1921, an American lawyer from Los Angeles named Elmer E. Gardner sent a letter to the National Desertion Bureau (NDB) in Manhattan that contained a commitment by his client, Henry Camley, to support his wife if she agreed to divorce him for a one-time payment of 4,000 francs in accordance with her ketubah, and for an additional sum over a period of ten years for his eight-year-old daughter until she reached adulthood.

Camley had left Palestine in 1909 and migrated near the residence of his brother-in-law Rahamim Kamshin in Rochester, New York. He lived for five years in close proximity to his brother-in-law until he decided to break off contact with his family and to begin an independent life in a place where no one knew him and where it would be difficult to locate him. He changed his place of residence from the East Coast to the West Coast and arrived in Los Angeles on the eve of World War I. He opened a restaurant there and began a new life that was completely different from the one he had been given in Palestine. The estrangement from his family was absolute, and all attempts to trace him were in vain. The outbreak of World War I and the closure of the sea routes led to a cessation in the search for the missing husband. During those years, his wife, Rachel, suffered from deprivation, hunger, and illnesses while trying to maintain herself and her child in the nearly unbearable conditions in Jerusalem during wartime.

When the war ended, Camley's wife applied to the Joint Distribution Committee that was active in Palestine and transmitted all the details known to her in order to trace her husband's whereabouts and to let him know that she wanted to join him. Naturally, the first application made from Palestine was to the NDB.[135] The letter of the Joint Distribution Committee in Palestine was terse and requested that the NDB representative apply to

Rahamim Kamshin, who would certainly know one or two details about the fate of the missing husband. It became clear through the investigation that the husband had not only moved to the West Coast but also changed his name and identity. Henry Camley turned out to be in fact Haim Abushdid, who was living in Santa Monica, California. When Abushdid (or Camley, in his new identity) was told that his wife had located him and that she was interested in joining him together with his daughter, he chose to contact her through his lawyer, who was in charge of dealing with the case. He wrote,

> I wish to inform you that I have recently met a friend of mine who told me of his meeting with your brother-in-law Rahamim and that the latter asked him for details about me. My friend answered with the intention of provoking him that I was about to get married. Your brother-in-law threatened him that he was prepared in such a case to bring you to America and to prove to the world that I was a married man and also gave him our photograph as bride and groom which was taken eight years ago to show to my new wife. When I heard this from my friend and saw our picture, I burst out laughing, and such words went in one ear and out the other. I am sure that I cannot love you any more or bring you to America in order to live like a family. Since I do not love you, no one can force me here in America to live with you. . . . It is already eight years since we have been apart from each other and you have suffered far more than I have since I am a man and can easily manage anywhere. It is good that you are in another corner of the world because if you were here or your brother-in-law had brought you here, who knows what would happen to you.[136]

The letter sent by Abushdid to his wife shows that he had totally adopted the American way of life: his contact with his wife through a lawyer, his trust in American law that would protect him, and the importance of love in the decision to marry. Although the reply of his wife is not available, it may be assumed that this new world of ideas was strange and unknown to her. The alienation was total and unbridgeable.

In the case of *agunot* still in Eastern Europe, the third reason—the search for work in other cities—was not a valid one, because the man's family was far away and it made no difference if he was searching for work in New York or some other city. This was not the case when the whole family was already residing in New York. The reasons for deserting wives in Eastern Europe were often incompatibility or the desire to live with another woman in the new country.

Due to the increasing number of *agunot* in Eastern Europe and among the immigrants in the United States, Jewish charitable organizations, especially in the United States, began to assist these poor women. In 1911 the National Conference of Jewish Charities established a special department (the Desertion Bureau) to deal with the matter. A year later—as the numbers multiplied—the department became an independent organization called the National Desertion Bureau under Charles Zunser.[137] YIVO's card catalogue of *agunot* contains the names of many Jewish women in Russia whose husbands had deserted them. According to the information in this card catalogue, most of the husbands were located and explained their desertion by saying they had found another woman and had started a new family.[138]

The primary reason for desertion was the difference between the old world that the husband had left and the new one he had entered. The longer he remained in the new land without his family, the more deeply alienated he became from his family and the Eastern European world he had left behind. In most cases, the reason for marriage in Eastern Europe was not young love but force of circumstance and traditional society's disapproval of young women leading independent lives. For her book *The World of Our Mothers,* Sydney Weinberg interviewed forty-six women who had immigrated to the United States during the period of the great migration. One of them told the author that she had married a sick distant cousin due to constant pressure from her mother, who wanted to see her settled with a family and children.[139] In his memoirs, *A Dreamer's Journey,* Morris Cohen describes how his mother had met her husband: it was not a case of romance (hardly known in her circle) but the standard procedure in which a marriage broker brought the couple together. He explains how she found out about her upcoming nuptials: "She was in charge of a booth at an annual fair, selling some linens, when my father, his father and the marriage broker approached and pretended that they wanted to buy some of the things that she was selling. She realized what they were after and said to my father: 'What is the use of pretending? I know why you came. Do I please you?'"[140] But despite the forced introduction and their character differences, they lived together for sixty-seven years in mutual devotion and total loyalty: "The love that grows out of devotedly living together in common efforts proved at least in their case more enduring than romantic love that is often only temporary attraction."[141]

The mass emigration led to a real crisis in the structure of the Jewish family in Eastern Europe. The delicate relationship between man and woman was ruptured when the husband left. A more liberal society and encounters with women—both Jewish and non-Jewish—without the mediation of a marriage broker placed some men in the face of temptation that they could not resist.[142]

Alone in the United States, a man could build a new life, a life completely different from the one he had led in Eastern Europe. The old-fashioned woman he had met through his parents and a marriage broker was exchanged for another woman he met under less restricted circumstances. Meanwhile, the *aguna* remained in Eastern Europe waiting in vain for her husband or saved up money and followed him to the destination country to search for him there. YIVO's card catalogue of *agunot* contains records of many women who, after five or six years, went to the United States with their children and, with the support of Jewish and other organizations, began searching for their husbands.[143]

It is important to keep in mind that the vast majority of men who emigrated by themselves brought their families over and did not desert them. But their experience upon reunion was indicative of the alienation created by prolonged separation. Quite often the family members found their husband/father almost unrecognizable when they landed at the port: his external appearance, his fashionable clothes, his clean-shaven face, and sometimes a changed name accentuated the difference between them.[144] In the case of husbands who deserted their wives and children, the sense of alienation that was an inevitable aspect of the separation was accompanied by an abandonment of morality and responsibility for their families. A popular Yiddish song expresses the misery of the abandoned wives:

Oy, ongeshpart on elnboygn,
Zitst zich a froy, shept baynacht,
Taychn trern rinen fun ire oygn,
Zi zitst doch k'seyder un tracht.

Mayn man iz geforn glikn zuchn,
In columbuses land.
Hal'vey volt er mir chotsh a get geven shikn,
Ich zol nit zayn in aza bitern shtand.

Oy mentshn, mentshn, ir fort doch avek,
Ir fort mit shifn un mit a ban.
Fregt dortn vos er hot mir gelozt a viste agune,
Oyb ir zet ergets mayn man.[145]

Conclusion

Three events changed the nature of the Jewish people in modern times: the Holocaust, Jewish nationalism (including Zionism and Israeli independence), and the mass Jewish migration from Eastern Europe westward. The first two events have been the subjects of extensive, in-depth historiographical discussion and have been perceived—rightly so—as having created profound and far-reaching changes in the Jewish people. But Jewish migration has been pushed aside as a formative historical event. It is no exaggeration to say that the emigration of hundreds of thousands of Jews from Eastern Europe was a formative event on the same scale as the Holocaust and the establishment of the state of Israel. This is because the situation of the Jewish people at the end of the great migration was totally different in all respects—economic, political, social, and cultural—from its situation on the eve of the westward migration.

More than 2.5 million Jews left Eastern Europe for destination countries overseas and began a new, more secure life. The letters published in this book bring into sharper focus what every migration scholar knows. Behind the impressive numbers of Jewish migration hides the ordinary Eastern

European Jew who hesitated and vacillated, trying to decide whether to remain or to emigrate. Every emigrant had a name. The attempt to get to know the people embodied by the statistics and the quantitative data has uncovered personal stories—sometimes heartrending ones—of individuals and families that found themselves in the throes of a migration that changed the Jewish people immeasurably. Alter Perling, Mashe Zilazne, Moshe Leyzerovitsh, Dobe Khaykl, Miriam Leskes, Moyshe Zelnik, and Itzik Blum represent hundreds of thousands of others who did not leave behind written documents yet had similar experiences and coped with the same difficulties on their way to their new land.

The letters in this book are significant because they provide the opportunity to learn about the initial stage of the drama of Jewish migration from primary sources. Much has been written about the lives of immigrants in the destination countries and about their social integration, but very little has been written about what took place behind the scenes before the decision was made to emigrate and during the move to the new country. The letters from women who remained behind reveal the crisis that families underwent during the prolonged absence of the husband/father. Many men moved to the destination countries, overcame the difficulties described in this introduction, brought over their wives and children, and began to sink roots in the surrounding society. But many more, who were unable to gather the emotional and financial strength required for this venture, chose to remain. In retrospect, they made the worst decision that a European Jew could have made at that time.

Moreover, the letters from prospective emigrants to the information bureaus provide for an interesting combination of quantitative and qualitative research. The statistics regarding the tens of thousands of letters can give us a broad picture of Jewish migration, its demography, the migrants' occupations, and the role of the pogroms in the decision to emigrate. The letters enable us to understand Jewish migration "from below," and the analysis reinforces the conclusions drawn from the findings of the statistical and quantitative research. The micro (the letters) does not contradict the macro (the demographic characteristics of the migrants) but rather complements it. Nevertheless, despite the fact that the two perspectives complement each other, the sixty-six letters printed in this volume demonstrate that emigration from Eastern Europe was not a collective experience. It was a composite of personal decisions made by hundreds of thousands of individuals. Hence, in order to understand better the migration process, it should be examined in inductive ways that will result in deductive conclusions and interpretations.

For many of the migrants, the initial period of adjustment to the new country was difficult and fraught with crises. But within a short time most of them achieved the desired freedom, and their economic conditions and social standing improved exponentially. Thanks to the integration of the Jewish immigrants in the destination countries, their migration is a dramatic and fascinating success story, albeit one that is not perfect. The mass migration of Jews, as it turns out, was not sufficiently large. Six million Jews who had not left Europe were murdered in the Holocaust. Nevertheless, migration led the Jewish people onto a new path, and at its end the Jews found themselves stronger and with more standing and influence than ever before.

Notes

1. See, e.g., Jocelyn Cohen and Daniel Soyer, eds., *My Future Is in America: Autobiographies of Eastern European Jewish Immigrants* (New York, 2006). Their book presents the stories of nine immigrants who wrote their memoirs many years after arriving in the United States. Conversely, the letters published in the present collection were written in real time. A comparison of primary sources (the letters) and secondary sources (memoirs) can contribute not only to an understanding of Jewish migration in the early twentieth century but also to a discussion of the significance of memory as a historical source.
2. Irving Howe, *World of Our Fathers* (New York, 1977), 57.
3. Haim Avni, *Mi-bitul ha-inkvizitsya ve-ad "hok ha-shevut": Toledot ha-hagira ha-yehudit le-argentina* (Jerusalem, 1982), 106.
4. Philip Taylor, *The Distant Magnet: European Emigration to the U.S.A* (London, 1971), 27.
5. Samuel L. Baily, *Immigrants in the Land of Promise: Italians in Buenos Aires and New York City, 1870 to 1914* (Ithaca, N.Y., 1999), 35.
6. Dudley Baines, *Emigration from Europe, 1815–1930* (Cambridge, 1995), 26.
7. Ibid., 11, 12, 25.
8. Ibid., 9.
9. Ibid., 9, 13.
10. William I. Thomas and Florian Znaniecki, *The Polish Peasant in Europe and America* (repr., Urbana, Ill., 1984), 3.
11. David Fitzpatrick, *Oceans of Consolation: Personal Accounts of Irish Migration to Australia* (Ithaca, N.Y., 1994), 3.

12. See Withold Kula, Nina Assorodobraj-Kula, and Marcin Kula, *Writing Home: Immigrants in Brazil and the Unites States, 1890–1891* (New York, 1986).
13. Robert Rockaway, *Words of the Uprooted: Jewish Immigration in Early Twentieth-Century America* (New York, 1998).
14. Ibid., 3.
15. Liebman Hersch, "International Migration of the Jews," in *International Migrations*, ed. Imre Ferenczi and Walter Willcox (New York, 1931), 471–520.
16. Mark Wischnitzer, *To Dwell in Safety: The Story of Jewish Migration since 1800* (Philadelphia, 1948), 291–92.
17. Gur Alroey, *Immigrantim: ha-hagirah ha-Yehudit Le-Erets Yisrael be-reshit ha-me'ah ha-esrim* (Jerusalem, 2004), 113–33.
18. Wischnitzer, *To Dwell in Safety*, 293.
19. Samuel Joseph, *Jewish Immigration to the United States from 1881 to 1910* (New York, 1914), 87–94.
20. Simon Kuznets, "Immigration of Russian Jews to the United States: Background and Structure," *Perspectives in American History* 9 (1975): 42.
21. For many years historians have been debating the number of Jewish immigrants to the United States in 1870–80. The numbers range from 15,000 to 45,000. In an article titled "Di erste rusishe yidishe masn imigratsye un di amerikaner yidn," *YIVO bletter* 4–5 (December 1932): 312–29, Ezekiel Lifschitz states that 40,000 Jews arrived in the 1870s. This number is based on data presented in the *Evreiskaya Entsiklopedya*, published in St. Petersburg in 1907. The basic assumption of the editors of the encyclopedia—which Kuznets later showed to be erroneous—was that most of the emigrants from Russia and Poland were Jews. This error, adopted by Lifschitz, recurs in Moses Rischin, *The Promised City: New York's Jews, 1870–1914* (New York, 1962), 20, and in Salo Wittmayer Baron, *Steeled by Adversity: Essays and Addresses on American Jewish Life* (Philadelphia, 1971), 158. Baron estimates the number of Jewish immigrants at 45,000. Kuznets was the first to try to separate, based on the census, the Russian and Polish Jews from the non-Jews and to obtain a more realistic estimate.
22. Ira Glazier, ed., *Migration from the Russian Empire* (Baltimore, 1995–97, and Baltimore, 1995–98), vols. 1 and 2, v–xxi.
23. Hasia Diner, "Before the Promised City: Eastern European Jews in America before 1880," in *An Inventory of Promises*, ed. Jeffrey S. Gurock and Marc Lee Raphael (New York, 1995), 43–62. See also Jonathan Frankel, "The Crisis of 1881–82 as a Turning Point in Modern Jewish History," in *The Legacy of Jewish Migration: 1881 and Its Impact*, ed. David Berger (New York, 1983), 9–22.
24. Diner, "Before the Promised City," 44, 59, 61.
25. England should also be included on the list of destination countries, as approximately 120,000 Jews moved there, although this is merely an estimate. The historian Lloyd Gartner claims that it is not possible to isolate the Jews from the statistics on people classified as Russians or Polish Russians; nor can it be determined whether England was their preferred destination or merely a transit station on the way to North America, South America, South Africa, or Australia. Gartner calls this problem one of the great mysteries of the period of the great migration. See Lloyd Gartner, "Notes on the Statistics of Jewish Immigration to England," *Jewish Social Studies* 22, no. 1 (1960): 97–102.
26. Hersch, "International Migration of the Jews," 483.

27. Jonathan Sarna, "The Myth of No Return: Jewish Return Migration to Eastern Europe," *American Jewish History* 71 (1981): 256–68.
28. See Hersch, "International Migration of the Jews," 502.
29. See Eli Lederhendler, *Jewish Immigrants and American Capitalism, 1880–1920: From Caste to Class* (Cambridge, 2009), 16–17; see also 44–45. Lederhendler also looked at the memoir literature and found a disparity between occupations in Eastern Europe according to the memoirs and the occupation statistics in the United States.
30. See Gur Alroey, *ha-Mahpekha ha-Sheketah: ha-hagirah ha-Yehudit meha-Imperyah ha-Rusit, 1875–1925* (Jerusalem, 2008), 86–87.
31. See Gur Alroey, "Galveston and Palestine: Immigration and Ideology in the Early Twentieth Century," *American Jewish Archives Journal* 56, nos. 1–2 (2004): 138–40.
32. Gur Alroey, "The Jewish Emigration from Palestine in the Early Twentieth Century," *Journal of Modern Jewish Studies* 2, no. 2 (2003): 111–31.
33. The few studies that have dealt with this aspect are Zosa Szajkowski, "The Sufferings of Jewish Immigrants to America in Transit through Germany," *Jewish Social Studies* 39 (1977): 105–16; Pamela S. Nadell's pioneering study "The Journey to American by Steam: The Jews of Eastern Europe in Transition," *American Jewish History* 71 (1981): 269–84; Pamela S. Nadell, "En Route to the Promised Land," in *We Are Leaving Mother Russia,* ed. Kerry M. Olitzky (Cincinnati, 1990), 11–24; Pamela S. Nadell, "From Shtetl to Border: East European Jewish Emigrants and the 'Agents' System, 1868–1914," in *Studies in the American Jewish Experience,* vol. 2, ed. Jacob Rader Marcus and Abraham J. Peck (Cincinnati, 1984), 49–78.
34. Yanovsky Archives, Central Zionist Archives, Emigration, A156, file 26, 4.
35. Ibid., 6.
36. Samuel Yanovsky, *Divrei ha'arakha, zikhronot, ketavim nivharim* (Tel Aviv, 1947), 15.
37. Ibid., 14.
38. Ibid.
39. Ibid.
40. "Aberatung fun di murshim," *Der yidisher emigrant,* March 2, 1909, 13.
41. "Mitoch ha-tehum: rishmei masa," *Ha-zeman* 143 (July 16, 1907), 3.
42. Meir Dizengoff, "Me'et ha-va'ad ha-palistinai be-odessa," *Ha-tsofeh* 658 (March 20, 1905): 3.
43. The Hibbat Zion movement (or Hovevei Zion, the societies that made up Hibbat Zion) was founded in the Russian Empire in 1881. The ideological basis for the movement was expressed by Leon Pinsker in *Autoemancipation,* published in 1882. In 1890 the czarist administration gave its official imprimatur to the movement's activities throughout Russia, and the movement's central committee, known as the Odessa Committee, was founded. When Herzl came on the scene and the Zionist Organization was established in August 1897, the vast majority of Hovevei Zion societies and their activists joined the Zionist Organization. Nevertheless, the movement remained active, working in cooperation with the Zionist Organization's institutions on behalf of Jewish settlement in Palestine.
44. Sheinkin to Otto Warburg (1908?), Central Zionist Archives, A24, file 52.
45. Moshe Leib Lilienblum, "Derekh la-avor golim," in *Ketavim otobiografi'im,* vol. 3 (Jerusalem, 1970), 14.
46. M. Shilo, "Changing Attitudes in the Zionist Movement towards Immigration to Eretz Israel," *Cathedra* 46 (December 1987): 109–22.

47. Ibid., 111.
48. Alroey, *Immigrantim,* 75.
49. Menahem Sheinkin, lecture, January 5, 1913, Central Zionist Archives, A24, file 52.
50. On the Galveston plan, see Bernard Marinbach, *Galveston: Ellis Island of the West* (New York, 1983). See also Gary Dean Best, "Jacob H. Schiff's Galveston Movement: An Experiment in Immigration Deflection, 1907–1914," *American Jewish Archives Journal* 30, no. 1 (1978): 43–79.
51. Di vikhtigste tnaim un yedios der emigratsye durkh galveston, Central Zionist Archives, A36, file 95b, 1.
52. Israel Zangwill, *Land of Refuge* (London, 1907), 20.
53. "Ha-nedida ha-yehudit veha-temikha la-nodedim," *Hed ha-zeman* 169 (August 2, 1908): 1. See also Wischnitzer, *To Dwell in Safety,* 100–105.
54. "Ha-nedida ha-yehudit," 1.
55. Ibid.
56. On the attitude of the German Jewry to Eastern European Jews, see Steven Aschheim, *Brothers and Strangers: The East European Jew in German and German Jewish Consciousness* (Wisconsin, 1982); and Jack Wertheimer, *Unwelcome Strangers: East European Jews in Imperial Germany* (New York, 1987).
57. Baines, *Emigration from Europe,* 8.
58. Arcadius Kahan, *Essays in Jewish Social and Economic History* (Chicago, 1986), 118.
59. Many of their publications can be found in the National and University Library in Jerusalem.
60. Yanovsky Archives, Central Zionist Archives, Emigration, A156, file 26, 10.
61. Ibid., 13.
62. *Emigrantn un agentn: Nit keyn oysgetrakhte mayses* (St. Petersburg, 1912).
63. Ibid., 20.
64. S. Bloch, "Fun bremen kan argentina," *Der yidisher emigrant,* December 16, 1910, 6.
65. Ibid.
66. On this methodological problem, see Baines, *Emigration from Europe,* 9–10.
67. Letter to Arthur Ruppin, August 25, 1914, Central Zionist Archives, L2, file 138.
68. Letter to the IRO (1913), American Jewish Historical Society, I-91, IRO, box 122.
69. Letter to Arthur Ruppin, August 25, 1914, Central Zionist Archives, L2, file 138.
70. Letter to Arthur Ruppin, May 12, 1914, Central Zionist Archives, L2, file 138.
71. Letter to the IRO, July 6, [1907?], American Jewish Historical Society, I-91, IRO, box 122.
72. Letter to the IRO, January 19, 1905, American Jewish Historical Society, I-91, IRO, box 122.
73. Letter to Israel Zangwill, November 6, 1905, Central Zionist Archives, A36, file 53b.
74. Saul Stampfer, "The Geographic Background of East European Jewish Migration to the United States before World War I," in *Migration across Time and Nation,* ed. Ira Glazier and Luigi de Rosa (New York, 1985), 220–30.
75. The internal distribution within the Pale of Settlement is based on a database of about 6,000 people who wrote to the ICA information office and emigrated. See http://mjmd.haifa.ac.il.
76. See www.levyinstitute.org/publications/?docid=791. See also Nancy Green's study *The Pletzl of Paris: Jewish Immigrant Workers in the Belle Epoque* (New York, 1986). Green

emphasizes the economic reasons for Jewish immigration to France and notes that on the eve of World War I there was a demand for workers in France.

77. V. V. Obolensky, "Emigration from and Immigration into Russia," in *International Migrations,* vol. 2, ed. Walter F. Willcox and Imre Ferenczi (New York, 1931), 521–80.
78. Ben Zion Rubinstein, *Galitsye un ir bafelkerung* (Warsaw, 1923), 27–37.
79. See Gur Alroey, "Patterns of Jewish Migration from the Russian Empire in the Early Twentieth Century," *Jews in Russia and Eastern Europe* 2, no. 57 (2006): 24–51.
80. Isaac M. Rubinow, "Economic Condition of the Jews in Russia," *Bulletin of the Bureau of Labor* 72 (September 1907): 487–583 (reprinted as a book, New York, 1970, 500).
81. See Ezra Mendelsohn, *Class Struggle in the Pale: The Formative Years of the Jewish Workers' Movement in Tsarist Russia* (Cambridge, 1970), 1–26.
82. We do not know how many Jews lived in Zakharino at the beginning of the twentieth century. The nearest city was Mstislavl (in the province of Mogilev), which according to the 1897 census had 8,516 inhabitants, including 5,076 Jews (59.6 percent). We may assume that the number of Jews in Zakharino was much smaller (fewer than 1,000 inhabitants). See Jakob Segall, *Veroeffentlichung des Bureaus fuer Statistik der Juden* (Berlin, 1914), 62, 78.
83. A low-ranking officer (roughly equivalent to a sergeant).
84. David Koheleth to Arthur Ruppin, November 11, 1913, Central Zionist Archives, L2, file 133/3.
85. A review of 391 letters to the Palestine Office indicates that 60 percent of the writers were advised not to go to Palestine, 20 percent were advised to make their own decision as to whether to go, and 20 percent were encouraged to go. A correlation was found between the financial capital noted in the letter of inquiry and the answer given. The less money a potential emigrant had, the less likely that he would be advised to move to Palestine. For more information on this subject, see Alroey, *Immigrantim,* 60–77.
86. See Central Archives for the History of the Jewish People (CAHJP), file 34a. See also "Vi azoy bakumt men an oyslendishn pas?" *Der yidisher emigrant,* December 24, 1907, 9. The process described was that required in the northwestern portion of the Pale of Settlement, but the procedure in other regions was similar.
87. "Vi azoy bakumt men an oyslendishn pas?" 9.
88. Ibid., 10.
89. Jacob Lestschinsky, "Hashkafot kalkaliot," *Ha-olam,* January 12, 1912, 5. The ICA's data indicate that 75 percent of the emigrants crossed the border illegally without passports.
90. See Korrespondenzblatt des Centralbureaus für jüdische Auswanderungsangelegenheiten, Berlin, September 1909, Central Zionist Archives, A36, file 95b, 7. The border stations mentioned here were in Galicia while those in parentheses were in Russia. The names are written in German transliteration as they appear in the original.
91. Ibid. The border stations mentioned here were in Germany; those in parentheses were in Poland. See also Yanovsky Archives, Central Zionist Archives, n.d., 156, file 26, 22.
92. J. Teplitzki, "Reisebericht," January 1907, CAHJP, ICA/34c, 6. For more on Wirballen, see D. R., "Verbalen," *Der yidisher emigrant,* February 15, 1909, 10–11.
93. Teplitzki, "Reisebericht," 7.
94. Ibid., 9.

95. A. A., "Di daytshe kontrol stantsyes," *Der yidisher emigrant,* July 15, 1909, 3.
96. Teplitzki, "Reisebericht," 8.
97. A. A., "Di daytshe kontrol stantsyes," 3.
98. Ibid., 4.
99. Szajkowski, "Sufferings of Jewish Immigrants," 108. According to Yanovsky, emigrants with tickets from the Belgian shipping company Red Star Line were the only ones allowed to cross into Germany. See S. Y. Yanovsky and A. I. Kastelyansky, *Spravochnaya kniga po voprosam emigratsii* (St. Petersburg, 1913), 11–12.
100. Szajkowski, "Sufferings of Jewish Immigrants," 105.
101. Alexander Harkavy, "Diary of a Visit to Europe in the Interests of Jewish Emigration, 1906–1907," Harkavy Papers, American Jewish Historical Society, 2.
102. Mary Antin, *The Promised Land* (New York, 1912), 169–70.
103. Ibid.
104. Cecil Lamar, *Albert Ballin: Business and Politics in Imperial Germany, 1888–1918* (Princeton, N.J., 1967), 18.
105. Kurt Himer, *Die Hamburg-Amerika Linie im sechsten Jahrzehnt ihrer Entwicklung, 1897–1907* (Hamburg, 1907), 52.
106. Migrants who did not have the appropriate documents could not cross the border through the supervision stations. Many made use of the services of professional border smugglers who helped them to cross over the borders illegally.
107. Letter to Albert Ballin (n.d.), Central Zionist Archives, A36/3.
108. Ibid.
109. "Virbalen," *Der yidisher emigrant,* February 15, 1909, 11.
110. "Fun der preysikh-rusisher grenits," *Der yidisher emigrant,* January 28, 1909, 3.
111. Ibid.
112. Ibid.
113. "Halalei ha-emigratsya," *Ha-zeman* 144 (July 17, 1909): 2.
114. *Emigrantn un agentn,* 17.
115. Ibid., 15–16.
116. Letter to Arthur Ruppin, March 1, 1914, Central Zionist Archives, L2, file 133, 3.
117. "Le-toledot provokatsya ahat," *Ha-tsefira,* February 12, 1914, 2.
118. For further information on fears of crossing the border, see the Spievak file, YIVO Archives, RG 102, file 35. In the 1940s, YIVO, under the direction of Max Weinreich, put a notice in the Jewish press asking Jewish immigrants to answer two questions: Why did they leave Europe? What had they obtained in the United States? More than 350 autobiographies were sent to YIVO; some of them describe sneaking across the border. A few of these autobiographies have been published in a collection edited by Jocelyn Cohen and Daniel Soyer. See Cohen and Soyer, *My Future Is in America.*
119. Letter to Israel Zangwill, November 18, 1908, Central Zionist Archives, A36/97.
120. Ibid.
121. For the dollar exchange rates at the beginning of the twentieth century and today, see http://oregonstate.edu/cla/polisci/faculty-research/sahr/sahr.htm.
122. Letter to Sam Rosenberg (n.d.), American Jewish Historical Society, I-91, IRO, box 122.
123. Ibid.
124. Ben Eliyahu, "An erneste frage," *Der yidisher emigrant,* March 18, 1909, 2.

125. Ibid.
126. Mark Baker, "The Voice of the Deserted Jewish Woman, 1867–1870," *Jewish Social Studies* 2 (1995): 98–123.
127. Several studies have addressed the issue of women deserted by their husbands during the great migration. See, e.g., Ari Lloyd Fridkis, "Desertion in the American Jewish Immigrant Family: The Work of the National Desertion Bureau in Cooperation with the Industrial Removal Office," *American Jewish History* 71 (1981): 285–99. See also Aaron Rakeffet-Rothkoff, "Rabbi Yitshak Spektor of Kovno: Spokesman of Agunot," *Tradition* 29, no. 3 (1995): 5–20; and Reena Sigman Friedman, "Send My Husband Who Is in New York City: Husband Desertion in the American Jewish Immigrant Community," *Jewish Social Studies* 44, no. 1 (1982): 1–18.
128. Eliyahu, "An erneste frage," 1. See also "Agunot," *Der yidisher emigrant,* January 1, 1912, 13; *Der yidisher emigrant* (U.S.), May 1, 1912, 10.
129. National Conference of Jewish Charities, 1901, 56.
130. National Conference of Jewish Charities, 1912, 70.
131. Ibid., 64.
132. Sore (Sara) Sherman to the IRO, November 4, [1906?], American Jewish Historical Society, I-91, IRO, box 122.
133. Mashe Zilazne to the IRO, January 26, [1906?], American Jewish Historical Society, I-91, IRO, box 122.
134. Miriam Leskes to the IRO, n.d., American Jewish Historical Society, I-91, IRO, box 122.
135. On the application of Rachel Abushdid to the National Desertion Bureau, see YIVO Archives, RG 297.
136. Letter of Haim Abushdid to Rachel Abushdid, September 22, 1920, Central Zionist Archives, L3, file 162.
137. Fridkis, "Desertion in the American Jewish Immigrant Family," 291–92.
138. Card catalogue of the National Desertion Bureau, YIVO Archives, RG 297.
139. Sydney Stahl Weinberg, *The World of Our Mothers: The Lives of Jewish Immigrant Women* (Chapel Hill, N.C., 1988), xv–xvi, 23–40.
140. Morris Raphael Cohen, *A Dreamer's Journey* (Boston, 1949), 12.
141. Ibid.
142. Howe, *World of Our Fathers,* 180.
143. The names of women who arrived in the United States appear in the records of the NDB (YIVO Archives, RG 297). In order to protect their privacy, the archives do not allow their names to be mentioned.
144. Fridkis, "Desertion in the American Jewish Immigrant Family," 287.
145. *Oh, leaning on her elbow,*
A woman sits late into the night,
Rivers of tears flow from her eyes,
She sits there thinking, thinking.

My husband has gone to seek his fortune,
In Columbus's land.
Oh, if he had only granted me a divorce first,
I wouldn't be so miserable now.

Oh, people, people, you are leaving,
You are going on boats and on trains.
Ask him why he deserted me,
Should you meet my husband there.

Ruth Rubin, *Voices of a People: The Story of Yiddish Folksong* (Philadelphia, 1979), 343.

The Letters

Author's Comments

THE LETTERS WERE WRITTEN in Yiddish and Hebrew by Eastern European Jews who were considering migration. It is not known whether they made the decision to migrate to one of the countries that received migrants. Since a considerable number of the letters were written in a state of distress and emotional turmoil, the handwriting was not always legible. The deciphering of the letters took many long months, and there were instances (not many) in which it was not possible to make out certain words. In those cases, "[illegible]" has been inserted into the text. Also, throughout the text there are many endnotes that will help the reader better understand the letters. In addition, since in Eastern Europe in general and in the Russian Empire in particular there were many variations of a person's name, sometimes the letter writer spelled his or her own name differently within a single letter. The letters printed here retain the spellings of persons' names exactly as they were written in the original letters.

The translation of the letters was not an easy task. Over the past century, Yiddish and Hebrew have undergone many changes, and the spoken language today is different from what it was a hundred years ago. However, an attempt was made during the course of translation to maintain the style of writing of the Eastern European Jews. The translators, Yankl Salant, who translated the letters from Yiddish to English, and Deborah Stern, who translated the letters from Hebrew to English, showed solicitude for the text and a sensitivity toward the letter writers. I believe that the reader of the letters in English (in spite of translation) can feel the writers' distress and strong desire for any bit of information about the country of destination and generally perceive the spirit of the times.

The original letters are located in two main archives: the Central Zionist Archives in Jerusalem and the American Jewish Historical Society in New York. Sometimes the replies to the letters were preserved in the information bureaus. In those cases the answer would appear at the end of each letter. Most of the letters were sent from towns and cities in the Pale of Settlement and in Galicia, and their distribution closely reflects the dispersion of the Jewish population in Eastern Europe.

Letters 1–66

• 1 •

Central Zionist Archives, A36/97

Firma (Postcard)
F. Missler[1]/Bremen
Bahnhofstrasse 30
Bremen, November 18, 1908

Honorable President of the Jewish Territorial Organization[2]
Mr. I. Zangwill,[3]

The writer of this letter is a "Jewish emigrant," that is, a homeless wanderer,

---

1. Friedrich Missler was one of the big travel agents in Bremen who sent migrants from Germany to the United States, Canada, South America, and South Africa. He used to give his clients, together with the sailing ticket, a small bag with his name engraved on it and official notepaper of the company with its address on 30 Bahnhofstrasse in Bremen printed on it. Missler had good relations with the shipping company of North-Deutscher Lloyd. The letter by Alter Perling was written on Missler's official notepaper.
2. The ITO was founded in August 1905 after the Uganda proposal was taken off the agenda of the Zionist Organization at the Seventh Zionist Congress. The supporters of Herzl, headed by Israel Zangwill and Max Mandelstamm, resigned in protest from the Zionist Organization, and in a side room at the hotel in Basel they announced the founding of the ITO, which was intended "to procure a territory upon an autonomous basis for those Jews who cannot or will not remain in the lands in which they at present live."
3. Israel Zangwill (1864–1926), Anglo-Jewish writer and the president of the ITO. His best-known literary works (*Children of the Ghetto, Dreamers of the Ghetto*) are characterized by their documentation of the lives of Jews in the Jewish ghetto of London. But *The Melting Pot*, in contrast, describes the lives of the Jews who migrated to America. As the president of the ITO, Zangwill searched for a territory for the Jewish people. He conducted negotiations with Canada, Australia, and Britain, and according to him he turned every stone in his search for territory without success.

a true wandering Jew. For a year I have been far from my home—the Jewish ghetto in Russia—and have been roaming through Germany. I have been thrown out of Berlin and Koenigsburg many times, and finally, with great difficulty, I obtained a ship ticket from one of my cousins in New York, but in Bremen I was stopped with a mild case of trachoma.[4] In short, I had to stay in Bremen to have my eyes treated, and now they are healed and I should be able to go to America, but the doctor told me that he could not guarantee that I won't be sent back because in America they are very strict right now. Many of those that the European doctors had let through were sent back from New York and Baltimore—then the ship ticket is lost. And if I were to be sent back from America I would be devastated. I can never go back to Russia and it is impossible for me to remain in Germany. Then the only option left for me would be to jump off a bridge.

I myself am a healthy, young man of twenty-one—robust, full of courage and energy. I'm missing only one thing: "a home," a country, a place on this great planet where I can focus my strengths on making a living for myself. I'm not seeking any fortunes, I'm not chasing after luxuries—only what the patriarch Jacob prayed for: "bread to eat and clothes to wear."[5] We Jews have *borekh-hashem* 689,000 organizations which "provide for" Jewish emigrants. All of them beat the philanthropic drum: we must care for the Jewish emigrant. We must help the Jewish homeless. We must find a home for the Wandering Jew. Everyone is doing something, everyone is working, each one on his own part, within his own system . . . and the Jewish emigrant?

I have been here in Bremen for quite some time now. Thousands of Christian emigrants come through on their way to all parts of the world. Many were stopped with trachoma but they leave anyway: for Brazil, for Argentina, not including the thousands that are leaving for Brazil without a penny to their name—basically they leave without emigration

4. Trachoma is a contagious eye disease that can lead to blindness. Migrants who were found to be infected with the disease were not permitted to enter the United States. A considerable amount of literature was created on the subject of the medical examinations that described the migrants' fear of this examination and their dread that they would be forced to return to Europe.

5. Gen. 25:20.

offices . . . without relief organizations. But the unfortunate Jewish emigrant? He ends up bone-weary. He ends up deracinated. He suffers beyond measure and without an end until he loses hope and the will to live—we are worse off than any other people! The tragedy of our exile is boundless. It is not my intention to reproach our organizations. I am not a newspaper writer, and my articles have never been buried in an editor's inbox.

I turn now to the ITO so that I can be sent somewhere where I can live—and where I will be allowed to live. Send me to Galveston, Texas.[6] Send me to Brazil! I don't care if it's in the remotest place in the world, just get me a home!! In a word: help a miserable Jewish emigrant!!

My ship ticket was to be from Bremen to Baltimore and then New York. Four weeks ago I sent the ticket back to America and today I have just received the 120 MK that the ship ticket cost. Therefore I am requesting that the ITO send me to Galveston, Texas, for the 120 MK. My eyes are completely healed, not a trace of trachoma remains. And the Bremen ship doctors would let me through but I am afraid that America would send me back from Castle Garden. In Galveston I have no one who might take me in. I also have no money to show, I do not even have an address or a friend in Texas. I only request from the ITO that they escort me off the ship and procure work for me. It doesn't matter to me what kind of work, whether factory work or agricultural labor, just so I can earn enough to live on.

I am a healthy man who can—who wants to—work, as I have written before. But since there is a ship for Galveston that departs a week from Thursday, the 26th of November, I must have an answer by Wednesday the 25th of November. I believe that you will be able to give me a

6. The Galveston plan (1907–14) was the result of a meeting of interests between Israel Zangwill and Jacob Schiff. The aim of the plan was to divert Jewish migration from the crowded cities on the East Coast of the United States (New York, Philadelphia, Boston, Chicago, and Baltimore), where job demands were low, and to send the Jewish migrants to places where job demand was high and where it would be much easier to establish a livelihood. Galveston was chosen as the port of entry to the United States. The ITO was responsible for mobilizing the migrants in Eastern Europe and sending them to the port of Bremen. The Hilfsverein der deutschen Juden took care of them in Bremen, and Jacob Schiff arranged to disperse them in the western part of the United States. About 8,000 Jewish migrants participated in this plan.

1

Bremen den 18 November 1908

צום געעהרטען הערר פרעזידענט פון
דער יודישער טעריטאריאל ארגאניזאציאן"
הערר י. זאנגוויל.

29617

דער שרייבער פון דיזען בריף איז א יודישער עמיגראנט",
דאס הייסט א היימאטהלאזער וואנדערער און יאמערליכער [illegible].
פון וועלכער זייט זאגט איך בין פערטריבען פון מיין
היימאטה - דיזע יודישע געהעטא אין רוסלאנד" און איך וואנדערע
זיך ארום אין דייטשלאנד מען האט מיך שוין וויפיעל מאל
אויסגעוויזען פון בערלין, און פון קעניגסבערג, און מיט
צרות האבע איך בעקומען א שיפס קארטע פון אונזער [illegible]
אין [illegible] אבער אין ברעמען האט מען מיך פערהאלטען
און [illegible] טראכאמא, בקיצור; איך האב מיך געוואלט
לאזען קורירען מיינע אויגען אין ברעמען און
[illegible] פון מיינע אויגען אויסגעהאלט און איך

precise and correct answer within this amount of time. Therefore I ask that you answer me right away, I am counting on it. Because if not November 26, the next ship for Galveston does not set sail for another six weeks.

I end off with the good hope that the honorable Jewish Territorial Organization will direct all its resources to help an unfortunate Jewish emigrant, so that my voice is not "a voice that calls out in the desert."[7] In case this letter does not arrive on time, or your letter arrives after N. [November] 25, perhaps the local committee of the Hilfsverein der deutschen Juden can send me to Galveston. I ask that you write from London to the Galveston Immigration Bureau telling them to escort me off the boat there (I will also write them myself).

Respectfully,
Emigrant Alter Perling

P.S. There is another emigrant here who has been having his eyes treated for a while. The trachoma is cured, but he is left with painful aftereffects. In addition it is very difficult to get to the New York Baltimore harbor [*sic*]. He also wants to go to Galveston and has money for a ship ticket. So, he is hereby also requesting a reply saying that the ITO will send him to Galveston.

Perling A.

My address:
Alter Perling
Bremen
Auswanderhalle 5

7. Isa. 40:3.

•2•

Central Zionist Archives, A36/9

The letter from the emigrant Sheyne-Gadye Mendelson of the twenty-ninth Galveston[8] group to her brother in Kovno.[9]

Burlington, July 28, 1909

My dear, dear brother!

I can finally write you a letter and share everything with you. I did write you a postcard from Galveston. That was on Saturday. We arrived here Monday evening at nine o'clock. Someone was already waiting for us here and had already taken care of everything. We have free room and board for a week, which is naturally being paid for by the ITO. Next week we'll start working in a button factory, where we'll start making 4 or 5 dollars a week and we can work our way up until each of us can earn 10 dollars a week.[10] Burlington is a country [*sic*], that is, a small city that has about twenty-five thousand residents. The city is growing, has train connections with the biggest cities, and is 175 English miles from Chicago. The climate here is temperate, that is, not too hot and not too cold. It's not too expensive to live here. I hope we'll be able to work our way up. Other than that, we're healthy and cheerful. Now, my dear brother, I will write you about how we got here.

---

8. For Galveston plan, see footnote 6. As living conditions for Jewish immigrants on the East Coast deteriorated, Schiff reached the conclusion that the diversion of immigration to inland towns in the American West should take place in the immigrants' countries of origin, i.e., before they reached New York. On this point there was agreement between Zangwill, who was searching for land for Jewish settlement, and Schiff.
9. A town in the province of Kovno. According to the census of 1897, there were about 71,064 inhabitants, including 25,441 Jews (35.8 percent).
10. The rate of exchange between the dollar and the ruble at the beginning of the twentieth century was 1 dollar = 2 rubles. The migrants earned 5 dollars a week, which equaled 10 rubles. In real terms this was a significant economic improvement over their earnings in Russia.

We were in Bremen for a week until July 1. We had a very good time there. We didn't have to pay for room and board. Those who weren't going through the ITO naturally had to pay 75 kop. a day each! Shloyme went to an eye doctor in Bremen and found out he had a slight inflammation and should take a week to let it get better.[11] Naturally that's what we did, it cost 11 marks, but because of that he didn't have any problems with doctors. July 1 at 6 in the morning we rode out of Bremen to the Port of Bremen, a four-hour trip. There we boarded the great ship *Frankfurt* and at 11 in the morning we set sail.[12] Yes, my dear brother, leaving the shore was pretty tragic. We had no one to escort us, no one to wish us bon voyage. We sailed off completely alone. Then when we reached the open sea, I wished that everyone had been there to say good-bye, but unfortunately . . . The first day, the weather was very beautiful, but after only a few hours in the sea air, I started to feel bad. The rocking of the ship and the unfamiliar sea air caused dizziness and nausea. I started vomiting and I was beginning to feel better by evening. Then Shloyme started to repeat the same thing, but for him it passed quickly, only on the first day, whereas I was sick the entire week, mainly in the mornings. The ship was not among the best, there were 150 people in just one section. The food was not very good either, they served four times a day: 8 in the morning—coffee and a roll with something else, 12 noon—meat soup, herring, 3 in the afternoon—coffee or tea with biscuits, 6 o'clock dinner—dairy soup and something else along with it. Yes, they put effort into giving us food, but mostly it got thrown overboard. It was a good thing that we had money; for money you could get anything, for example, eggs, milk, sardines, and other such things. We spent a nice bit of money on the journey. Shloyme bought himself a 10-ruble clock in Bremen and then we had [80] dollars left. Saturday, July 3, we sailed out of the English Channel into the Atlantic Ocean, past the Isles of Scilly which

11. The American immigration authorities used to make migrants who had eye infections and contagious diseases go back to Europe, and the shipping companies were responsible for the cost of the return passage. Therefore the shipping companies conducted thorough eye examinations of the migrants before they boarded the ship. By doing so they reduced to a minimum the losses that the migrants might cause them.

12. The ship SS *Frankfurt* was owned by the Nord-Deutscher Lloyd shipping company. Its maiden voyage occurred in 1869; it weighed 7,431 tons and was 300 feet long and 39 feet high.

belong to England.[13] We had bad weather Monday evening and Tuesday. There was a storm. It didn't calm down until Wednesday morning and the lovely weather lasted until Saturday. Saturday and Sunday, another storm and Sunday evening a return to nice weather which lasted until Baltimore. Thursday [*sic*] morning, July 16 we arrived in Baltimore where we stayed for one day and sailed again on Saturday morning the 17th.[14] The entire journey to Galveston was very nice, but it got hotter and hotter by the day, so much so that we would walk around barefoot in our undergarments and sleep on the deck. It was impossible to stay in the cabin because of the heat. But aside from that, we had a good time on the ship. There were [330] emigrants, about 200 Jews, most of them going to Baltimore. To Galveston there were [43] of us. So we finally arrived on Saturday the 24th in Galveston. It's hard to imagine how much the ITO did for the emigrants. Picture this, as we disembarked from the ship, the representative of the local committee, Mr. Greenberg, was already there waiting for us and had taken care of everything for us.[15] The ITO emigrants don't have to pay the 4 dollar head tax for each person that enters America. They picked up our baggage and drove us in cars to the committee's center, a big, beautiful house with all the comforts, even bathrooms; we each got to take a bath. They gave us only the best food. The same day, they specified where each of us was going to go. No one settles in Galveston. They sent the heavy baggage ahead and gave us free train tickets to wherever each of us was going—Burlington for us. They also gave us food for the trip: eggs, sardines, bread, and other such things. We were on the train for thirty-two hours. The trip here from Galveston costs around 25 dollars per ticket per person. The baggage costs money as well. When we got here there was someone waiting for us in the train station who had set everything up for our first week. That also costs money and it was all paid for by the ITO. The only thing left to wish for is that the ITO would be able to influence the entire flow of Jewish emigration and systematically organize it. Then

13. I checked all names of English islands, and this was the only one similar. It could be that the writer heard "Scillys" (plural) and thought the name was the singular for one island: "Selias."

14. That particular Thursday in 1909 was actually July 15. She meant either Thursday, July 15, or Friday, July 16.

15. The reference is to Louis Greenberg, a member of the Jewish Immigrants Information Bureau office staff in Galveston.

we could hope to be able to concentrate rapidly in one place and live as a normal people, like all others. Dear brother, I now believe I've written you all the details. I will only be able to write about what life is like here after a few weeks when we are better acquainted with this place. In the meantime, we are resting up from the long trip, taking walks. Burlington is a very lovely city. There are not many Jewish families here—maybe all told, twenty families—but everyone is making a nice living. So, now I will end my letter. Heartfelt wishes and kisses from your sister Sheyne . . . Warm wishes to Bashele . . . warm greetings to Mr. Filman, who does so much for the emigrants . . .

Address: "Mister Simon Mendelson, [c/o] Lyeo Cohen. Burlington, Iowa, America."

·3·

Central Zionist Archives, A36/3

Open letter to Mr. Ballin[16]

In light of the role that you play in the German port, we are addressing the following questions to you, Mr. Ballin:

1. Do you know, Mr. Ballin, how the Jewish emigrants in the holding camps are being abused and harassed?[17]

---

16. Albert Ballin (1847–1918) was one of the most talented directors of the shipping company HAPAG (Hamburg Amerikanische Packetfahrt Actien Gesellschaft). After years of training in the business of his father, who was a travel agent in Hamburg, Ballin—who was a Jew by origin—was appointed as head of the travel department of HAPAG. In 1891 the company changed its name to the Hamburg Amerika Linie, and eight years later he was appointed as general director of the company. Under his management, HAPAG became the largest shipping company in the world. The outbreak of World War I and the closing of the shipping lanes led to the cessation of trans-Atlantic migration, and the shipping company faced a crisis. Ballin's nerves did not stand up to the strain, and on November 9, 1918, he died after taking an overdose of sleeping pills.
17. Following a cholera epidemic that broke out in Hamburg in 1892 and led to the death of about 8,600 people, it was decided to set up supervision stations along the German-

2. Do you know that the German shipping companies support the holding camps along with their agents in Russia both morally and financially and that they are responsible for all the crimes and acts of shame that this band of thieves and robbers has committed?
3. Do you know, Mr. Ballin, that the holding camps [and] a wide network of agents in Russia support the trafficking of emigrants over the border with all the associated dangers to their lives?[18] They compel them and do everything within their power to get this defenseless mass of illegal emigrants over the border in order to get at them to blackmail and fleece them while they are in this condition, without rights, under the threat of being handed over to the Russian border patrol.
4. Do you know, Mr. Ballin, that this year at the holding camp Illowo[19] there were two suicides: Mr. Vaznyansky advised a desperate Jewish man to hang himself and the man did hang himself in the synagogue of the holding camp; out of desperation another Jewish man attacked the officials with a knife, wounded several, was captured and brought to a [military] prison where he hanged himself?
5. Do you know, Mr. Ballin, that Jewish men, women, and children who were waiting to go to France were held in the holding camp for a long time living in filth until the children got lice, scabies, and scurvy?
6. Have you ever, Mr. Ballin, seen a holding camp? Do you know what one looks like? Don't they call Castle Garden in

---

Polish border. The supervision stations were set up in 1893 at the initiative of the German shipping companies (HAPAG and Nord-Deutscher Lloyd), which, by order of the authorities, conducted medical examinations of the migrants and prevented those with contagious diseases from entering Germany territory. At these supervision stations, the German shipping companies exerted great pressure on the migrants to purchase sailing tickets from them.

18. Migrants who did not have the appropriate documents could not cross the border through the supervision stations. Many made use of the services of professional border smugglers who helped them cross over the borders illegally.
19. A border station located about 100 kilometers northwest of Warsaw.

> New York "the island of tears"? So must one call your holding camps "the islands of the devil." No other name is right for this place. As was Dreyfus on Devil's Island, immigrants are tormented there, women abused, and people hear only disparaging insults and are very often slapped around.

Other people are treated no better than the Jews, but their governments can stick up for them. We Jews are an orphaned people. Who will stick up for us? But you, Mr. Ballin, even though a Jew, must answer for the troubles of a Jewish immigrant at the holding camp. Can it be true that you do not know what a holding camp is really like? It is impossible! The holding camps are an important and dominant factor in the business that the German companies have with the emigrants. It is a devilish discovery and wide net into which all of the fish of the immigration stream must swim. And you, Mr. Ballin, must know about the regime in power there and the vile and mean acts that your agents like Mr. Weichman, Vaznyansky, and others carry out, shaming the Jewish people. If only they were at least not Jews. Yes, Mr. Ballin, you know about all this and must know about it all and being "half responsible" is a crime against humanity and your own people. Gather up the tears spilled in a single year on this demonic island and from them you will be able to make a long, wide stream on which you, Mr. Ballin, will be able sail out on a nice yacht trip.

Emigrants' signatures:
A. Bukshteyn
A. Talalyevski
Dovid Nissenkorn—sailed to Philadelphia
Yoyne Khvalavski
Ezriel Shirer—tormented in Illowo eleven weeks
Moyshe Leyzerovitsh—in Tilsit harassed by Klein, 15 rubles too many were taken from him, and when "I didn't want to give them, they wanted to send me and my eight children back to Russia"; going to Philadelphia
Motl Lemelzohn—I sailed to Buenos Aires and I was held for eight days and I didn't have a single pfennig of money and I missed the ship on which I was supposed to sail and now I must wait here in Bremen for the next ship and they want to charge for food

Dobe Khaykin—sailed to New York or Philadelphia
Avrom Lubkin—sailed to Chicago
Borekh Fiver—sailed to Philadelphia
Yoysef Ben Tsiyon Arinovitsh—sailed to England
[illegible] Batovski—I was harassed in Illowo, an agent took 35 rub. from me. I'm sailing to Africa
Rosenzweig in Illowo—they took 3 rubles from me as graft
Moyshe Avrom Khelmunski—I was supposed to travel through Hamburg to Liverpool, but they sent me via Bremen, London, Liverpool—Lost 42 rub.
Shmuel Kupernik to Galveston—tormented in Illowo for fifteen days, missed the ship
Avrom Shteynberg—went through Illowo
Yekhiel Khazan
Mendel Khaladnyak
Yudel Klein
Noyekh Movshovitsh Guterman—sailed to Cleveland
Nakhman Narnski
Levi Vladimorov—from Odessa to New York, held in Illowo six days
Volf Aronoff—from Lodz to London, held five days in Illowo, they took 10 rub. too much
Leybe Slavin—from Sene to New York, held in Illowo twelve days, 30 extra rub. taken from me
Raphael Zaslavski—to New York, 15 extra rub. taken from me
Avrom Nakhum Makerevitz—sailing to Jaffa, held in Prostken, 82 rub. taken from him, sent through Portugal
Berel Karnov—sailing to Bellingham via Illowo, 2 extra rub. taken
Hershel Zimmerman—to London through Thorn from Chelm, traveling with passport, stopped and locked up for three days, traveled to Paris, 244 marks were taken, sent to London, taken for examination, abused, and they wanted to report him for insulting the government
Salam Bistritsky—from Elisavetgrad through Illowo to New York
Binyomin Orlovsky—from Elisavetgrad through Illowo to New York
Yankev Leltton—held in Illowo for three weeks, money denied, found out about it through the mail, then they finally let him go starving, abused, his telegrams intercepted. The postmaster told him that the money had been there for quite a while.

Tsemakh Fox—was going from Petrikov to Hull via Rotterdam, bought tickets to Rotterdam and Breslau, express train, third class, two people[,] 64 marks and 60 pfennig. Had on him 19 rub. They took him off [the train] in [Rovno], sent him to Postav, took 19 rub. and the tickets, and sent him to Bremen at his own expense. He is here in total desperation.

Binyomin Shapiro—went to Berlin, detained in the train station. Was sent back to Roteburg, where he was examined, paid the doctor 7 marks. Paid 37 marks to get to Hull. Came to Bremen, they demanded more money so he paid another 9.35 marks and 7.50 to the committee.

Simkhe Gelman—was in Illowo five weeks, they denied his money, intercepted his telegrams. The man made a detailed complaint to Lloyd.

• 4 •

American Jewish Historical Society, I-91, IRO, Box 122

Dear Sir,

Even though I don't know you, I would like to thank you for your kindness in informing me that you didn't know the address of my husband Khayim Kalikovitsh, whose whereabouts we wanted to find out. In my previous communication to you I wished you to do me the favor of finding out once and for all where he was. But since it seems that he used to write often to his parents in Rovne[20] and now it's already been two years since his parents received the last letter, they actually think he might have died.

Therefore I ask you to take pity on me and write to Santerdev[21] where he was living two years ago. Perhaps it is written in some record book where all deaths are recorded, so that I can, through your good heart, be released

20. Rovno, a city southwest of the Pale of Settlement (Ukraine) in the district of Volhynia. According to the census of 1897, there were 24,563 inhabitants, including 13,780 Jews (45.9 percent).

21. "Santerdev" is an unidentified place name. It is clearly a mispronunciation. Although the correspondent relayed the request to St. Joseph, Missouri, the dev at the end may be a Russified pronunciation of *Dieu*; thus "Santerdev" is likely to be Centre-Dieu, Quebec. I am grateful to the anonymous reviewer who pointed this out to me.

[from my marriage], because I am a young woman in my twenties, and my husband was only with me for somewhat more than two months and he's already been gone for five years and my life is miserable now that I can't establish where he has disappeared to. About two years ago I was told that he was working in a slaughterhouse in Santerdev.

Perhaps you could be so kind as to rescue me, and to the best of your ability find out how to inquire there, so that I will be able to be assisted by you and you will forever be in my prayers to God. Please, I beg you, please save me. And if you answer me, please answer in Yiddish because we cannot read English. It was not easy for us to find someone who could read your response in English.

From me, yours, a stranger who awaits your answer.
Miriam Leskes

My address is:
Mariya Leskes
Town of Vladimiretz Volinsk[22]

February 18, 1909
Mrs. Mary Leskes,
Wladimir Vohliner Gub. Russia

Dear Madam:

Upon receipt of your letter of Dec. 21, we wrote to the Board of Health of St. Joseph, Mo., making inquiry regarding your husband. Not receiving any reply from them we wrote to our representative in St. Joseph Mo., and have received from him a reply, copy of which we enclose.

Yours very truly

22. Vladimir Volinsk, a town southwest of the Pale of Settlement, in the province of Volhynia, with 8,804 inhabitants, including 5,869 Jews (59.4 percent).

•5•

American Jewish Historical Society, I-91, IRO, Box 122

I wish all the best to my dear, good, as yet unacquainted friends, that is, the dear people who know where my d[ear] husband is. I beg you, dear people, from the bottom of my heart, to have pity on me, a forlorn young woman, pity on my young years which are flying by as if in a dream. I can hardly even tell if I am alive or not, dear people, when I'm reminded of how great my sorrow is that I have not heard from my d[ear] husband for six months and I cannot understand the reason. Since I have heard from a man who came to Neswizsch,[23] he told me to write to you because you are the ones who sent him from your office, therefore only you know where he is. I beg you from the bottom of my heart to take pity on me, without knowing me, pity on a forlorn, young woman whose desolation is so great that I don't know who to turn to anymore besides God, as before, and then to you, so that you take pity on me and find him and give me a real answer. I would like to know where he disappeared to, whether or not—God forbid—he is dead. Or on the other hand, maybe he wants nothing more to do with me, this I also want to know. My dear people, I am not writing this letter with ink, but rather with the hot tears flowing from my eyes, so much that I cannot describe how huge my sorrow is that I don't even have enough to live on one more day, and I pawned everything when he went away and I still haven't been able to get my things back because I gave birth and I had to spend money on that too and so from the stress and strain I've become ill. My eyes are never dry from all my crying. My dear good friends, I beg you to forgive me, a poor woman, for putting you to any trouble. Therefore I hope, dear people, that God makes sure that you never know sorrow. God should grant health to you and your wives and your dear children and all your families. I will [pray] to God for you.

I will never forget you for my entire life, now I must wait for your help, because the man who came from America described you to me as the kind

23. Neswizsch, a town northwest of the Pale of Settlement, in the province of Minsk, with 8,460 inhabitants, including 4,687 Jews (55.4 percent).

of people who love to do a favor, especially in such a difficult situation like mine, for such a troubled woman like me with a bitter heart that cannot be compared to anyone else's. Briefly I beg you to take the trouble and do my bidding for me and search him out. He is called Bune Milshteyn. I believe he is in your records.

So, I ask you, dear friend, take my current situation on faith, that I have been put out of my apartment, and I've been left completely alone and I cry over my years, and lament the day I was born destined for such dark misery that has happened to me. Things look completely hopeless to me now, that's how bad things are for me. I'm writing you so much. I'm writing you and all it really amounts to is a drop in the bucket. It is impossible to fully describe my current misery [and] only now have I finally quieted down my nerves, which do not let me rest. And in what kind of situation I have ended up. I hope to God that you will receive this letter of mine, dear people, and maybe I will actually get the help from you that the man who came from America was telling me about you, that you don't have to be asked for [help] because you have very kind characters. Therefore I'm writing you this letter now, and there are actually tears pouring from my eyes. But my heart is telling me that I will get a good answer from you, mainly that you will write me about my d[ear] husband. Please heed my request and do what I ask you and have pity on my young years, which have been taken away by great misery. Why should I start writing the whole story about my previous situation, up to the time when I had to marry myself off, a lonesome orphan girl, when I had to work myself to the bone for my few rubles, [and before, when] he was living here there was practically no income, and then when God finally helped and he made it to America, I finally believed that [my luck] would [finally] change for the better. He sent me money every month and wrote lovely letters, as is normal to a young wife, and suddenly the letters stopped, and the money, and one has to endure it, if I had the money, I would go myself to see what happened to him. My dear, good friends, I will try to get money for you if you will fill my request and write me about him, and maybe you can send me his address if he is still alive. With that I will stop writing. May you stay healthy, along with your wives and children. From me, your as yet unacquainted and best friend, Sore [Sarah] Milshteyn. Be so kind as to address your letter to Peysakh Milshteyn. Of course you know how one writes to Neswizsch: Peysakh Milshteyn. It will arrive right away, and forgive me, dear people, for sending it without a stamp. I think it will be more likely to arrive. I hope to God that my letter may find you in the [best health.]

To Town of Neswizsch
Minsk Province
Mister Pesakh Milshteyn

·6·

American Jewish Historical Society, I-91, IRO, Box 122

Dear and Loyal Husband Sam Rosenberg,

first I owe you news of my health and our dear, lovely, clever, perfect children's health, and I pray to God that we'll always hear the same news of you. And second, I just wanted to tell you, dear husband, that I haven't yet picked up your dear letter from Montgomery, Alabama, with the 50 rubles. The reason is because my father is not at home. So, what can I write you? I have done enough. The biggest householders in the community were deciding the matter of membership in the synagogue council and when the head councilor finally had someone who died, he didn't want to give it to anyone else, but rather to the same person whose name was there, and my father will not come before Passover, he wrote me a card. Since they refused him the license, he went back to that one. He has never sold himself to that one, but I think maybe he will come for Purim, because I write to him just what's going on. So, I'm writing you this letter so that you know, because I'm thinking that the money will be returned to you. I don't want you to get scared. It's only because my father is not at home. So just imagine, dear husband, how good it is for me now. Believe me, before I was destined to lay my eyes on the money, I was going out of my mind with anxiety because from one sum of money to the next it took two months, calculated to cover just what I need with two small children. But there is one God and he is not punishing me completely. If I hadn't had the jewelry to save myself, I would have starved to death with my children. I beg you most urgently, my dear husband, that the minute you get this letter from me, you answer me right away and send me double the amount of money care of Shaye Kaytelgiser, for God's sake, be sure to send it to no other address than to Shaye Kaytelgiser. You shouldn't think anything of it that I'm writing to you from this address. I'm sure he is a fine person, my money is as good as your money and your money is as good as mine. He is a very fine person, a wealthy man and a Hasid.[24] He is a writer for the Radziner Rebbe. Send only money to his address, and you should send letters to me at my father's address. They do bring letters to me at my father's address. Dear husband, I've already written you one letter to this new address. You wrote me that when you receive a letter, you would write me. I beg you urgently to write me news because I'm very curious to know. I'll close my letter here. Be well and stay strong, from me, your wife, Libe Rosenberg. I will write you more news: I had a dream, twice already the same dream. I can't describe to you what the dream was, but if God helps us see each other again, I will tell you in person. And I'm writing a double letter to Mindl in Vengerove that she should write me what's happening with them. If she writes to me, I will send your mother a letter from you that I just received from America. And I also sent one of your letters to my brother in Warsaw. Shloyme-Velvele sends you loving regards, and Khayiml sends you heartfelt regards. He has no peace without you—he has to hold your tender letters while eating and sleeping. I just bought him a hat for 50 kopeks and a pair of shoes for 5 gilden. And I wish you could hear, dear husband, how Shloyme-Velvele is learning to write [on ruled paper]. I just gave his teacher a ruble. Please send money to this address, and if you have received this letter, and letters to my father's address.

The following is an additional letter from the same woman to her husband. The two letters were photocopied together.

Dear and Loyal Husband Sam Rosenberg,

at the beginning of my letter I bring you news of my health and our dear, lovely children's health: that we are all—thank God—completely well, and I pray to God that we'll always hear the same news of you. And second, you

24. Hasid, a pious Jew who practices the trend in Judaism of being close to God at all times.

should know, dear husband, that I happily received your dear letter from Mongomre [Montgomery] with the 50 rubles, and I'm answering you the same day, and I can't read your letter. I don't understand at all why you are suddenly praising Warsaw to me. My dear husband, I beg you to be patient and take the time to write me a real letter. You have nothing more to write than a half a yellow page, and you write me that when you receive a letter from me, you'll write me news. I think you should keep your word. You should have written news in your letter to me precisely because you wanted to receive a letter from me. Dear husband, you should write me whether you think you will send me the ship ticket before Passover, because I need to know if I should rent an apartment. Now, I'm staying in my father's apartment and the apartment goes for 60 rubles without firewood.[25] That is very expensive for me since my father is just a melamed.[26] I give half and he gives the other half. You should know this because I wrote you that the other Hebrew teachers betrayed my father, and no one wants to give him a license. In short, he's actually in Ljublin[27] today trying very hard [to find work]. May you earn in a week what it has cost him so far. Believe me, dear husband, if I were with my father, I swear on my life that I would just live out my years with him and not go to America. But I see that God wills me to go to America. It wouldn't be so bad for me if I had a home. If you write me a real letter right now saying yes or no, I will rent an apartment here for a year in that one's building. And this year is now ending after Passover and I'll have to move out of the apartment eight days after Passover. In short, I beg you, dear husband, to answer this letter right away because it is really horrible to have to wander around all the time with two children. Don't think that I'm like you: a person that can feel so much, and you should know that you are not acting like yourself, what are you thinking, my dear husband? I care a lot about you. Do you see how you made me unhappy by selling the house in Vengerove?[28] What wouldn't I have there today? I would be living in my own apartment. All you wanted was to sell. It was a terrible, dark moment

25. Without wood means that the rent for the apartment does not include wood for heating.
26. Term used for a teacher who taught young children the Hebrew alphabet in Jewish traditional society.
27. Ljublin, a city in Poland in the Ljublin province where, in 1908, there were 62,394 inhabitants, including 31,721 Jews (50.8 percent).
28. Wengrow, a town in Poland in the Sdeltz province where, in 1908, there were 12,102 inhabitants, including 8,136 Jews (67.2 percent).

that I let you sell it. Today the house would have been completely ours because your Grandmother is no longer among the living. Dear husband, I'm thinking of writing your mother a letter and sending her the photograph of you that I just got from you. I'm begging you, do you hear me? If you do, write me right back. That's all the news I have to write. Stay healthy and strong, from me, your true wife, Libe Rosenberg. Shloyme-Velvele sends you loving regards, and Khayiml sends you heartfelt regards. They hold on to your letters and send you kisses and say "my daddy" [cut off]

•7•

American Jewish Historical Society, I-91, IRO, Box 122

Honorable Society![29]

Having nowhere else to turn for a satisfactory answer, I have the honor to write to you and I believe that you will not refuse me and will answer my questions below. By my profession I am a liquor distiller, that is I have served in factories that make various sweet liqueurs and spirits, now I have decided to leave for America as a result of the terribly critical situation in our area. But before I commit myself to the journey, I want to know whether there will be something for me to do in America connected to my profession, and therefore, I would need to know the following:

1. Do people in America drink a lot of liqueurs, or do they mainly drink unsweetened spirits like Gin or Whiskey and liquor distilled from wheat, corn, rye, and such?
2. Are there many distilleries in the United States of America and is it possible to quickly obtain a position in such a distillery?
3. If you happen to know, how much does the government get

29. The reference is to the Industrial Removal Office (IRO) established in 1901 by the Jewish banker Jacob Schiff and Jewish philanthropic organizations in the United States. The aim of the IRO was to reduce the density, congestion, and poverty in the cities along the East Coast by sending the migrants to the western part of the United States and providing for their livelihood in their new place of residence.

for each level of alcohol percentage per one hundred liters of liquor? If this is not practiced there, then I don't need the information.

4. Especially this one: How does one go about getting work and what does one need to do to obtain such a position? Is there a reputable bureau or society that can fill such positions or does one have to advertise oneself in a special journal devoted to my line of work?

And awaiting your honored reply, with the deepest respect, I remain
Moyshe Zelnik

I'm sending my address separately:
Town of Dubossary,[30] Kherson Province
Mister Moisey Ikhelyev Tsyulnik
Post Office Box No. 3

P.S. Would you please write me if perhaps you know of the address of an American journal devoted to liquors and spirits? I believe that it can be found in the American "address book."

I will do everything you advise me to do.

• 8 •

American Jewish Historical Society, I-91, IRO, Box 122

Kretingen[31]
July 6

Please give your courteous attention to the following message: Since I'll be setting out soon for America, I would like to know which region is

30. A town south of the Pale of Settlement, in the district of Kherson, where there were 12,109 inhabitants, including 5,219 Jews (43.1 percent).
31. Kretingen, a town northwest of the Pale of Settlement, in the district of Kovno, where there were 3,418 inhabitants, including 1,203 Jews (35.2 percent).

more suitable for me and how prevalent my profession is there. I am a druggist. I have worked for many years in drugstores (pharmacies). I know the business and the work very well.

So, I'm requesting your help in answering these urgent questions for me:

1. What region or city is more suitable for me, considering my profession?
2. Can a person in this field find work in these kinds of businesses: drugstores, pharmacies, hospitals, drug warehouses, etc.?
3. What are the average earnings of someone working with these kinds of products?
4. What would a person coming from Russia be required to know to attain this goal?

I believe that this honorable organization for assisting Jewish emigrants will not [refuse] me and will send me this information that I need so urgently and I send you [my] greatest thanks for it.

In awaiting your swift reply
Respectfully and faithfully,
Moyshe Burgin

My address is:
Movshi Burgin
Shtetl of Kretingen
Kovno Province
Telshe County

• 9 •

American Jewish Historical Society, I-91, IRO, Box 122

Loyal Brothers of the Removal Office,

My dear brother, with tears in my eyes I turn to you and I beg you from the bottom of my heart that you not take offense and I ask that you excuse me for this letter that I'm writing you. And I ask, my friends, that you not take offense at everything that you are going to read in this letter because my hardship brought on all this that led me to commit this crime against you, my dear brothers, and against myself. This is the story: Last week I went to you with a request that you send me somewhere for work. I noticed that the man who signs people up recognized me as I had been there once before. So I got scared that I wouldn't be sent again and it is so bad for me here, God help me. Soon I will have nothing to eat, so I was forced to say that my name is Mordkhe Kaplan because my real name, Leybl Kashelevits, is already in your book. Dear brothers, please don't think that I gave myself another name because I committed another crime. No, I have—God forbid—done nothing else, only this mistake, because I was afraid that you would not want to send me again. Dear brothers, I can say that you are doing the right thing by checking up, because of course there would be people who should not be sent and I among them because I already went through you once. But I must tell you, my friends, if you sent me now you would definitely have the same mitzvah as before because I am worse off than the time before. It is true that I was in America for four years. During that time I saved 300 Russian rubles. I usually also sent some to my family to live on. It didn't go that well for me here. I had 300 rubles, so I thought that if I returned home, I would perhaps be able to make an easier living there than here in America. After last Passover I left for my city of Brest Litowsk.[32] I went home, saw that no one's life was secure and on top of that, the workers would not let me work. I saw that if I stayed at home any longer, I wouldn't even have enough to escape back to America. So in twelve weeks I went back with the

32. A city northwest of the Pale of Settlement, in the district of Grodno, with 46,621 inhabitants including 30,527 Jews (64.9 percent).

thought that God would help me now and if I could just make enough for travel costs I could soon send for my family. I came and worked a whole winter baking matzah and I didn't make out badly. I sent my family money and I saved something for myself as well, but now it turns out that I've been out of work for twelve weeks and the whole time I didn't want to go to you because you had already sent me once. I had a few dollars so I thought that there would be more work later, but in the end I still don't have any work and my money is already gone, and I don't even have anything left to send my family, so things are really bad now. So I decided to go to you so you would send me wherever you wanted as long as I would have the possibility of making a living. In the end I was recognized and I was afraid to say my real name because now they wouldn't want to send me. Therefore I tell you that I am now adrift like a ship in the middle of the ocean. I have no idea what I should do now. The money is all spent and God only knows when there will be more work. I don't know anyone else to turn to now but you. I beg you, dear brothers, to have compassion for me and to send me this one time anywhere you think I will be able to make a living for my family and I hope I will not want to go home again, but it would be better if I could bring my family here. For more about my honesty, anyone that knows me will give me the best reference. I beg you, dear brothers, have pity on me and forgive me and send me wherever you think makes sense because I am very desperate. I am also sending you a couple letters from my wife so that you'll be convinced that what I'm writing you is true, and that hardship was what forced me to change my name, but never again—God forbid—for any reason. I wanted to send you my wife's receipts for the money, but I don't have them anymore. However, I am sending you one receipt. It is for several rubles which is what I often send my mother. In the office that this receipt is from you can see that I also send my wife money but now things are very bad for me. I beg you to forgive me. It is not my fault; my hardship brought it on. May you all be well.

From me, your friend who hopes that you will recognize the truth,
Leybl Kashelevits

My address is
Mr. Karp
7 Forsyth St.

• 10 •

American Jewish Historical Society, I-91, IRO, Box 122

Office
Joseph Shmulevich
Taran
Cherkassy, November 7, 1906
Committee of ICA
to New York

Cherkassy, Kiev Province
Staro-Sobornu Spusk N 10
Joseph Taran from Kiev[33] to the IRO
November 1906
Cherkassy Representative
Jewish Colonization Association

Esteemed Gentlemen of the Committee!

Since I have found out that America is the source of the merchandise paraffin, I therefore request that you esteemed gentlemen, members of the committee each one of you, please do me the favor of answering the question, if it is at all possible, whether this type of merchandise is available in America and whether that is really the source, and [of providing me with] several addresses of factories located there, if it is at all possible, at least one address of one factory.

Even though this work has nothing whatsoever to do with the work of our group . . . nonetheless, as members of a group, I beg that you do me the favor of answering as soon as possible.

This type of merchandise is called paraffin. If possible, please write the prices of this type of merchandise. My address is Russia

Joseph Taran
Cherkassy,[34] Kiev Province
Russia

33. Kiev, a city southwest of the Pale of Settlement. According to the census of 1897, there were 246,519 inhabitants, including 31,801 Jews (12.9 percent).

34. Cherkassy, a town southwest of the Pale of Settlement, in the district of Kiev. According to the census of 1897, there were 29,595 inhabitants, including 10,950 Jews (37 percent).

• 11 •

American Jewish Historical Society, I-91, IRO, Box 122

Sunday, Sivan 17,[35] the 1837th year of our exile, Ljubischow[36]

Dear Sirs!

It is a time of trembling now for the Jews. Every malicious evildoer is tormenting and oppressing this nation, which people have been persecuting and trampling on unmolested for thousands of years. Such crushed, downtrodden, tormented people, men and women under duress, are commonly found only in this oppressed nation. For this reason the flow of emigration has increased so dramatically these days that in the entire Pale of Settlement there is no home where there is not someone who has died/emigrated.[37] Every Jewish family has a limb in the land[?]! The character of the emigrants varies. Each of them had a different reason for moving far away. Most of them are avoiding military service; I myself, your correspondent, am one of these.

I am currently twenty-one years old, and I have to report for the army this year. For the past three years I have been in the city of Ljubischow, in the district of Pinsk, province of Minsk, teaching "Hebrew in Hebrew," running a second-rate reformed heder.[38] I am fluent in Hebrew. I did general

---

35. Unless otherwise stated, all dates given in the footnotes are Gregorian. The dates in the letters themselves are Julian if written in the Russian Empire and Gregorian if written elsewhere.

36. Libosha (Ljubischow), a town northwest of the Pale of Settlement, in the district of Minsk. According to the census of 1897, there were 2,739 inhabitants, including 1,888 Jews (68 percent).

37. This is an allusion to Exodus 12:30, which describes the killing of the firstborn (one of the ten plagues) in Egypt: "There was no home where there was not someone dead."

38. The heder is a term used for a teaching institution in traditional Jewish society. This was a private institution where the melamed received his salary from the parents of the pupils. The pupils in the heder were usually boys, who began their studies at the age of three to four years old and finished at the age of thirteen (bar mitzvah). The pupils who wanted to continue their studies went to a yeshiva. The Heder Metukan was a more advanced institution of learning in which Hebrew and other subjects were taught.

studies in my youth but by now have almost forgotten [what I learned]. I do not know foreign languages, except for reading and writing a very little bit of German and English. I have 300 rubles in cash. And now, because, as I mentioned above, I have to report to the army, I am compelled to flee, but I will not do so until after reporting for the army at the end of the month of Heshvan 5667.[39] I turn to you, honorable gentlemen, to ask what country I should go to and what I should do there. I want to study technology—after enrolling in some polytechnic institute, of course. Were it not for the frequent searches and interrogations in Germany, where they investigate all the doings of every person and demand that every immigrant coming from Russia produce a provincial certificate or even a simple passport, I would have gone to Germany to enroll in a polytechnic institute. But because I do not have the required papers, I would be a refugee, and under the present laws and customs Germany deports immigrants of this sort. So I have to move to America and fulfill my sacred aspiration there. The question is: How? As I have been told recently by various people in answer to my many questions, in America the polytechnic institutes only accept people who have worked in a factory for at least a year. I was advised to go to America, work in a factory for one year, and learn the trade. During that year I would also earn money because the factory owners pay the workers wages, and I would be able to save up a little money. Of the money that I have now, I would have no less than 75/80 U.S. dollars left, because I would have spent half of my money (300/400 [rubles]) on travel expenses. And after finishing my work at the factory, I would go to night school daily and study English. Thus I would be preparing doubly for the polytechnic institute—both with money and by doing the technical work and learning the necessary language of the country. Honorable gentlemen, as an institution that stands at the right hand of young Jews in both material and spiritual matters, please fulfill your sacred duty to heed my words in this letter and give me an accurate, honest answer: What should I do? Are my presumptions groundless? Am I building castles in the air? If you don't like my plan, please show me a different way to achieve my goal, and specify it to me in writing, saying to whom I can turn for help, how to start, by what means to go to America, and to what city. For 90 percent of the emigrants from Russia, including the Jewish emigrants, go to New York, the Jewish

39. October–November 1906.

ghetto has grown even in America, and destitution and poverty result from the journey to New York. So what other city can I go to? Please, honorable gentlemen, reply to me quickly, answering all my questions clearly so that I know what lies ahead of me, so that I am not a lost traveler, a blind man groping in the dark. In the hope that you will not turn me away empty-handed, I conclude respectfully and with the blessings of Zion,

A. Papish

My address:
Ljubischow, Minsk Province

to G. L. Papish

· 12 ·

American Jewish Historical Society, I-91, IRO, Box 122

Dear Sirs!

On the fifteenth of Sivan I dispatched a letter to you, asking you various questions. No doubt you received my letter, and by the time this letter reaches you, I may have received an answer from you. But if this letter reaches you before you reply, I ask you again to answer me quickly. I will repeat my questions.

I am twenty-one years old. This year I have to report for the army, and it will be a shame. I must leave Russia, but I don't know where to go—what country to go to and what to do there. For the past three years I have been in Ljubischow, in the district of Pinsk, province of Minsk, teaching "Hebrew in Hebrew," running a second-rate reformed heder. I know Hebrew fluently. I can read and understand an intermediate-level book in Russian. I didn't do general studies, and I don't know foreign languages except that I can read and write German and English. I have 300 rubles that I have earned by working. Of course, after I arrive in whatever country I will be spending a considerable amount of my money.[40] Furthermore, I can't leave Russia until I have reported for the army and they have given me an exemption—if only they will. I do not have a provincial certificate and I might not have a simple passport either. What do you think a man like me can do in a foreign land? My aim and ambition is to study technology, and if not, then I would like to study a different field. Honorable gentlemen, as knowledgeable residents of your land, give me advice and a strategy for achieving my goal. As I told you in my letter, I have discovered that in America the polytechnic institutes only accept people who have worked in a factory for a year. After arriving in America I will have about 70–80 U.S. dollars left. During my year working in an American factory I will get perhaps a few dozen dollars more. I will listen to you: What night school should I attend in the meantime to learn English—the language of the land, which is very valuable to immigrants from Russia? By the end of the year, I will know a little of the technical work, I will have a bit of ready money, and I will know a little English. Perhaps I will be accepted to the polytechnic institute, and thus I will be able to achieve my goal. But if you don't like this plan, then please, good people, fulfill the sacred duty of every Jew who can do so: stand at the right hand of a native of Russia fleeing living death and seeking asylum. Please give me good advice that is right for me and my financial and physical situation. If you know that I would be better off going to some other country rather than America, let me know that, too, because the Jewish soul now in Russia is imprisoned and shut in on all sides: (1) the Pale of Settlement; (2) restrictions on engaging in commerce and industry; (3) I cannot get into any school. And there is much more that there is no room to describe here. Please, honorable gentlemen, heed these words of mine and my first letter and send me a proper reply quickly.

Respectfully and with the blessings of Zion,
A. Papish

town of Ljubischow
To L. Papish [illegible] Minsk Province

40. Although this is what he says, he probably means "by the time I arrive . . . I will have spent," given that in his previous letter he anticipated that travel expenses would use up half of his 300–400 rubles, leaving him with 75–80 dollars, and given that later in the letter he says he will have 70–80 dollars left after he arrives.

• 13 •

American Jewish Historical Society, I-91, Box 122

October 9, 1913
09 Oct. 1913 Zhovnino[41]

Esteemed, prominent gentlemen of the Removal Office. I can thank you many times over for saving a family from the miserable life of being tormented by hunger because my husband left me in Russia with five children and came to New York and was unable to make a living even for himself. Imagine, dear friends, what it was like with him unable to help my five children and me. Then we found the benevolent Removal Office which was our savior. Perhaps you remember that on April 22 you sent my husband to Milwaukee, Wisconsin. And since he has been staying there my eyes have been opened. He started to earn money little by little and started to send me money to live on. His name is Yoysef Bogoslavske. But, my dear friends, I have one more urgent request for you. Perhaps you can do my children and me a great kindness and help us out with the ship tickets. Although my husband is now earning $12 a week, he must still keep enough to live on. My children and I must live, and everything is so expensive now, we barely have enough for food and for the children to study Yiddish at the very least. But it costs good money and the children are becoming ruined because I can't put them with good teachers, and their aptitudes are very good. And my husband writes that in America it doesn't cost anything for children to study. Therefore, my dear gentlemen, please have pity on my children and save them from this cursed place Russia. Dear gentlemen, best friends, how could I have dared to go to you with such an urgent request? Because my husband writes me frequent letters and I have yet to receive one in which he doesn't thank you for doing him so much good. So I figured that you won't refuse my request and you will do me a favor. I think my children will be forever grateful to you and if you won't do this for me, I don't know how I will ever be able to bring my children to America and whether I will be able to make respectable people out of them.

41. No details were found regarding the town.

The names of my family: my name is Hasi Bogoslavske, I'm thirty-four. My oldest child, a girl, Yate-Mirl, eleven years old, my son Borekh, nine years old, my daughter Menye, seven years old, a little boy Shmuel-Meyer, five years old, and a little girl Nekhome, one year old. This is my family. I beg you not to be cut off from your good hearts and that you do for my children the good that you do for the whole world and we will not forget you. There is no one here in Russia who we can count on for a favor, so I have my hopes pinned on you.

Be well, from me, Hasi Bogosklavske

This is my husband's address:
Mr. Joe Bogoslawsky
481-3-St. Milwaukee
Wis.

And this is my address:
Shtetl of Zhovnino
Zolotonosha County
Poltava Province
Khasye Boguslavska

• 14 •

1913 12 [December]

Shtetl of Zhovnino
Zolotonosha County
Poltava Province
Khasye Boguslavsk
Removal Office

Best friends in the Removal Office. I received a letter from you on November 7 and I am grateful that you answered me. But, my dear friends, please understand that I cannot read English, so I don't know how you responded to my request that you save a family from torment in cursed Russia, that you help me out with ship tickets, and only God knows if we will be able to make our goal, since we are so defenseless. The only hope I have is with you, that you pull my children out of this terribly dire situation. But according to how my husband wrote about you on more than one occasion, I'm certain that you will be my rescuer. I'm not talking about myself at all, but about my little children who have to live in such a savage place and in such poor conditions, where we have nothing to offer them. And however much my husband may earn, if we were all together, that would be enough, but since he has to live there and I with five children here, it is not enough and everything is so expensive now, and now that it is winter everything costs even more. Please don't ignore my request, and send me ship tickets for my family. I have heard from many newspapers that your office helps Jews. I request that you also include me in the list of all the unfortunate people, and have pity on me and on my children, and send me ship tickets. I have one more request of you, please forgive me, that you write me letters in either Yiddish or Russian because there is no one in our shtetl who can read these letters that I have received from you. I feel terrible that I do not know what you wrote me, but no one can read it. End.

Khasya Bogoslavske

Mrs Chassje Boguslawska
Shownino, Poltava Gub., Russia

Dear Madam:

We regret to advise you that this office does not extend its benefits to people residing outside of the city of New York, and for that reason it would be impossible for us to send you steamship tickets for a journey to America.

Very truly yours,
Industrial Removal Office

• 15 •

American Jewish Historical Society, I-91, IRO, Box 122

Odessa,[42] August 8, 1910

Esteemed Gentlemen and Friends of This Office,

I beg you to consider this letter that I am writing you now. My brother-in-law, Mr. Royz, writes me that the money owed to me for the furniture that was broken on the move from New York to Alabama and since then in the meantime I have become very depressed.[43] After that, we went back to New York from Alabama and my husband died during that time and I am left with four children and I was forced to go back to Russia because my family lives in Odessa, then my brother-in-law has been trying the whole time to get the money from your office, and you won't answer him because you must think that he's making the whole thing up. So, I'm writing to you: Tsivye Rotsumer, the wife of the deceased Izzie Rotsumer. I beg you to take into consideration this miserable widow and send me the 10 dollars to the address that I will now indicate. I hope that you will fulfill my request and take pity on an unfortunate woman. With respect, Tsivye Rotsumer. I request that as soon as you receive my letter you send out the money.

Odessa
Kherson Province
Yekaterininskaya Corner
House No. 42
Apt. c/o Koshevatskii

Tsivya Rotsumor

42. Odessa is a city on the shores of the Black Sea, in the province of Cherson. According to the census of 1897, there were 403,882 inhabitants, including 138,835 Jews (34.4 percent).

43. The previous sentence seems incomplete in the original Yiddish too. The writer must have omitted something after the word *Alabama*.

· 16 ·

American Jewish Historical Society, I-91, IRO, Box 122

The Ministry of Interior Affairs
Rabbi of Ekaterinoslav
15/28 of March 1912
town of Ekaterinoslav

Highly Esteemed Members of the "Removal Committee" in New York,

In the name of an old Jewish woman, I am writing to the esteemed members of the committee in the full hope that you will fulfill the request of this unfortunate woman.

Fifteen years ago her son Yankev Raskin and her son-in-law Aba Milner and their families immigrated to Brooklyn. For twelve years they were writing their mother, but for the last two years she has not received any more letters from them. This elderly woman therefore requests with tears in her eyes that the committee find out if they are still alive or if they are long dead. Their last address was

J. Raskin
119 Harrison Ave. Brooklyn, N.Y.

Kindly supply an answer as soon as possible.

Crown Rabbi of Yekaterinaslav[44]

Chief Rabbi of Ekaterinoslaw
Russia

44. Jekaterinoslaw, a city in the south of the Pale of Settlement. According to the census of 1897, there were 121,216 inhabitants, including 36,600 Jews (29.7 percent).

Dear Sir:

In reply to your esteemed communication regarding Jacob Raskin who you say known to live at 119 Harrison Avenue, Brooklyn, we beg to inform you that a thorough investigation by us revealed the fact that no one in the house has any knowledge of any such person as J. Raskin having ever lived there at any time.

Very truly yours,

• 17 •

American Jewish Historical Society, I-91, IRO, Box 122

Jewish Colonization Association[45]
(ICA)
Ponevezer Committee Information Bureau for emigrants[46]
Ponewesch,[47] Kovno Province, May 3, 1909

Highly Esteemed Gentlemen

According to the wishes of the poor relatives of Mister Joseph Cohen whose exact address we provide here, we kindly request current information about this man, because they have not had any news from him in four years. Before that he used to write them all the time, send them small amounts of money, and inquire after them. He even promised to send them ship tickets

45. Jewish Colonization Association (ICA) was founded in 1891 by the Jewish baron Maurice de Hirsch. The aim of the ICA was to help Russian Jews migrate to their countries of destination in general and to South American in particular.
46. The information office in Ponewesch was part of a network of local information bureaus established at the initiative of the ICA throughout the Pale of Settlement and in Poland. The central information office of the ICA was located in St. Petersburg, and it supplied the funds for the offices and instructed the local officials how to help and guide Jewish migrants.
47. Ponewesch, a city in the district of Kovno. According to the census of 1897, there were 12,972 inhabitants, including 6,564 Jews (50.6 percent).

and take them in. But for four years he has not answered their letters. Therefore they certainly would like to find out about him and please write us a precise response.

Our address is:
J. Radin. Ponewesch [Kovno] Province
This man's address is
Joseph Cohen et Co. dealers in wines and liquors
199 Division St.[,] New York

With great respect from
J. Radin and Ja. Bril

Mr. I Radin
Kovno Prov., Russia

Dear sir:-

We have yours of the 3rd inst. And beg to state that we will make every effort to locate Joseph Cohen, and if we should succeed we will inform you.

Yours very truly, Industrial Removal Office
For Investigator

Try to locate Joseph Cohen whose address was c/o Joseph Cohen & Co., dealers in wines and liquors, 199 Division St. He has not written letters to his relatives in Russia for the past four years. Locate him or find out what happened to him. E. M.

June 2, 1909
Ponewesch, Kovno, Prov, Russia

Dear Sir:
I beg to inform you that we have discovered the whereabouts of Mr. Joseph Cohen, in regard to whom you wrote us on the 3rd of May last. He is at present

located at 149 Watkins St., Brooklyn, N.Y., and is in Liquor business in partnership with Mr. Meisel. He has promised to write to his relatives in Russia. He is living at the above address together with his wife and children. Hoping this information will be satisfactory to you, we are,

Yours very truly
Industrial Removal Office

• 18 •

American Jewish Historical Society, I-91, Box 122

Esteemed Society!

Today, having received a letter from the Warsaw branch of the ITO in which they counsel me to write to you for advice, I have the honor of requesting a rapid response from you. I am a *shokhet, moyel,*[48] as well as a Hebrew teacher, a capable young man of thirty, a specialist in my field. But since in the Russian provinces where Jews are permitted to live, there exists the cursed meat-tax, [and] where the number of *shokhtim* is limited as well as the number of teachers, all sorts of teachers are springing up like mushrooms and make the fees drop so that is impossible for even the smallest family to earn enough to live on.

Therefore I am forced to emigrate from Russia to search out bread for my family, which consists of eight members. For travel expenses I have 600 rubles. So I request that you, dear friends, let me know if it is possible for someone like me to settle in some city in the United States of America, and if it is possible for you to find me a position in which I can work in my field, or be a correspondent for some Yiddish or Hebrew newspaper. And you will not—God forbid—have any grief from me if you do write me to tell me that I should come.

48. *Shokhet*, a person qualified for the slaughtering of animals and fowls according to Jewish ritual laws; *moyel*, circumciser.

Respectfully, Elyakum Getsl Froykin
P.S. Physically I am healthy and I have good prospects.

My address:
Minsk[49]
Corner of Zakharyevska and Kolomensk
for Paretsa Druikin

• 19 •

American Jewish Historical Society, I-91, Box 122

Keydan, January 22

Dearest Sh-D[50]

May your life abound in joy, I am—thank God—in total health. I received your postcard of January 16 about your health and may God assure that it stays that way. Last week I wrote you a letter and I wrote you about everything. This week nothing new has happened with me. I will write you about everything next week. How is your time in America now?

I don't have anything else that's new to write about. Stay healthy and be happy. From me, your wife who hopes to hear [illegible] Etel Zis[man] [illegible] very friendly [illegible] from me, your [illegible] hopes for much goodness [illegible] Zisman.

49. Minsk, a city northwest of the Pale of Settlement. According to the census of 1897, there were 90,938 inhabitants, including 47,561 Jews (52.3 percent).
50. These are probably the initials of the man's name. For example, Shloyme-Dovid.

• 20 •

American Jewish Historical Society, I-91, IRO, Box 122

January 26, [1907?] Sjedletz[51]

I, wretched, poor Mashe Zilazne, come to beg your pardon many times over, you highly esteemed people who toil on the committee, forgive me my hardship which brings me to this, that I am forced to write to the gentlemen of the committee that they should be so kind as to have compassion and pity on me, a wretched woman with my two poor children.

I beg you to hear me out, dear people and gentlemen who are on the committee, ever since my husband who goes by the name Moyshe Zilazne left me and my two poor children, one of whom is called Avrom, and the other son Ayzele, and it has already been nine months since he left me and my two poor children, and six months already that he has not sent us one letter. I don't have any way of feeding my children and I'm as miserable as can be. It is terrible for my poor children and me. And the poor children miss their dear father. And I mourn my young years that I should—God forbid—end up an *agune* [abandoned woman]. Of course I have nowhere else to seek advice but first from dear God and then from the committee[52] which is well known also to my husband. He is a housepainter and is called Moyshe Zilazne. Please have mercy on me and on my children and announce it in the papers perhaps he is in Noviyorek [New York], and take the trouble for me and find out for me since I don't have any way of feeding my poor children and myself, and this letter is getting soaked with my tears. I will always pray that you may have long lives, dear committee, I beg your pardon again and again for bothering the gentlemen of the committee to do me this favor of writing in the newspapers. I am relying on the committee to take the time to find out as quickly as possible. My wretched children will always pray for you because I'm a miserable orphan with no parents who is forced [to ask for this] and for my weak, weak pen

51. Sjedletz, a city in Poland, in the province of Sjedletz where, in 1908, there were 25,432 inhabitants, including 13,944 Jews (54 percent).

52. The reference is to the IRO.

it is totally impossible to announce in the paper. And if I receive an answer from the committee and a letter from my dear husband, I will be forever grateful to the gentlemen who work so hard on the committee, certainly I am assured that the committee will definitely fulfill my requests. We have no bread to eat. I will end my writing now, from me, miserable woman Mashe Zilazne of Sjedletz.

Please answer to this address:
Sjedletz, the street is called Ogrodowa Ulica
c/o [Yudel] Markesfeld, number 29

Adieu

My husband's name is Moyshe Zilazne
I, his wife, am called Mashe Zilazne
One son is called Avrom, and the second son Ayze[le.]

• 21 •

American Jewish Historical Society, I-91, IRO, Box 122

"From Russia"

Please forgive me for not using your title, but I do not know to whom I am writing. As soon as I read in the newspapers that a committee was founded in America that sees [illegible] emigrants in the countries or [illegible] so that they don't become a burden and [illegible] there was an address where [illegible] with a letter I ask you if there is a place for a young man of thirty with rabbinical ordination from the rabbis in Russia, who knows how to preach, lead the prayer service, read the Torah in shul, where he can obtain a position as a rabbi and be able to survive because in Russia things are very bad since the war has ruined the country.[53] I request an answer as soon as possible and you will earn a great *mitsve.*

53. Russo-Japanese War (1904–5)

From me, Ayzik [Isaac] Blum.

And this is my address:
To the Town of Neswizsch[54]
Minsk Province
Mister Aizik Blum
Rabbi N. Kazilor

• 22 •

American Jewish Historical Society, I-91, IRO, Box 122

Plonsk,[55] 13 Shvat[56] Year 5665 [1905]

Honorable Administration!

We request an answer to several questions:

1. A single man of eighteen. He is familiar with the textile trade and his capital consists of two hundred fifty rubles (250 rubles). And he is fluent in Russian and Hebrew. Where in America should he go so that he can earn a living and learn the language?
2. A single man of twenty-three (that is, 23), a pattern designer, fluent in three languages: German, Russian, Hebrew, with capital amounting to one hundred fifty rubles (150 rubles). Where in America should he go to be able to earn a living?
3. A single man of twenty, fluent in Russian and Hebrew, with

54. Neswizsch, a town in the district of Minsk. According to the census of 1897, there were 8,460 in habitants, including 4,687 Jews (55.4 percent).
55. Plonsk, a city in Poland in the province of Warsaw where, in 1908, there were about 11,603 inhabitants, including 7,551 Jews (65 percent).
56. January 19, 1905. Shvat, a month in the Jewish calendar, usually corresponding to the months of January–February.

capital amounting to six hundred rubles (600 rubles). Where in America should he go so that he can enroll in a technical school where his capital will last him until he will be able to earn a living in his field?

4. A single man of eighteen, an agricultural worker, fluent in Polish and Hebrew, and his capital amounts to 200 rubles. Where should he go to be able to earn his living in agriculture?

Respectfully yours: Russian Emigrants

Our address:
Russland-Polen
A.B. 150
Russia-Poland
Plonsk, Warsaw Province
"General Delivery" A.B. 150
250 rubles

• 23 •

American Jewish Historical Society, I-91, IRO, Box 122

I Adar 9, 5665,[57] Oni

Dear Sirs!

I come from the province of Minsk in Russia, and I currently live in the Caucasus, in a small town in the province of Kutaisi.[58] Its name is Oni, and it is aptly named,[59] for it is poor in knowledge, poor in good factories, and also literally poor. I work here as a rabbi, *shokhet,* and *moyel,* but all this is not enough to support my household, because I earn 35 rubles per

57. February 14, 1905.
58. Kutais, a town in Russia. According to the census of 1897, there were 32,679 inhabitants, including 3,464 Jews (10.6 percent).
59. *Oni* (in the Ashkenazic pronunciation of Eastern Europe) is the Hebrew word for "poor."

month and it is very expensive here. But the main thing is that I don't have the right of residence here, so I have decided to move to America. Having seen something in the newspaper (*Hatzofeh*)[60] about your valuable endeavor, I am writing to you. I was ordained by one of the greatest rabbis to judge and teach, to write divorce decrees and officiate at weddings. I am also an expert *shokhet* and a wonderful *moyel,* as well as a great preacher who captivates my audience. Moreover, I am in the prime of life and can work like any common person, so long as I can support my family and live together with them without fear. As I love small towns and absolutely hate big cities, I am turning to you. I could not find a prepaid reply letter in my local post office, so forgive me if it costs you anything to reply. My address is:
Shtetl Oni Koutoisi Province
to Rabbi Sh. Teishov

Eagerly awaiting your reply, Shlomo Yehuda [surname illegible]

• 24 •

American Jewish Historical Society, I-91, IRO, Box 122

My dear friends, advocates of our cause, the great, illustrious men who are standing on the ramparts in the great city of New York to save our Jewish brethren, may you live well and happily forever.

Now that I have wished you well: I received your dear letter concerning the 200 rubles of R. Chaim Yosef Khelmetsky, in which you tell me that you don't remember when you received the money. I therefore inform you that the post office in my small community didn't want to send money to New York, so I sent the money to the ICA (Jewish Colonization Association) in Libava[61] on August 25, 1908. They wrote to me that after

60. A daily newspaper in Hebrew published in Warsaw during 1903–5 and edited by Eliezer Eliahu Friedman.
61. Present-day Liepaja, Latvia, known in German as Libau. A port city on the Baltic Sea in the province of Kurland. According to the census of 1897, there were 64,753 inhabitants, including 9,454 Jews (14.6 percent).

receiving the money they sent it to you in accordance with the conditions that I stipulated with them: that the aforementioned R. Chaim Yosef sent the money for his son Zvi Hirsch Khelmetsky and his wife and their small son so that they would have enough money to return to his father's house. And if he didn't want to go home, after the money arrived there it would be sent back to the aforementioned R. Chaim Yosef Khelmetsky. After the Sukkot holiday, I received a letter from Hirsch Khelmetsky in New York saying that the money had reached you, and that you wanted to give it to him so that he could buy himself a ticket for the ship. As his wife was then pregnant, and the doctors had told her that it would be dangerous for her to travel by ship, the money stayed with you. I, too, received a letter from you then asking what to do with the money, and I told you to hold on to it until he agreed to travel. But many months have passed, during which time he has written letters to his father saying that he is afraid to return home because he would have to serve in the army.[62] His father therefore wants the money back, together with the interest if there is any. Please don't ignore his request. Send it immediately to my address so that there are no complaints against me for having advised him to do this and for having promised him that you would fulfill his desired condition and that the money would remain intact. And your good enterprise will have honor and glory. And now I venture to speak to you. Please tell me what I need to know, partly for the sake of others to whom I have been a brother and helper until now in the ICA in the community of Loyev, overseeing the emigrants who go to seek their bread overseas. I have advised them how to get a provincial passport, and how to avoid the trap of the agents. Now I myself want to go to America, since I have two sons and a married daughter there. My household now includes another two big sons, one seventeen years old and one fifteen, as well as an eleven-year-old daughter and two small sons aged seven and six. And my wife yearns for us all go to New York to be together with our older children. Furthermore, I can barely make a living in my small community, and there in New York I have a lot of acquaintances who have promised to give me a respectable

62. According to czarist law, young men of eighteen years were obliged to enlist in the army. Any person who did not appear at the recruitment office was fined 300 rubles. Although the fine was for the individual defector, his family was often penalized by the authorities.

job as a rabbi and preacher, so with God's help I will earn a living there. But I have heard that the laws governing entry to the land of the free are now very tough, and many people have been sent back from Castle Garden,[63] having been denied entry into the country. Who can imagine the bitter fate of the people who sold all they had to pay for the journey, and were then forced to return empty-handed to their land? They would have been better off drowning in the deep sea than suffering their bitter fate. Therefore, please be so good and compassionate as to let me know the legal situation. Who is turned away? Is it just those who are suffering from trachoma in the eyes or who are sick—or is it that they don't have room for so many people so they have put a stop to the massive influx of immigrants? I am afraid to embark on the voyage, lest I be one of those sent back. Please, therefore, out of the goodness of your hearts, tell me the legal situation. If you recommend that some of my acquaintances and relatives come and guarantee me a livelihood, or if you have any other advice that is obvious to you, please let me know right away. Does one have to show money upon arrival? How much is needed? Please be so good as to tell me everything clearly in our language, Yiddish, or in Hebrew or Russian, but not in English, since no one here knows how to read letters in English. And as it would be a good idea to know the entry laws well, publish them in periodicals for the sake of our migrant brethren, so that they know who should stay home and who should go to the new land. And after you offer your good advice to myself and others, I will follow it and inform the masses, and I will never forget your kindhearted generosity.

With respect and high esteem from your friend, who awaits your prompt reply. May God exalt you and give you great honor.

With blessings from the bottom of my heart,
Yitzchak Darginski, head of the Loyev[64] rabbinical court

---

63. Castle Garden was an immigrant landing depot from 1855 to 1890. By the time this letter was written, it was actually the site of the New York City Aquarium, but the writer was apparently not aware of this.

64. Lojew, a town in the district of Minsk. According to the census of 1897 there were 4,667 inhabitants, including 2,150 Jews (46 percent).

My address:
To Shtetl Loyev, Minsk Province
To Chief rabbi
Yitzchak Darginski

· 25 ·

American Jewish Historical Society, I-91, IRO, Box 122

Jewish Colonization Association
(ICA)
Ponewesch Committee
Emigrant Information Bureau

Esteemed Gentlemen!

Since we have received your swift response to our earlier inquiry, we are writing to you with another inquiry on behalf of an old, sickly widow whose son has been there in New York for twenty-five years. But for the past eight years, she has had no news of him.

His last address is:

Mr. Mehr Fridman New York City
N. 232 Division St.

By profession he is a tailor. Please be so kind as to find out about him and inform us as soon as possible.

Respectfully we await your response,
I remain Y. Radin
A. Bril

Address Ponewesch, Kovno Province
J. Radin

· 26 ·

American Jewish Historical Society, I-91, IRO, Box 122

Andrashovka[65]
November 4

I request a response from the members of the committee[66] on the following matter!

Two years ago my husband went to America in order to earn his keep, [and] left me with a small child. The whole time he has sent me money to live on and good letters saying that he would soon bring me to New York. But now it has been three months since I have received any news of him, and I used to receive a letter from him every week. I am strongly convinced that he has had some kind of accident or misfortune, because his attitude towards me was extremely good.

He has been living in New York the whole time. But four weeks ago a young man from New York came here and told me that my husband left New York with the idea of going to Boston or Chicago. I have no further information. My current situation is terrible. I don't have a penny and I haven't the faintest hope of getting anything and I'm even more frightened by the fact that I might not be able to find out anything about him in which case I am completely doomed. Therefore I wrote to Dr. Hefshteyn of the Emigration Committee[67] in Berdichev,[68] and he advised me to write to your committee. So, take pity on a beaten-down, weak woman and answer me. My husband was residing the whole time in New York at the following address

65. I did not manage to locate this town.
66. The reference is to the IRO.
67. The reference is to the ICA information office that was part of the network of information bureaus spreading throughout the Pale of Settlement and in Poland.
68. A city in the district of Kiev. According to the census of 1897 there were about 53,355 inhabitants, including 41,617 Jews (78 percent).

Mr. J. Goldsten
432–40 E. 79 Street
New York
For Sherman

My husband's name is Yankev [Jacob] Sherman and he was residing at the above address. I feel it is unnecessary to repeat my request. I assume that the members of the bureau will find it urgent to answer me right away.

So, I remain your as yet unacquainted friend, Sore [Sarah] Sherman

My address:
Shtetl of Chervonnoye (Volin Province)
Andrushovka County
Sara Sherman

December 2, 1908
Mrs Sarah Sherman
Andrushefsky, Wolosk, Russia

Dear Madam:
In reply to your inquiry of the 4th of November regarding your husband we beg to say that we have no one on our records by name of Jacob Sherman who was sent to either Boston or Chicago. We have no means of ascertaining the whereabouts of your husband, but we should suggest that if you do not hear from him you might advertise in the Yiddish newspapers. If, however, you have any further inquiries to make you might address them to the Hebrew Immigrant Aid Society[,] 234 East Broadway, this city, who are better able than we are to obtain such information.

Yours very truly,

• 27 •

Central Zionist Archives, A36 53b

Mitglied des direktorium der
I.T.O.
Dr. M. Mandelstamm[69]
Member of the board of the Jewish Territorial Organization
Kiev, November 6, 1905

Our great president, head of the Jewish [Territorial] Organization, great author, crown of Israel, Mr. Israel Zangwill!

Not in ink but in blood and tears are we composing these words to you! The hand trembles, the eyes tear, the mind is confused, and we cannot organize our thoughts and express them to you! A shout [is heard] outside in our city of Kiev.[70] The soldiers, Cossacks, and police are slaughtering our brothers and sisters in the company of hooligans, and there is no one to protect them. The defense societies have become disheartened; they cannot stand up against the battle-hardened armies with their amazing tactics. Shouts outside, screams in the homes, in the basements, in the attics, in the caves. The screams of children and infants, the sound of women fainting, the groans of the dying, and the breaking of the bones of old people thrown from the upper floors deafen the air of Kiev! Infants and children are being torn up, ripped in half, and thrown to the dogs! They are slicing open the stomachs of pregnant women, cutting out organs from healthy people, and flaying them with iron combs. If the heavens don't explode at the sound of the cries, they must be made of iron and brass! If the earth doesn't shudder at the sound of the wails, then it is a bloody earth, a wasteland full of the fire of the inferno!

69. Max Mandelstamm (1838–1912). He was one of the founders of the ITO and headed the company for Jewish migration in Kiev that sent migrants to Galveston.

70. Between the years 1903 and 1906, violent pogroms broke out against the Jewish population. Most of the pogroms occurred in the southern districts of the Pale of Settlement (Chernigov, Poltava, Jekaterinoslaw, Kherson, Podolia, Kiev, and Bessarabia). More than 3,000 Jews were murdered in the pogroms of 1905–6. In Kiev, a number of pogroms occurred during which 485 Jews were killed and more than 400 were injured.

Oh! All the property of the Jews has been plundered! The damage totals fifty million. All the merchants and shopkeepers in the city have been left naked and destitute, with only their shirts on their backs. Starvation is rampant in the city. We are all dying of hunger, including our infants and children! Thousands of people are crying out for bread but there is none. The children are fainting from hunger. The committee distributes loaves of bread and herring every day, and like locusts they all fall upon the distributors, pushing and shoving, shouting and weeping loudly, "Give me! Give me bread! Give me herring!" Like predatory wolves they fight over a loaf of bread and grab the herring away from each other! You will see a terrible tragedy in Kiev, an unprecedented tragedy. The theaters and community centers are crammed like [chicken] coops with men, women, and children, ill and wounded, heads bandaged, screaming in pain! Every day, many of them die horrible deaths in terrible agony!!!

In every community center and every theater are seven hundred families lying on the floor, seven hundred families without a pillow under their heads or bedding to lie on—just the hard floor. They are beset at all times by fear of death. None of us has faith in life!

There are no words in the dictionary of any language to describe the terrible tragedies being perpetrated now in our land of "evil."[71] The railroad brings slaughtered Jews, maidens tortured and killed, children with shattered limbs. It is hair-raising to see the hooligans wielding axes and picks, knives and swords to chop off the heads of men, women, and children! The heart lurches at the sound of the wild shouts, the cries of joy from the murderers, delighted to see Jewish blood being spilled like water! The army, police, and hooligans get special pleasure from hearing a Jew or Jewess screaming, "Help!" They laugh with glee when they hear, "Oh! Alas!" and they mimic these cries. We heard with our own ears how one young officer, wanting to please his young "love" with Jewish cries of "Help! Oh, alas!" honored her by bringing her to the site of the pogrom and ordered that a Jewish family be beaten severely. Their screams rent the heavens, and these people applauded and cheered!

But what are all the evils that I have described so far compared with the great evil that we want to tell you about here? So many people are fleeing Kiev and the vicinity that in four days eight thousand received provincial

71. *Risha* (or *Rasha*) is "evil" in Hebrew. A play on the word *Russia*.

papers from the provincial officer to go abroad, in addition to those sneaking across the borders, who are seven times that number. All the transports are crammed with men and women like herring in a barrel. The tickets for all classes of the train are sold out a week in advance! The panic is so great that emigration on this scale has never before been heard of. It exceeds all waves of emigration in the history of the world! Thousands of people are coming to Mandelstamm, crying and asking for territory. They scream, "We'll go not just to Uganda,[72] but even to the Mountains of Darkness—anywhere as long as we can get away from here!" "We will make do with meager bread and water for the rest of our lives, we'll wear rags, if we can only breathe the air of a Jewish land."

Our purpose in writing this letter is as follows: Please, honorable President! Please, crown of Israel! Print our words in the English newspapers! We ask and plead that the great Jews in England approach the King of England and the ministers, with you, Mr. Zangwill, our president, at the head of the deputation, and ask them to give us Uganda immediately, because the entire Jewish nation wants Uganda. The "Zionists of Zion"[73] turned down the offer on their own initiative without consulting their people. If necessary, we will provide you with a hundred thousand signatures from a hundred thousand Jews in Kiev and its suburbs, plus the signatures of millions from Odessa, Warsaw, Minsk, Bialystok, Vilna, Elisavetgrad, and so on. We all want Uganda! We all want to escape from the bloody land! We are not sure of our lives! Please, great Jews in England, please, Mr. Greenberg,[74] return to Territorialism for the sake of the spilled blood of

72. The writer of the letter is referring to the Uganda plan that Herzl had brought in 1903 to the Sixth Zionist Congress. At the congress it was decided to send a delegation to the designated area and only afterward to decide whether to accept the offer or reject it. In July–August 1905 (four months before the letter was written) the Seventh Zionist Congress was held—the first to be held after the death of Herzl—and the British plan for Jewish settlement in the Guas Ngishu heights, in Kenya of today, was rejected by the Zionist Organization and was removed from the public agenda. Against the background of the pogroms, the writer of the letter requests the president of the ITO, Israel Zangwill, to revive the plan.

73. Zionists of Zion (Tsionei Tsion), the opposition to Herzl in the Zionist Organization that rejected the Uganda plan. It was headed by Menahem Ussishkin.

74. Leopold Greenberg, a Zionist activist in England. He was born during the 1860s and served as the right-hand man of Herzl while that individual was engaged in negotiations on Uganda with the British government.

Д-ръ М. Е. Мандельштаммъ

Mitglied des direktorium der

„I. T. O.“

№

ד"ר מ. מנדלשטאמם

חבר הדירקטוריום של

ההסתדרות היהודית

הטריטוריאלית

קיוב, יום 6 לירח נויאבר שנת 1905

לשמעו הגדול, ראש ההסתדרות היהודית, הסופר הגאוני

עטרת ישראל, הר ישראל זאנגוויל!

לא בכדי כי אם בדם ובדמעות הננו עורכים אליך את הדברים האלה! דמה ילדות והעינים דומעות, הרעיונות נבוכים ואין אנחנו יכולים לסדר את המחשבות ולהפסיק לפסק! צעקה בחוצות עירנו קיוב, אנשי הלגיון, הנוצרים והפוליציא שוחטים את אחינו ואחיותינו בחבורת החוליגנים, ואין מי שיגן עלינו, חבורות ההרגה הרפו את ידיהן ולא מעטות לעמוד נגד צבאות החיל המלומדות אלה והמסודרות בתכסיסים! עולמים! צעקה בחוצות, צעקה בבתים, במרתפים, בעליות הגגות, במערות. צוחת ילדים והמשכבות, קולות נשים מתעלפות, אנקות חללים ושברי עצמות רקעים הנשלכים מהקומות העליונות מתרוששים את אויר קיוב! עוללות ותינוקות מרוטשים ונקרעים לגזרים ונשלכים לרחוב! פוצעים בטני נשים הרות, כורתים אברים, עוקרים עינים מחוריהן ומסרקים בשרם במסרקות ברזל, אך לא יתפלצו השמים לקול הצעקות האלה שמי ברזל ונחושה הם! אף לא תתפלץ האדמה לקול היללות – כי אורך הדמים היא, על אלה האלוה אש תאכל! [illegible] סוחרי הציר והכנעני אהה! שבת כל רגש היהודים! הנערים עולים לאולינים חמשים, [illegible] פתו מתים ברעב יחד עם שאר בריות ונמסר כי, רק בשלוחים לעזר, הרעב כבד בעיר, [illegible] עוללינו וטפנו! אנשים נעלפים צועקים ללחם ואין, הילדים מתעלפים מצלצלות רעב, [illegible] לחם כפרות לחם ודגים גלויים בכל יום, ובאורבה יתעלפו על הבחורים, ידחקו ולחצו, צועקים ובוכים בקולות: "לחם! לחם! פת לחם! לחם רק דג עזה!" כאמרו [illegible] ורבים על כבר לחם, ונורפים [illegible] רצחו את הדבים האלה! טרגדיה נוראה תחזינה

your brothers and sisters. Please, good-hearted, honest Mr. Cowen,[75] the sword is hovering over our heads; we have been declared fair game! The senders of the letter may not be alive tomorrow. The sound of swords, shots fired by the army, the clang of knives, the wails of the slain, and the shouts of hooligans fill the air of our land and the air of Kiev! Mass emigration by a million families is under way now in our country and we need a land! Go to the government and ask it to give us Uganda, improve its offer to us slightly, just say the word, and all the emigrants will go there now! The reply should be sent to:

Kiev Bolshaya Vasilkovskaya 74
to Moshe Rosenblatt
In the name of thousands of families, Moshe Rosenblatt[76]
I have written on Mandelstamm's letterhead to show that I am an associate of Mandelstamm's and am known to be a reliable man whom you can trust.

• 28 •

Central Zionist Archives, A36 53b

December 6, 1905, Kiev

Our great president, head of the Territorial Organization,
crown of our Jewish people, Mr. Israel Zangwill,
may God protect and save you!

From the mountains of Kiev, from the vale of tears of the land of evil,[77] we cry out to you for help!

Please, prince of Israel, hurry up and save us from the teeth of the predatory beasts that are opening their jaws wide to swallow us alive! The pogrom ended back in October only officially; it is still going on, not

75. Joseph Cowen, the London delegate at the Sixth Zionist Congress.
76. A rabbi and public activist in Kiev, who was a member of the Mizrahi movement.
77. See note 71.

noisily or tempestuously but slowly. Not a day goes by without hooligans or police attacking Jews who are passing by innocently on the street—killing them and robbing them of all they have, and even stripping off their clothes! Not a night goes by without murders, thefts, and robberies! The fear is escalating; none of the Jews living in the city can sleep at night due to fear! We sit here in groups at night, trembling at the sound of a driven leaf, and the sound of a mouse scratching at the wall freezes our blood!

More and more people are being killed! The panic and flight have reached tremendous proportions here; emigration is increasing daily; almost half of the Jewish population has left Kiev! And the poor people who remain are starving to death! Blood is increasingly fertilizing this polluted soil, and brains are being mixed in with the earth! Not one of us has faith in life, for our lives hang in the balance! Every hooligan and every barefoot person beats Jews on the street and no one protests. The police and soldiers laugh at the sight and cheer. Almost all the civilian inhabitants of Kiev are members of the Black Hundreds,[78] and they incite the people against the Jews!

In brief, Mr. President, we are like a sheep among seventy wolves. We dwell among scorpions!

In this letter I speak on behalf of thousands of Jewish families among whom I live. They have charged me with appealing to you and beseeching you to ring the bells in England, move heaven and earth in the London newspapers, beat the great drum and call for assistance, help the nation of six million who are in terrible distress, in life-threatening danger!

We don't want protests! We aren't demanding that the English government intercede in this matter and fight our battles. We don't even want protest meetings by our brethren. We want redemption! In other words, we want to go to the wilderness—anywhere as long as we can escape from this bitter exile! We even want to go to the Mountains of Darkness, coal mines, salt mines, a land whose soil is iron and brass—as long as we can breathe air, sleep in peace, eat dry bread unmolested, and not have our flesh cut with knives and axes and our blood spilled like water!!!

78. The Black Hundreds is the general name for the small, right-wing, anti-Semitic groups in Russian society who attacked and murdered Jews under the guise of patriotism and loyalty to the Russian homeland.

The chronicler who gathers material to compile the annals of these terrible happenings will compare our troubles to the troubles of our forefathers. He will find that the torments that the Egyptians inflicted on our ancestors, the torments of Nebuchadnezzar[79] and the Chaldeans, the torments of the Romans in the time of the destruction, and the suffering that the medieval inquisitors caused our ancestors are like a drop in the ocean compared to the torments and suffering of the present age! Now they are killing, slaughtering, cutting to shreds old and young, pampered infants and sucklings; they are strangling women and grinding them in the mill, sinking their claws into them like beasts of prey. In every home you will see a slaughterhouse, rivers of blood as in the slaughterhouse for beasts and fowl!

Oh, Mr. President, where shall we go?! We have no asylum or place of refuge! The poor people who still remain in Russia and have not fled the country are considered fair game, like sheep to be slaughtered!

All the Jews in Russia now lift their eyes to you and only you! The day when you tell us about some territory will be a holiday, a day of redemption and salvation, a day of deliverance and reprieve! We all agree to Uganda! Anything as long as we can get out of here!

We plan to send fifty delegates from Kiev to Brussels[80] for the Congress, representing the poor Jewish proletariat. They are prepared to move heaven and earth there, and to cry out bitterly so as to evoke mercy for us and our wives and children. Our delegates will melt the hearts of stone of our satiated bourgeois such as Wolffsohn,[81] Marmorek,[82] Montefiore,[83] and

79. The King of Babylon (630–562 BCE) who destroyed the First Temple in Jerusalem.
80. The reference is to the Brussels Conference that took place on January 29, 1906. Following the pogroms and the rising tide of migrants, the Zionist Organization concluded that it was its duty to offer suitable solutions for the sufferings of Russian Jewry. The aim of the conference was to gather together under one roof the various Jewish philanthropic organizations and to try to solve the many problems that had arisen as a result of the migration and to consult together over the question of the rights of Russian Jewry. But nothing came of this cooperation.
81. David Wolffson (1855–1914), the second president of the Zionist Organization and one of the initiators of the Brussels Conference.
82. Alexander Marmorek (1865–1923), Member of the Zionist Actions Committee.
83. Francis Montefiore (1860–1935), one of the most active leaders of the Zionist movement in England.

Gaster![84] Our delegates will soften the hearts of rock of the stubborn men who trade on the Jews' troubles in order to amuse themselves with ideals, such as Ussishkin[85] (the Jewish Trepov), Temkin[86] (the Jewish Durnovo), Rosenbaum (the Jewish Pobedonostsev), and Greenberg (the Jewish Witte, who leans in both directions)! The fifty young people going to Brussels are destitute, without even enough food for one meal. Nevertheless, they have decided to pawn everything they have, even their clothes, go on foot and take along moldy, dry bread—so long as they can persuade the conference to go the right way, not straying after distant ideals in a place where immediate salvation is needed as desperately as air to breathe! They will show everyone that if they are silent now, then—Heaven forbid—they will be dooming their brethren to annihilation!

Our great president, Rabbi Israel Zangwill! And our elder brother, the leading light of the generation, Dr. Zalkind,[87] do not be silent! Stir up public opinion in London! Choose delegates from among the partisans of our cause to go to the conference in Brussels, traveling with you and camping under your banner. Send a circular to all the Jewish-populated cities to choose delegates en masse from the various countries, so that we can turn the platform that they are building in our direction! For this is a matter of life or death!!! It is a historic moment, and we have no right to let it pass with indifference!

Finally, I have some advice: "Sholem Aleichem,"[88] the popular author known for his great talent, lives in our city. He is the storyteller of the ghetto, a writer who sketches and depicts all the slight movements of Jewish life in exile. This author's every artery and drop of blood are of ghetto life.

---

84. Moses Gaster (1856–1939), one of the most active leaders of the Zionist movement in England. In 1887 he was appointed hakham of the Spanish and Portuguese congregation in London.

85. Menahem Ussishkin (1863–1941), a notable Zionist leader and one of the leaders who forced the abandonment of the Uganda plan.

86. Ze'ev Temkin, born in 1861, a member of Hovevei Zion and a representative of the Odessa Committee in Palestine during the 1890s.

87. Alexander Zalkind (1865–1931), a physician and Zionist activist in czarist Russia. He was the head of the Jewish community in St. Petersburg and took part in the self-defense organization in Gomel and Kishinev and in connection with the blood libel that was fabricated around the Bayliss case.

88. Sholem Aleichem (1856–1916). This is the pen name of Shalom Rabinovitz, an important Yiddish writer.

The nation loves him for his wit and style, and he has tremendous authority. I recently converted him into a Territorialist, and I tried to convince him to go to Brussels, because I know that when Sholem Aleichem speaks onstage, even the walls will have ears. The walls of the building will be moved by his voice, and his authority will have an enormous amount of influence on the nation. He promised me, but nevertheless, to reinforce the matter, I recommend that he be sent an invitation from ITO headquarters in London, which is under your jurisdiction, honorable President. Then I am sure that we'll catch this big fish. Don't make light of it.

I bow down to you from afar with humility and endless respect.

Moshe Rosenblatt

My address for a reply:
Kiev, Bolshaya Vasilkovskaya 74, to M. Rosenblatt
The address of Sholem Aleichem:
Kiev, Bolshaya Vasilkovskaya 35, To Sh. Rabinovich

• 29 •

Central Zionist Archives, L2 133 I

The American Shirt Waist Co.
Manufacturers of
Ladies' and Misses' Dresses
151–53–55 West 25th St.
New York, March 2, 1914
Dr. A Ruppin[89]

89. Arthur Ruppin (1876–1943), an economist and sociologist who was a member of the Zionist Organization since 1905. In 1908 he was sent by David Wolffson to Palestine to set up the Palestine Office, which represented there all the Zionist societies dealing with settlement. Among the different departments in the Palestine Office was the information office, which provided information about the possibilities of employment and settlement in Palestine.

Honorable Rabbi Dr. A. Ruppin [illegible]

I was advised by someone here in New York that I could find out the full particulars and details from you about settling in Jaffa or Tel Aviv, or in some area that you know. I am a sixty-year-old man with a wife, both of us born in Russia. My children are all married. My assets are 6,000–7,000 American dollars. The question is whether my capital will be enough to build a respectable life, because here in America one must work hard and I cannot do that anymore, because the twenty-seven years we have been in America have robbed us of our health. I was quite wealthy, but bad people ruined us. So the question is whether that amount of capital will be enough to make a nice life, so we won't have to live off of the cash. Here in America I was always involved in business and made out well, but bad people ruined us. So we want to leave this country and settle in Jaffa. Therefore, I am seeking instruction.

With great respect and esteem, your as yet unacquainted friend, Yitskhok Goldberg.

I. Goldberg
639 Williams Ave.
Brooklyn
America

· 30 ·

Central Zionist Archives, L2 133 I

Medanos,[90] May 25, 1912

Distinguished brothers who honor our nation and esteem our land, we have a question for you. You are no doubt aware of the terrible plight of our

90. An independent colony in Buenos Aires province. Near the city port of Bahia Blanca. In 1914, of 14,000 inhabitants living in Medanos, nearly 100 families were Jews.

brethren in Russia, which forced us to go where the poor people went. Now the time has come to leave Argentina. Now we have a question: Where should we go? It would pain us greatly to return to our families in Russia. To bring our families here and stay in Argentina, in the country where our children are being raised without human knowledge,[91] without knowing their roots, and without nationalism would be very, very upsetting. If we could earn a living in some other way in the city, things would still be as they were, but as it is we are just farmers working the land. And since we don't know how to make a living by any means other than the land, we all, the sons of ten men—some with their families here and others with their families in Russia—are joining together to go to Palestine, where whatever happens we will know that we are working for ourselves and for our children, and our children will know that they will remain Jewish, and our hope will not yet be lost. In a word, here in Argentina there is nothing to do: working for years carrying burdens like a donkey is not for a human being. But as we know that there are people among you who can give us good advice, we are asking you a question before we go to Palestine. We want to purchase land and houses and pay for the [illegible] in cash.[92] We have more than enough. We do not need a loan. We can immediately pay whatever amount is agreed on. We each have between 4,000 and 8,000 francs, and we all are men with family members who work, including our daughters. We just need advice: show us where we can get land and houses that we can pay for in cash.[93] If we have no choice we will buy land without houses and build our own houses. Also, when should we go to Palestine? Should we go to Haifa or straight to Jaffa? As for the remaining questions, we know clearly about everything from a reliable source.

Our address:
Republica Argentina
Estancia Medanos
Provincia de Buenos Aires
F. C. Sud
Senor Poalei Defro

91. Alternatively, he may mean "without knowing anyone."
92. Alternatively, he may mean "in installments."
93. Again, he may mean "in installments."

Distinguished Representative of the Jewish nation,
Because there are not among us very educated men, we come to ask your forgiveness for our very not good writer. There is no one better among us. We [have for this] an aphorism: "the hand is bad, but the mind is good"

Respectfully,
[Poalei Defro]

• 31 •

Central Zionist Archives, L2 133 V

Ljublin,[94] September 14, 1913

Greatly Esteemed Gentleman Dr. A. Ruppin in Jaffa, Palestine!

I come to you with a big request?

Namely, when the Agudah Mizrahim-Tsiyonim was founded, I joined the ranks as a Mizrahist[95] and have placed all my hope on being a colonist in Palestine in the very near future. At that time, I had no money and my profession up until the Russian Revolution was gaiter-maker. In German it is called *Oberteilenmacher.* And on account of the strike in the days of the revolution, I closed the workshop and ended up as just a shoe-buttonhole-maker and had to start dealing in black market goods from Austria. At that time, someone turned me in, but—praise be to His Blessed Name—they didn't find anything on me. Further business of this sort is out of the question. I have turned over a new leaf.[96] I have 1,000 rubles. Therefore, my request is the following: inasmuch as 1,000 rubles is not enough to

94. A town in the province of Ljublin. According to the census of 1908, there were 62,394 inhabitants, including 31,721 Jews (50.8 percent).
95. Mizrahi, a religious Zionist party within the Zionist Organization, founded in 1902. Its leaders were Rabbi Samuel Mogilever and Rabbi Jacob Isaac Reines.
96. *Ikh hob gemakht a remonent* (Yiddish). The word *remonent* which means "tools, implements," makes no sense here. It appears that the writer meant to write "remont," which means "renovation"—in this case a renovation of self: "I have turned over a new leaf."

enable someone to come to the colony, I therefore request that you come up with some kind of exception so that you can take pity on me. Because if you cannot assist me, then I will have to keep on dealing with the cursed black-market goods, I'll probably end up in jail and won't be able to realize my pious vision for my life. Now, I am a thirty-four-year-old man with two children,—long may they live—one six years old and one five years old. So if you have mercy on me, I will certainly be able to endure the initial hardships that will have to be faced. But if you turn me down, then I'll be a doomed *Goles-yid* [Jew of the Exile]. I figure that it is possible that if you put your mind to it, you could strive to come up with something for me. Jewish institutions do, in fact, exist. In addition to the 1,000 rubles, I still have three machines to sell along with a little of my household furniture. I can probably make another 300 rubles from that, but not more. One needs, of course, money for expenses. I intend to leave right after the holidays—may they go well for us—and will expect nothing more than to receive word from you that there is a possibility for me, then I will begin to tighten my belt. It would probably need to take six months.

I beg that you answer my letter soon. My neighbor, a tailor, would like to go with me. He also has almost 1,000 rubles but does not intend to work in that trade if he goes. He proposes that we be made partners and be given a parcel of land as a loan so that we will have what to live on, and maybe, he says, make a partnership in a dairy farm and bring the milk to a nearby city and in this way make a living. He's going in the middle of the winter with his wife and a girl of sixteen. Therefore, if I receive a response in time he will include me on his passport as a helper.[97] Please let me know if they let people go down to Jaffa without a government passport.

From me, Yankev-Sholem Kats Shidlover

My address for the answer
Ljublin, Russia-Poland
Kowalski Street, No. 14
Jakob-Szulim Szydlower

97. According to Russia's law, the passport listed all family members irrespective of age—wife, children, other relatives, and sometimes fictive family.

Please note!
I myself was born and raised in the countryside, which means that I know how to plow a little. I won't need much time at all to learn everything. My neighbor, in addition, has always been a fruit-grower. He used to lease fruit orchards [farms], so he is also not far off from this.

• 32 •

Central Zionist Archives, L2 133/III

Nisan 5, 5674,[98] Chabno[99]

Dear Sir![100]

Forgive me for being so bold as to disturb your work or your rest and tire you out with words and questions that have nothing to do with you or anyone but me, a simple young woman whom you don't know! After all, what am I to you? Is my letter worth taking a few moments of a busy man's time? I am sure it is not. So why am I writing?

I will tell you the truth. I thought a lot and hesitated before writing to you, but finally, finding no other option, knowing no one who can answer my questions, I forced myself to turn to you, sir.

And I beg of you: forgive me this trespass.

Before I ask you my questions and present my doubts regarding myself in relation to Palestine or vice versa, in order for you to know how to answer me, I think it necessary to describe my character to you.

Eighteen years have passed since I was born to my shopkeeper parents, who lived in a small, remote town in the province of Kiev.

My father is a decent householder of good lineage, a good, honest man. He fears God, observes the Sabbath, and is meticulous about all the

98. April 1, 1914.
99. A town in the province of Kiev. According to the census of 1897, there were 2,719 inhabitants, including 1,721 Jews (63.3 percent).Present-day Polesskoye, Ukraine.
100. The reference is to Arthur Ruppin, director of the Palestine Office.

commandments. My mother, too, is a modest, decent[101] woman, although she is more freethinking than my father.

Of course, our home is a God-fearing Jewish home, and it was in this home that I was raised.

As a child I attended the dear old heder together with the boys, studying the Bible with various commentaries. Then, when I was a little older, I started studying the [Hebrew] language as a language and grammar.

Until my tenth year I spent all my time on these studies because I did not enjoy playing, I did not make friends with children, and I studied nothing else.

When I turned ten, I embarked on general studies and spent less time studying [illegible].

I attended school until my twelfth year, after which I studied only two hours a day for another two years. I finally stopped because my parents were unable to teach me Hebrew and Russian. And there was another reason: I had entered an environment that treated our nation, our language, and our Torah with scorn and inspired me to prepare better to obtain a certificate for several departments or to enroll in a gymnasium. This started making me apathetic about what was dearest to me in life, which in the secret recesses of my heart had never stopped being dear to me. I never enrolled in the gymnasium and didn't earn a diploma because my father wouldn't let me go, as he was sure that I would write on the Sabbath there, and nothing I did helped. Even then I did not entirely forget the Hebrew language. I read books, and in these books I found things that spoke to me much more and were much dearer to me than I would have found in Turgenev[102] and Tolstoy,[103] which I consider precious and lovely.

And while I sat listening, almost absentmindedly how they ridiculed to my nation and its Torah[104] being disparaged, I never stopped studying them. Finally I decided to fight their battle.[105] I realized that these people

101. The handwriting is not clear. It may say "a modest, honest woman."
102. Ivan Sergeyvich Turgenev (1818–83), a Russian writer and dramatist.
103. Lev Nikolayevich Tolstoy (1828–1910), one of the greatest Russian writers in modern times.
104. Pentateuch.
105. Alternatively, she may mean, "I started fighting their battle."

are sick. With a pained heart, I understood—or rather, I felt—that no, a wise man speaks the truth. I did not feel their souls in their words. I realized that these people would find no peace of mind and would wander forever from place to place without friends or family. And the sight of their souls ripped to shreds frightened me and filled me with fear. Finally I left them and went my own way. I again started spending many hours studying the language and reading. But one thing pained me greatly: It was almost impossible to obtain Hebrew books, whereas Russian books were [illegible], and of course I read Russian more than Hebrew. Only in the past year have I been able to get books to read. The days that I spent in foreign surroundings influenced me slightly, too, and tore my heart a bit. This little tear gave me no rest. I would go from our town to Kiev, from Kiev to our town, thinking about stopping everywhere, at every house.

I wandered from place to place, from house to house, from person to person. I exchanged one book for another and found no rest. Something [illegible] inside me, in my very being, gave me no rest; I could not get rid of it and even now cannot do so.

Once, a year ago, in a moment of agony and grief, I sat down and contemplated what I had been through in my life. With heavy, troubling [illegible] my heart, I sat there and thought about the purpose of my life, about Lilienblum's[106] book *Derekh la-avor golim.* Suddenly, I felt relieved. I understood that I would rest in our land, in the land that I never stopped thinking about, whether voluntarily or involuntarily, day or night. Even back in the heder, when I had sat with the Pentateuch or a verse and learned the beautiful, dear stories, I had yearned for it, for the holy places, for the graves of our forefathers, for the tombs of the Maccabees. I remember the impression made on me by the story by David Shimonovich[107]—the dear, young author with the sensitive, refined heart—about his visit to the tombs of the Maccabees, that was printed in *Ha'olam*[108] in 5670[109] (I don't remember the title).

106. Moshe Leib Lilienblum (1843–1910), a leader of the Hovevei Zion movement in Russia.
107. David Shimonovitz (1891–1956), poet, writer, and Hebrew translator.
108. Die Welt (Ha-olam), the official bulletin of the Zionist Organization.
109. 1909/1910.

With special emotion I soak up everything having to do with Palestine.

From that day on, I realized that I will not be silent and will not rest until I go there, to the land of my dreams.

For an entire year I have been fighting with my parents, who refuse to let me go for fear that I will have to work hard, since I don't have the means to support myself in a foreign land.

Finally they told me to ask someone if I can be supported there.

Personally, I am not afraid of hard work. There is one thing that I want to know: whether I can also study. I don't know what trade. I imagine that I won't get classes to teach, because there are enough teachers in Palestine, and I doubt I will find an intellectual position. I will undoubtedly have to work the land. I am slightly familiar with this work, because we have a large garden and an orchard, and I have loved working in it ever since I was a child.

At present this work does not appeal to me. I would very, very much like to study, but without money I won't be able to, so I've decided to work by day and study at night. Please honor me with a reply and tell me whether I will find work and whether I can also study. If I have to work hard to do so, that's fine, for "God also commanded us to work and suffer."[110] Please answer these two questions of mine.

I am certain that you will calm me down and honor me with a reply, which I eagerly await. For the third time I ask you to forgive me for my letter.

Respectfully and with blessings of national rebirth,
Teyvl Kardash

My address:
Chabno, Teyvl Kardash
Kiev Province

P.S. [illegible] in the envelope even though I don't know if [illegible]

110. This is a line from Bialik's poem "Igeret Ktanah."

1

לכ' נשיא המדינה

אדון נכבד!

סליחה בעד זה, שהעזתי אני להפריע לעבודתו

על ענינים להתעסק בדברים של שאלות, כאשר נוגע

על לשאול אותך, כי אין לי עצה פשוטה, אי ודאי לי!

ודאות זה לי ולי? האם שזה הוא נכתב זה, כי אני

טפד יאבד עליו רגע מהדעת? ובטחוני, כי בודאי לא.

ובכן למה אני מדברת?

את האמת אגיד לו, כי הסבה תשובת [illegible]

[illegible], ובלי [illegible], אבלי הכל [illegible]. שיענני

על שאלות, הכרחיות לפנות אליך, איש נכבד.

ומאד מאד אבקש את כבודו לסלוח לי על עניני זה.

בטרם הערך לפניו את שאלות [illegible], הנוגעות

לי כמו לארץ ישראל, או להפך, וכבודו יודע זה לענין!

לא [illegible] מחשב. [illegible] את אפי.

שמונה עשרה שנה עברו מאז הולדתי לבית החנוני,

גם עירה קטנה ונדחת בפלך [illegible].

אבי הוא בעל-בית הגון ומחשב איש ישר וטוב, ירא

אלהים, שאוהב את השכנות ומדקדק על כל המצוות

ואמי גם היא אשה צנועה וישרה, [illegible] כי [illegible]

April 30, 1914
To Mrs. Teyvl Kardash
Chabno
Kiev District

We received your letter and read it attentively, and we earnestly desire to assist you. Since you have no profession, you have no other choice but to be an agricultural worker. Details regarding this can be found in the booklet attached to this letter. But the season for this work is in the winter and you should postpone your voyage to that period. After the day's work you can study in the evening. Lessons are given nearly everywhere for free. Yet one cannot hope, of course, for much success at studies after the labors of the day.

There is another way—to become a school or kindergarten teacher. Teaching requires training either privately or in a school. In Jaffa there is a seminary for school and kindergarten teachers and if you can obtain a certain monthly sum from your family for your upkeep, it is worth coming here and learning the Hebrew language so that you may finally receive a position in a school or kindergarten. The seminary in Jaffa belongs to Hovevei Zion and you may apply to the Hovevei Zion Committee according to the address attached here regarding the terms of acceptance.[111]

Yours truly,

111. The Hibbat Zion movement (or Hovevei Zion, the societies that made up Hibbat Zion) was founded in the Russian Empire in 1881. The ideological basis for the movement was expressed by Leon Pinsker in *Autoemancipation*, published in 1882. In 1890 the czarist administration gave its official imprimatur to the movement's activities throughout Russia, and the movement's central committee, known as the Odessa Committee, was founded. When Herzl came on the scene and the Zionist Organization was established in August 1897, the vast majority of Hovevei Zion societies and their activists joined the Zionist Organization. Nevertheless, the movement remained active, working in cooperation with the Zionist Organization's institutions on behalf of Jewish settlement in Palestine.

• 33 •

Central Zionist Archives, L2 133 III

Zakharin,[112] November 11

Dear Sir:

I am writing to you on behalf of one family, asking you to express your opinion if you have the chance. I am sure you will not turn me away, because your reply is important and valuable to me.

This family, in which the writer of these lines is one of the sons, comprises ten people, seven males and three females, that is, a father, mother, six sons, and two daughters. The parents are fifty-three years old. The eldest son is twenty-seven. The child of their old age is a six-year-old girl. The family's situation is as follows: The eldest son completed the Grodno[113] pedagogical courses two years ago and is now the principal of a talmud Torah[114] in a small town in the province of Mogilev. The second son, who has now returned home after three years of military service, works in the office of a lumberyard for 25 rubles per month. The third son is in a similar situation. I should add that these last two were shoemakers until recently and knew the work thoroughly; they only left it about three years ago because it does not provide a living. The fourth and fifth, aged fifteen and seventeen, are at home. The youngest son is eight years old and attends school. The two girls, aged six and twelve, are at home.

The father of the family is a shoemaker whose trade—due to the large number of craftsmen engaged in it and the intense competition

112. No data has been found about the town Zakharin (Zakharino). However, the nearest city to the town was Mstislaw, in the province of Mogilev in the district of Mstislaw (Uezd). According to the census of 1897, this city had 8,516 inhabitants, including 5,076 Jews (59.6 percent). It may be assumed that the number of Jews in Zakharino was much smaller than in the largest city of that province.

113. Grodno, a city in the province of Grodno. According to the census of 1897, there were 46,965 inhabitants, including 22,684 Jews (48.3 percent).

114. The Talmud Torah resembles by definition a heder but was intended for children whose parents could not pay for the tuition.

among them—brings in barely enough for food, and even that with great difficulty.

Everyone in the family is healthy, strong, and hard-working.

Five years ago, the family lived a life of poverty, barely earning enough for their dry bread, because the children were still small. Only recently, when the boys grew up and started helping out, one here and one there, did things improve a bit.

About six years ago, the family moved to a village in the province of Mogilev[115] because they thought it would be easy for them to make a living in the village.

In the village the family leases vegetable gardens in the summer and sells the produce and also engages in petty commerce.

All the family members are hard-working, quick, capable of all sorts of work, and not deterred by any kind of work, as long as it pays. And although the family earns its bread, albeit with difficulty, it is not content with its present situation, as disaster can be expected and there is no way to provide for the future.

The family does not feel any solid ground under its feet, and its [members'] lives are in danger. Being completely dependent on the *uryadni,*[116] who could evict them at any moment, they must suffer insult from the village farmers and must flatter them while they bleed at the sight of such cruelty. The family aspires to a quiet life, a life full of work and emotional satisfaction.

The family members are innocent and honest, brotherly peace prevails among them, and they have no differences of opinions.

In light of all this, the family is thinking about leaving this country and heading for another country that will treat them in a more welcoming fashion. We family members are aware that it will not be easy to attain our goal, but we trust that with hard work we will succeed. We are not aiming for a life of luxury or asking for easy work; we just long for a quiet, satisfying life. We are not idealists, but we are willing to make sacrifices—

115. In the province of Mogilev there were eleven districts (Uezds): Mstislavl, Chausy, Gomel, Cherikov, Klimovichi, Mogilev, Bychov, Seno, Orsha, Rogachev, and Gorky. There were all together 190,000 inhabitants in the district. Apparently the family moved to Zakharino.

116. A low-ranking officer (roughly equivalent to a sergeant).

provided that we are assured that our future will eventually be secure and stable, and that the ground under our feet will not collapse. If we see that there is no way for the entire family to leave the country all at once, then we have decided that the older sons—that is, the second and third sons—will emigrate first, and after a while the rest of the family will go.

We currently have 800 rubles.

Sir! If possible, express your opinion on this matter. Please help us by sending us your instructions and your advice: Would we be able to move to Palestine and settle on the land or even in some city? Will we find what we are looking for in the Land of Israel? Or would we better off heading for other countries, because the living conditions in Palestine are not suitable for us?

We are afraid that we will fail and ruin our already-precarious position. Please do not delay in replying.

Respectfully,
in the name of the entire family,
D[avid]. Koheleth

Address:
Shtetl Zakharin, Mogilev Province
to D[avid]. Koheleth

• 34 •

Central Zionist Archives, L2 137/2

Andizhan,[117] March 22, 1913
Friday, the week of the Torah portion Tazria, Andizhan
In honor of the special issue of *Hatsefira* of the
Jewish community of Jaffa, may it be rebuilt

117. A city in Fergana district. Today in Uzbekistan.

To the great and noble rabbi whom I don't know, A. Ruppin,
may he live long:

I entreat you, Your Honor, although I do not know you. I beg of you, do not turn me away. Have mercy on me and answer me, for you are aware of the present persecution and oppression in Russia. There are new edicts every day—may God save us. They oppress us every step we take, especially regarding the right to live outside the Pale of Settlement. And I, miserable soul, live outside the Pale without the necessary right of residence, and I am liable to be expelled at any moment. Therefore I resolved that, no matter what, I will leave this dreadful country and go to the holy city of Jaffa or someplace that seems suitable to me, where I will raise my children in accordance with the holy Torah and proper behavior. I myself am a good tailor, and I earn between 80 and 90 *perutot*[118] a month here because here they take [illegible] for work. But better dry bread in tranquility, as you know, and especially in the case of raising children, into which I put all my efforts and strength!

And you know about the education here!

Therefore I set my request before you. Have tremendous compassion and answer all my questions. Is my trade—that of a tailor, the work of sewing—considered an important trade there? How much would I earn there each month? Would I be able to support my family—three boys, the oldest seven years old and the youngest three years old, a one-year-old girl, and my wife, may she live long—and pay for the children's education? The main question is how much [illegible] how much the boss keeps for himself, and how much he pays the worker. Tell me everything. Please feel my anguish and fulfill my request. It will be considered a great mitzvah. Answer me in detail. I asked the editors of *Hatsefira*[119] but they told me to ask you and said that you would provide a detailed answer. I thought about enclosing stamps with this letter for your reply, but it wouldn't help because

118. He may be referring to 15-kopek coins. Alternatively, the abbreviation may stand for "francs."
119. A Hebrew newspaper that appeared intermittently between 1862 and 1931 in Warsaw and Berlin. At the beginning it was issued as a weekly and then, from 1886, as a daily. For most of the years, its editor was Hayim Zelig Slonimsky, and from the 1880s it was Nahum Sokolow.

the stamps from our country are not valid there. So please be so good as to send it without any stamps and I'll pay for it here, because I don't want you to incur any costs on my behalf. Give me strength. I strongly hope and trust that you will fulfill my request, perform a mitzvah for a friend, and sustain an entire family so that they don't have to suffer the agony of expulsion.

Your friend who doesn't know you, who always wishes you the best and eagerly awaits your reply,
Shalom Khanin

My address:
An'dizhan', Fergana Province
To Mr. Solomon Khanin
Build. Apt. Zabramnom

• 35 •

Central Zionist Archives, L2 133 III

Herrn Dr. A. Ruppin in Jaffa [March 1, 1914]

Esteemed Gentleman!

I believe that you already know about the misfortune that has befallen the better people of the small shtetl Zvanits [Zhvanets]. Our shtetl is located close to the border of Austria! Where our poor emigrants cross the border—naturally not with government passes, but through the corrupt "agents."[120] We could not stand by and watch our own brothers be robbed, swindled by Jewish "agents," so we wanted to fulfill the commandment "and you shall burn out the evil in your midst" and we ended up being cleared out ourselves. That is, we were sentenced to five years administrative exile in

120. Migrants who did not have passports were forced to cross the border secretly with the help of agents.

Narimsky Territory, Siberia. This misfortune happened to twelve families. Of [them], eight are now in prison (along with Mr. Sholem Altman, a certain Zionist), and four escaped over the border, and we are now on Austrian soil. We truly fell victim. I am in an extremely desperate situation that is indescribable, I cannot figure out how to conduct myself, so that I won't become completely ruined. Please read *Ha-Tsefirah,* no. 25–26, and you will familiarize yourself with the story of our misfortune and you will see how innocent we are.[121]

I wrote to my brother-in-law, Mr. David Roshovski (former secretary of Mr. Tshlenov[122] of the National Treasury) in Moscow, wanting to get advice from him about my plan to immigrate to Palestine. He replied that I should get in touch with you. That is why I'm writing you this letter. And since I want to have a "proper reply" from you, I will get right to the point, so I will describe my situation in detail:

My name is Fishl Koyfman, I'm thirty-nine to forty years old, a healthy person, raised by orthodox parents. I don't know any languages, I can read the Hebrew newspapers, but writing Hebrew is hard for me. I have read a lot of Jargon [Yiddish] literature. I count myself among the intelligent young people. My father—rest in peace—was a lumber dealer, and I have also worked with that my whole life. Lately I have also been dealing with flour and milling. I made the deals with other people's money more than with my own, so I had a good deal of liquidity. I was running the business in partnership with one of my brothers and he is now running it without me. The trades pay out more or less 2,000 rubles to each of us. If I am not there, I can expect half of that amount. I have 6,000 rubles of my own capital. If I want to sell my rights to my brother he might give me 1,500 rubles for it, so I will have approximately 7,500 rubles. I can possibly count on having the support of some good friends who believe in me, since I will not take even a kopeck from someone I don't know, so that's 1,500 rubles. It could come to 9,000 rubles all together. I will only be able to come up with the whole sum within eight to ten months, in other words, I'll be able to start taking the money out little by little, because if I demand the money

121. See "Le-Toldot Provokatzia Ahat" [History of a Provocation], *Hazefira*, December 2, 1914, 12.

122. Yehiel Chlenov (1863–1916), a Zionist leader and member of the Bank Otzar Hahityashvut of the Zionist Organization.

from my brother right away, it could damage the business. And I don't want him to have to liquidate it. My family consists of a wife, younger than me by two to three years, not a healthy woman, and three daughters. The oldest is eighteen to nineteen [years old], educated at home. The second is fourteen to fifteen years old and actually goes to Yavne high school. I send her 30 rubles a month. And she has also cost me 150–200 rubles this year in addition to the monthly allowance. She is now in the fourth level. She doesn't yet know of my plans. The youngest is seven years old and has also just started studying Hebrew. In "matters of commerce," I count myself among those who get it. As far as other ways of earning a living apart from commerce, I do not even have an inkling. I ask you now, after everything I've described, what should I do? May I come to Jaffa right away and look for an occupation? Will I not fail? Or maybe I should buy some land either as a vineyard or something else? Also, with this money, will I be able to expect to settle in Palestine? And will I be able to count on assistance, that is, to be able to borrow money to buy a bigger plot of land than my money would cover? And the main point, will I be able to make a living, will the soil or the vineyard provide income adequate to the needs of my household, so that I won't have to touch my capital? And which is better: to come for the first period alone or indeed to go right away with my wife and daughters? Please give me a detailed answer, the more detailed the better, then I will be able to make sense of your answer quicker.

Respectfully and with Zion's greetings,
Fishl Kaufman

My address:
Fieschel Kaufman
[Via Wien-Triest]
[If you establish] a bank with that objective in mind, and one could start buying land to settle poor Jews: and really, if such a bank were founded that could buy land and settle people that know what to do with land, and more so with the current situation of the Jews, immigration to Palestine would exceed immigration to America. I will add: whoever will and whoever can work on that, if a bank like that could be founded or a [illegible] and one could buy land! Then the settlement in the Holy Land could really become

stronger! And we additionally hope that—God willing—it will be that way and we poor Jews will be delivered from the dark hardships and the miserable exile, that on each one's heart weighs the burden of sorrow from the hardship of earning a living in the darkness of the exile! We place our hopes upon the One Creator! And upon you who work for the common good, his messengers. And we will be delivered, whenever it may be. And the people who work actively for the community today, whatever party they belong to, they are the messengers of the almighty God and we hope that you arrive in Zion and you will be blessed to live many years.

• 36 •

Central Zionist Archives, L2 133 III

Shevat 6, 5674[123] [illegible] Lodz[124]

To the honorable directors of the committee in Jaffa:

Now that the Zionist national idea has arisen among our people, this sublime, lofty idea has shot through all the ranks of our nation like an electric current. They have all awoken from the heavy, deep exilic sleep in which they were immersed until now, and they are all single-mindedly determined to return to their borders—to their ancestral land, the beloved land where they lived of yore. Oh, how sublime and lofty is this idea! Do the Jewish people have any aspiration more sublime and lofty than this—to return to their ancestral land? Hopefully, the joyous time will yet come and they will return there. But unfortunately and distressingly, only the wealthy members of our nation can go to the land of the Jewish people and realize this lofty aspiration, because they have the means and a lot of money to support themselves there in our ancestral land, if only a feeling of love for the nation and a feeling of love for the ancestral land prevailed

123. February 2, 1914.
124. Lodz, a city in Poland, in the province of Petrekow. According to the census conducted in Poland in 1908, there were 341,416 inhabitants, including 79,785 Jews (23.4 percent).

in their hearts. But what can a poor or middle-class man do who loves the nation and its ancestral land, whose soul longs and yearns to return to our ancestral land, but who lacks the opportunity and means to return to our ancestral land and to support himself there in our holy land. For example, I live in the city of Lodz. In Poland [illegible] a reformed heder from which I eke out my living meagerly and with difficulty. I do not have enough for my needs, because I have sons and daughters to support and do not have enough for them in terms of material goods. And who even talks about the spiritual aspect—educating them in a national-religious spirit while they are still small children and implanting in their hearts love for the nation of Israel and its land? This pains me, and it depresses me to think about boys and girls who will be swept up by the foreign trend current in Poland. For there are no words to describe and explain the economic hardship of the Jews of Poland, oppressed and harassed by the Polish people, and especially their troubles in terms of educating their sons and daughters, as it is impossible to give them a national-religious education that will keep them loyal to their nation and their land. And what is our hope if not our young generation? Therefore I, the writer of this letter, having had the idea stir in my heart of uprooting myself and my home from the exile and returning to my ancestral land, will make every effort and use every tactic not to remain in "exile." Although I have already resolved this in my heart, I am nevertheless writing to you, honorable directors of the committee in Jaffa, to ask your advice and consult with you. You can direct me as to the way to go and what to do. My entire family and I cannot go now, but I want to send my wife and family first to be supported there. I will remain in Lodz and send them enough to live on every month; it would be hard for me to go, too, as I don't know what is ready for them there. My plan is to stay in Lodz while my wife and family are there. That way I intend and hope to achieve the desired goal because costs in Lodz are very high, and the needs are even greater. And when my wife and family are in our land, where things are not so expensive and the needs are few, they will make do with little. In addition, my wife can earn some money by working because she is a seamstress. And then perhaps, with God's help, I will be able to save up a few hundred shekels and I, too, will be able to go to our land and purchase property there. That is my entire aspiration—to be able to settle there in our land already. Oh, how happy I will be with life if I attain this lofty aspiration. This is why I am writing to you and asking your advice. Please write back to me and tell me everything in great detail, including about the voyage and disembarking from the ship and in what colony one can best make a living.

With respect and reverence,
A Zionist who yearns to earn his living in our holy land

My address
Mr. Avraham Yaakov Litvin, Lodz
Province of Petrokov, 5 Sosnowa Street

• 37 •

Central Zionist Archives, L2 131 IV

London E.
July 10, 1912

Dear Sir,

Please be so kind as to answer these few questions. I am a man who is used to working and my wife is the same way. It doesn't matter what kind of work. My family is made up of exactly six sons and two daughters. The eldest son is fourteen years old and the youngest son, one. I have my mother-in-law who is fifty-five. I would like to settle my whole family in Palestine to raise chickens, milk, eggs, butter, and the like.

How much money would I need to get there, settle there and make a living?

Thanks in advance,
H. Finn

• 38 •

Central Zionist Archives, L2 133 I

B. A. Goldberg
Agent
Palestine Land Development Company[125]
January 7, 1914
Vilna, Tevet 9, 5674
To: Palestine Office, Jaffa

Dear comrades!

Two families that are about to be expelled from a small town have asked me whether they would be able to get by in Palestine.

The members of these families are blacksmiths, and as they lived near a village they also worked the land.

One of the families has a son who is also a blacksmith and three daughters who are seamstresses. The other has two sons who are blacksmiths and one daughter who makes corsets.

Please tell me how these families can manage in Palestine.

They are also asking whether work tools can be obtained there or whether they have to be brought from here.

I await your prompt reply.

With complete respect and the blessings of Zion,
B. Goldberg

Palestine Office
Jaffa, Tevet 22, 5674

125. Public society for the acquisition of land in Palestine and preparing tracts for Jewish settlement. It was established in 1908 by Otto Warburg and Arthur Ruppin.

To: Mr. B. A. Goldberg
Vilna, 18 Alek. Blvd.

Dear Sir:
In reply to your letter of the ninth inst.:
Master blacksmiths who are experts in shoeing horses may be able to find work and make a living from it. We therefore generally tell unmarried blacksmiths that they can come: they do not have the burden of a family, and they can move from place to place looking for work until they finally find it. But we cannot respond in the affirmative to people with a family who need immediate employment.

Expert seamstresses can earn between 60 and 70 perutot[126] *a month. If they really know their work well, the three daughters can support the family while the father and son look for work. The corset-maker may also be able to find work.*

If they decide to come, they should bring the tools of their trade with them.

Respectfully,

• 39 •

Central Zionist Archives, L2 138

Stryj,[127] Tishre 5, [year illegible, presumably 5669][128]

Very honorable Sir!

Relying on your faithful, holy work of replying pertinently to every questioner, I permit myself to ask you a small question. Here in Stryj

126. Alternatively, the abbreviation may stand for "francs."
127. Stryj, a city in Galicia in the Austro-Hungarian Empire. According to the census conducted in Austria in 1910, there were 30,942 inhabitants, including 10,718 Jews (34.6 percent).
128. Assuming that the year is 5669 (based on his next letter), the date corresponds to September 30, 1908.

and in almost every town in Galicia, there are factories that make sausage skins from the small intestines (*armen, kishkalakh*) of animals, which are afterwards filled with meat. In other words, they prepare the small intestines for making sausages. These skins are sent to Pest or Vienna or sold elsewhere.

And now I ask:

1. Is there such a factory yet in Jaffa or Jerusalem—or in some other big city that already has a railroad?
2. Are most of the slaughterers of meat Jews?

I hope you will send me a clear answer.

Signed respectfully and with blessings of national rebirth,
Yosef Wohlmann

Yosef Wohlmann, Stryj
Galizion

· 40 ·

Central Zionist Archives, L2 138

Stryj, Marheshvan 8, 5669[129]

Very honorable Sir!

Forgive me, sir, if I ask you my question again. Apparently you didn't understand my question properly, so your answer was not relevant to the question. And because I hope to support a Jewish family in our ancestral land, without any harm befalling anyone, I permit myself to ask again.

I was not asking about a sausage factory, but about a factory that makes

129. November 2, 1908.

sausage skins—in other words, a factory that prepares small intestines for use in sausages. I don't want to make the sausages themselves, just the skins. And by *skins,* I don't mean the pelt that is stripped off the animal, for which the authorities license certain people from the city, but sausage skins made from the small intestines. I am enclosing a piece of such a sausage skin as an example. After I process these sausage skins I don't have to sell them in Palestine; I can send them abroad.

And when I asked whether there are many slaughterers, I meant so that I could buy the small intestines from them. It would be especially good if there are many slaughterers of sheep. These skins are known as sausage casings.

In addition, please tell me if there is already someone in Jerusalem or Jaffa who collects bones and buys bones from bone collectors to send abroad. Also, how much does it cost to ship bones by sea from Jaffa to the German coast?

Please, sir, give me a clear answer to my first question. I bless you wholeheartedly.

With blessings of national rebirth, Yosef Wohlmann

• 41 •

Central Zionist Archives, L2 134

Grodisch[130] [illegible] Tammuz
[Esteemed] Gentleman

Dr. A. Ruppin,

Certain of your goodwill, and knowing your worthy name through our Zionist association as one of our greatest representatives, and especially

130. Grodisch, a town in the province of Warsaw. According to the census of 1908, there were 2,570 inhabitants, including 1,884 Jews (73.3 percent).

as meticulous with the multifaceted details about the Land of Israel, and also heeding the advice of Mr. Podlishevski, member of the great Action Committee, I am turning to you, Esteemed Doctor, with a request to receive from you a piece of information taking into consideration my current situation which I will describe in detail below. I am married, twenty-four years old, healthy, and I have somewhat more than an elementary education. The same in Jewish subjects. I work for my parents in their business, which consists of the following branches: wholesale kerosene production, Russian flour and grain. I am very skilled in these businesses. My capital amounts to three thousand rubles (3,000). My wish would be not to have to put the capital into purchasing land, but rather into setting up a business until I am familiar with the circumstances and conditions of the place. Then, in case I weren't able to get it off the ground, it would be easier to get the capital back than if it were invested in land. And speaking of buying land, I would like to know if there is a company that leases out the land for the first period, during which it can all be put in proper condition, and that, for the same period, allows people to come work for the same company on the same land as a day-laborer during the whole leasing period. I read in the newspaper that Haifa exports a lot of barley. I am very familiar with this commodity. I wonder if there is really something I can get my hopes up about. Thanking you, Doctor, for the answer that I hope to receive from you as soon as possible, I end my letter

With Zionist greetings
Avrom [Avraham] Tsverner

My address
Azryel Goldbard
Senior Barber-Surgeon
Grodisch
Warsaw Province
Abram Cwernir
Russia-Poland

• 42 •

Central Zionist Archives, L2 134

Byten[131]
June 2, 1914

Dear Sir!

I am writing to ask the bureau about the state of the animal business in the city of Jaffa or its environs. I intend to leave Russia and come to Jaffa and earn a living by engaging in some kind of commerce, and it occurred to me to ask you about the situation. I have always lived in the small town of Byten in the district of Slonim, and I trade in animals from all [illegible] But this is the second year[132] that business has dwindled, and I keep thinking[133] about going to the Holy Land, to the city of Jaffa, and engaging in this business to which I have been accustomed since my youth. My household is as follows: myself, my wife, and my seventeen-year-old daughter. I can bring a certain sum of money, about 2,500 rubles. Can I support my household with that? How much [illegible] can I earn and how much are the expenses of a house with animals? I am confident that I will receive a reply to my letter.

Here is the address for replying to my letter.

Respectfully, Aron Kopeliovich

Aron Kopeliovich Shtetl Byten'
Grodno Province
[In the margins:] Please deliver to Dr. Rupin [*sic*] at the Palestine Office

131. Byten, a town in the district of Grodno. According to the census of 1897, there were 2,682 inhabitants, including 1,614 Jews (60.1 percent).
132. Alternatively, he may mean "this past year."
133. Alternatively, he may mean "I am determined to go."

• 43 •

Central Zionist Archives, L2 133 I

Rozwadon[134] 6 Kheshvan 5674[135]

Highly Esteemed Doctor

I refer to the correspondence dated 24 Elul [5]673, No. 5285, from and to Mr. Mendel Hertslekh from here, and to our matter, and, as the party in question, I have the honor of inquiring with a precise piece of information to communicate in order to receive a satisfactory answer.

I am a master joiner (worker) [carpenter/cabinetmaker], my wife is from a village near Rozwadon, which is more or less known for agriculture; I have been working in this trade going on twenty years and (despite the fact that I have had journeymen and apprentices) am barely able to make a living for myself, my wife, and children. However, in the last two years, things have gotten much worse in Galicia, and carpentry work in general has diminished, both in construction and in (rustic furniture-making) household furniture-making. So we decided unanimously with our children (through the stimulus of my eldest son) that we should immigrate to Palestine and settle in a colony, buy land, and not have to become debilitated while waiting to get a bit of work. And now even if we get it, we don't earn enough to live on, because we have to do the work for a very low price, and live only from the fields. And if I do happen to get carpentry work, it will be good, of course, I will have enough to spend on the non-essentials—and I will also have time more or less to work on carpentry, because otherwise one is occupied in the fields, mainly when I am with a few children.

(I have approximately 400 crowns there [illegible] to have more)

Therefore, please do answer me and inform me:

If I will, after all, be able to survive in the way I have presented above,

134. Rozwadon, a town in Galicia. According to the census of 1910, there were 3,378 inhabitants, including 2,373 Jews (70.3 percent).

135. October 28, 1914.

I am a family of eight people, that is, my wife, three older sons, and three younger children.

What kind of field can be given to us and in what region?

What is the field like? Has it been overworked? Is it fallow?

How much (of course, this is directly related to what kind of field) does a dönüm [dunam] of land cost?

What percentage does the field produce there? (That is, according to the grains that the field produces.)

How exactly is the field transferred? That is, how much money does one have to pay initially? And how much credit is given? To be paid back over how long a period? And with how much—if any—interest?

Does the land come with a domestic economy? That is, a house, stables, stalls, machines, sheep, etc.?

What is a reasonable time to go there? So as not to get there before we would be able to take possession.

Most importantly, please inform me about everything that is essential to know in this regard.

In addition, I take the liberty of telling you that my eldest son is around twenty years old, has no trade, since he is not a carpenter, he is here [working] for a lawyer, a writer, and would very much like to go to Palestine, but does not know what kind of employment to look for there. The capital he has saved up is approximately 1,400 crowns, therefore I ask that you please simultaneously pass on to me what kind of employment my son could have in Palestine. Should he start some kind of marketable business or something else? Must he buy the field along with me?

I can also comment that if we are able to survive there, then many families from the region would go there.

In anticipation of receiving your satisfactory answer as soon as possible, I sign off

With respect
Yudl Oysubel

My address
Juda Ausubel
Rozwadon
(Galicia-Austria)

• 44 •

Central Zionist Archives, L2 140

With the help of God, Vitebsk,[136] Sivan 21, 5672[137]

To the very distinguished head of the inner executive committee,
the honorable Professor O. Warburg![138]

A young man left here for Palestine last week, traveling via Berlin. His name is Selik Mogilnitzky (Vitebsk).

Before setting out from our camp, Mr. Mogilnitzky came to me together with his friend Mr. Chaim Rubin to find out about aspects of life in Palestine, and it became clear to me from our conversation that his aim was to go to Palestine and work the land on a farm of the [illegible] or the Pal[estine] Land Dev[elopment] Co[mpany]. When he heard from me that in Palestine one has to make do at first with low wages, one franc per day, he even agreed to that. Since he is a tradesman, his trade being preparing leather for shoes—cutting and preparing the material for shoemakers—I asked him why he is switching from his trade, by which he earns enough to support himself, to farming, where he will have to suffer until he masters it. He replied that he hopes to become established as a colonist in Palestine. So when he told me that he is traveling to Palestine via Berlin, I advised him to visit you in Berlin. I gave him your address and promised to write a letter on his behalf requesting that he be given work someplace where the Palestine Land Development Company is currently active—that he be attached to a group of workers in some agrarian institution.

After Mr. Mogilnitzky left here for Berlin, I found out that he had done something despicable, and I must publicize it here: perhaps we can save the wretched woman whom he married about a month ago. Apparently

136. Vitebsk, a city in the province of Vitebsk. According to the census of 1897, there were 65,833 inhabitants, including 34,431 Jews (52 percent).

137. June 6, 1912.

138. Otto Warburg (1859–1938). A botanist of world renown, and one of the pillars of Zionism in Germany. He served as the third president of the Zionist Organization.

he intended to defraud her of her money, and he also deceived her in a crude and shocking manner, leaving here without her knowledge. She is crying and begging for compassion: If Mr. Mogilnitzky will not agree to take her with him to Palestine now, he should immediately send her a bill of divorce through the rabbis there and here. The address of the rabbi here is To rabbi Sh. L. Medalye, town of Vitebsk. By the way, I can bet that Mr. Mogilnitzky's wife could also work and earn a living in Palestine as a confectioner, cook, and baker.

Therefore, for the sake of honesty and justice, it is a mitzvah and an obligation to take an interest in this matter, so that a deceitful man does not roast his prey,[139] and for the welfare of Jewish women. Because when he sees that his deceit has succeeded, he may repeat it again and again, so we have to close up this breach.

If he doesn't want to give his wife a divorce, and if some assistance and help is needed from here, cable me at the following address:
Pekler, Witepsk
and we will try to have him arrested by the Russian [illegible].

Please confirm receipt of this letter. If possible, the reply should be in Hebrew.

With complete respect and the blessings of Zion, I am
Yitzhak Pekler

My mailing address:
Russland
To Y. Pekler
Town of Vitebsk

139. This is an allusion to Proverbs 12:27.

· 45 ·

Central Zionist Archives, L2 133

Radzyn[140]
Gub. Lubelska
[B' (scriptural weekly portion) Khukat, 1914]
[5]674 [1914]

Esteemed Dr. Ruppin!

I have the honor of asking you a few questions and request a prompt response. Since emigration to "Palestine" has won so many sympathizers in Russian Poland, there are many who would wish to have real information about various trades [or] businesses, which the emigrants could take up when settling there. Therefore, please be so kind as to inform me about the following questions,

1. Manufacture of cast brass and copper handles, doorknobs and the like for construction, the same production for machines such as ball bearings, commercial scales, and so forth; in general, all manufacture of brass and copper?
2. Can a good seamstress for women's outfits and dresses [get] high-end or mid-level work?
3. Can female hairdressers for women's wigs or falls find a position there or set themselves up in this respect? How much capital would be required? Would all the materials needed for this kind of work be available there? Or would it need to be brought in from abroad?
4. Would a young man with an intellectual profession, with capital amounting to approximately 2,000 [illegible], and additionally to 200 [illegible] be able to accomplish some-

140. Radzyn, a town in Poland in the province of Ljublin. According to the census of 1897, there were about 5,332 inhabitants, including 2,853 Jews (53.5 percent).

thing there? Doing what? In business or something else?

5. What kind of merchandise in general is imported there from England and specifically what kind of manufactured goods? And how about from Russia? Can any of this be imported in small quantities?
6. What are the details and the costs of the whole journey?

When is the best time of year to travel?

And as far as cast brass and copper production is concerned, [what] if one doesn't have the possibility of founding one's own small factory? Are there factories like that there, and can one get work in them?

I trust fully that you, Esteemed Doctor, will inform me well about everything.

[illegible] Thank you in advance.

With Zionist greetings,
[Fayvl Rotshteyn]

Address
Radzyn, Ljublin Province
Mister Abram Zilberberg
Russia-Poland

• 46 •

Central Zionist Archives, L2 133I

To the honorable gentleman, Dr. E. Ruppin!

I hereby ask the great gentleman, in his capacity as the director of the Palestine Office, to answer the following questions:

I live here in a village, not far away, and I earn my living by farming land that I rent and by working as a blacksmith. In general, however, material conditions are not good. Furthermore, these days every Jew is vulnerable to expulsion.[141] Also, I have little land, and blacksmithing work is not available all year round.

My family consists of nine people, five of whom can help me in the fields. One or two help with the blacksmithing as well.

Thus, I have a workforce. I want to leave my place of residence and move to our holy land. This is my request: As you see, I am moving for the sake of work. Therefore please give me all the information that I need, including whether it is worth leaving my present location. Can a blacksmith find work there all year round? Also, are there societies that give land to people like me and accept payment in installments? I can bring a little money with me, about 300 rubles.

As for [illegible] all the laws regarding the Ottoman Empire, please tell me what taxes have to be paid to the government on land and houses. Basically, please let me know all the information pertaining to Jewish settlement in Palestine. I eagerly await your reply.

Respectfully and with the blessings of Zion, [illegible] Elterman

My address:
To H. A. Gurvich
For A. Elterman
Town of Radoshkovichi[142]
Vilna Province

• 47 •

Central Zionist Archives, L2 135

Horodenka[143] [illegible] June 30, 1914

141. It is not clear whether this is what he means.
142. Radoshkovichi, a town northwest of the Pale of Settlement, in the district of Vilna, where there were 2,618 inhabitants, including 1,519 Jews (58 percent).
143. Horodenka, a town in Galicia in the Austro-Hungarian Empire. According to the census of 1910, there were 11,223 inhabitants, including 4,210 Jews (37.5 percent).

Dear Sir
Dr. Ruppin, Head of the Palestine Information Bureau

My dear sir!

Please fulfill my request and be kind enough to pass on precise information about the following.

I am a single, young man of twenty-eight years, living in Galicia, possessing a fortune of 7,000 crowns in cash, and have until very recently been working with wire netting and mesh, that is, I have solidly learned this profession after spending a few years in America. And now, returning to Galicia, I cannot earn a living for many reasons; first, having been in America, it is difficult for me to live in a land of various nationalities without equal rights. Second, big money is pressing forward in Galicia and therefore it is difficult for a person with a small amount of capital to accomplish anything in this area of fabrication. Thus, being nationally inclined, I want to try, perhaps something will work out for me, as well as for our Fatherland, something to accomplish [illegible] knowing that in a country where new settlements and colonies are being founded, various contrivances can be considered, such as new fencing, farming implements, poultry-yards, and since in Palestine wood is very expensive, one must certainly now utilize the modern and practical wire netting, here-named *Drahtgeflechte*. Being myself a bit of an expert in this I would like to request from the worthy In[formation]. B[ureau]. the following precise reply and advice.

1. Is the item (wire netting) very frequently needed there? What are the most marketable numbers, I mean diameter and width of mesh? And how much does a square meter cost, for example number 60 diameter 30 galvanized?
2. Is the above-mentioned article already produced by anyone else in the country [and if so] where exactly?
3. Or is it imported from abroad? From where?
4. How much is the import tax on ready-made <u>wire netting</u> and the difference from simple wire and <u>filament</u> [that are] <u>not processed?</u>

Approximately how much is consumed in a year?

I am hereby writing to the worthy Information Bureau for detailed advice about this because the conditions for a new immigrant over there are unfamiliar to me, [and] so as not to take imprudent steps by going directly to Palestine without having a clear picture. Notwithstanding I would like it to be noted that outside of my expertise in the area of wire netting, I also have knowledge of horticulture, cattle and poultry farming and I have no fear of any kind of work.

Thus, when I receive a prompt, favorable reply that there are some options for earning a livelihood in the land of our fathers; if I can earn like that, then I will come to Palestine right away and bring the necessary machines to establish a modern wire netting factory. I am also a maker of wire mesh—*Drahtgewebe*—which really is a separate line requiring a larger capital investment that would be utilized for these window frames, etc.

With full conviction that your worthy advice and reply will soon reach me.

With that I sign off respectfully,
Yehoshue Preminger

Osias David Preminger
Horodenka (Galicia)

Please also kindly let me know if there [are] also opportunities in the field of chemical items like shoe polish or metal polish and the like? What kind of packaging is utilized for it: a tin box or glass container? What countries are they imported from? What is the tariff on the above items?

I am most grateful from the outset for the attention that you will certainly pay to my inquiry and I remain
With Zion's greetings [Yehoshue?]

• 48 •

Central Zionist Archives, L2 133 III

Buguruslan, April 20, 1914
Doctor A. Ruppin
M. G. in Palestine
Jaffa

Since I am requesting to immigrate with my family to Palestine, I ask you to be so good as to write me whether it is possible for someone to buy an orange plantation which is already producing and would soon be able to provide enough income for a family of six people to live on. Because buying land and sowing an orange plantation and waiting four to six years until it starts producing is not possible for me because I do not have enough capital to be able to afford to wait such a long time.

Perhaps it is possible in Jaffa or Jerusalem to open a candy and gingerbread factory, a bakery, or a pastry shop. Would that work there? And would one be able to earn a living from that?

1. According to the information that I have assembled, Arabs with small boats ferry the passengers from the steamships that arrive in the city of Jaffa! And they charge the passengers 70 per person. Maybe a good business for me would be to place a small steamboat to ferry the passengers to the city. Obviously I would charge less than the Arabs, but I was told that the Arabs are bad people and they would not let a Jew run a small steamboat.[144]
2. Please write me your opinion about this. That is, if I were to set up a small steamboat in Jaffa to ferry passengers, would

144. Jaffa did not have a port. The steamships anchored at a distance of about 1 kilometer from the shore, and boats rowed by Arab porters reached the ship, brought the passengers down into the boats tossing in the sea, and took them to Jaffa. The writer of this letter wants to compete with the Arabs in this line of business. The plan did not succeed, and the Arabs kept their monopoly in this field.

that be a good business to make a living from? And is there reason to fear that the Arabs would kill [me] or destroy the steamboat? Do such things happen? And what measures can one take to protect oneself to avoid such an outrage?

3. Does one have to have a permit from the Turkish government to run a steamship on a small scale to ferry passengers to Jaffa or does one perhaps have to go to the municipal administration to lease the right to place a steamship in the harbor?
4. Does a Russian subject have the right to start a business in his own name in Palestine? Or does one perhaps have to open a Turkish subject company? Will I be able to accomplish this, because until this year I have been an agent of a Turkish bread company. Will I be able to do business under that company's name?
5. Will I be able to run several small steamboats on the Jordan to ferry passengers from one colony to the other, and can that be a good business? If so, we would set up a company—several steamboats to transport passengers with baggage/cargo.

I impatiently await your reply. I hope that you will write me detailed information in answer to my questions.

[illegible] Lipe Hertsbarg

My address
Town of Kremenchug,[145] Poltava Province
Sadovaya Street, No. 4
c/o Aron Shmulevitsh Tshudnovsky
L. M. Gertsberg
I attach to this letter a 10 kp. stamp for your reply.

145. Kremenchug, a city in the province of Poltava. According to the census of 1897, there were 63,068 inhabitants, including 29,768 Jews (47.2 percent).

• 49 •

Central Zionist Archives, L2 133 III

Dear Mr. [illegible]!
[May 10, 1914]
I am thirty-two years old. For seven years I have been a storekeeper here in our little shtetl Ille. My family consists of a wife and three children from age five down to one year. Until now I have made a living from the store. Now the Poles in the shtetl are opening a store that sells everything. That will without a doubt take the livelihood away from us Jews immediately and we have to take care of it early while there is still a chance to get out with something. Later there might be—God forbid—nothing left. And also I would very much like to educate my children in the Jewish tradition, which can be done more precisely in our fatherland. For people like me it would be impossible to send the children to study in Jaffa or somewhere else in Erets-Yisrael [land of Israel]. And also, beyond the practical [concerns], I want to leave Russia because of all the long-standing oppression that we're subjected to here. My capital amounts to approximately 2,500 rub. I reckon that, after expenses, I would still have 2,000 rub. I was born in the countryside, although I myself have not tilled the soil because I am also physically weak, although I am no stranger to the work. I also have an understanding of commerce.

I take the risk of impertinence by writing you, because I read in the newspaper *Hatsefirah* that you are the Ministry [*sic*] of Zionism and you will, I am sure, give sound advice as to what I should do. Therefore, please write me as to whether I will be able to earn a living in Erets-Yisrael with my small amount of capital [illegible] And doing what exactly?

Blessed be Zion and its revival.

Respectfully[,] Avrom-Yoysef Marinev

I understand Yiddish, Hebrew, and Russian.

My address
Iliya,[146] Vilno Province,
A. Marinov
Ille 25 Nisn 5674 [1914] here in Ille

· 50 ·

Central Zionist Archives, L2 135 I

Drugstore and cosmetic store
of Ya. Rabinovich
"Modern"
Peteburgskaya N22
Shevat 14, 5674
Dr. E. Ruppin
Jaffa
February 26, 1914
March 4, 1914[147]

Dear Sir:

I am writing to ask you, honorable Sir, if it is not too much trouble, to tell me the rules in Palestine regarding pharmacies. Can anyone who wants to, even someone who is not a licensed pharmacist, open a pharmacy in some village or town of Judea and Gilgal? And if no one will prevent him, what does he have to do? Is it necessary to obtain a special permit from the government here in Russia? And if only a licensed pharmacist can open a pharmacy, can a simple man known as a druggist open a pharmaceutical warehouse in Jaffa or in one of the cities of Judea and Gilgal? How much

146. Ilya, a town in the province of Vilna. According to the census of 1897, there were 1,431 Jews.

147. It is not clear why two different Julian dates are given here. To make matters even more confusing, Shevat 14 was actually January 27 according to the Julian calendar (February 10 on the Gregorian calendar), and not either of the Julian dates given.

money is needed to do so? Please tell me all this properly. Although I have a pharmaceutical warehouse here in the city of Jekaterinoslaw[148] in southern Russia, I am sick of my life in this land of new edicts, and with all my heart, being, and flesh I want to go to my ancestral land. But when such a thought occurs to me, a question immediately arises: What will you eat there, you and your household?! After all, you aren't trained as a farmer, and commerce and manufacturing have not yet developed in Palestine. So what will you do there? I don't want to go hungry anymore, not even in our ancestral land. Therefore, if it is at all possible to open a pharmaceutical warehouse so that I can earn enough for meager bread and water and a home, even if it is not a nice one, I would be the happiest man in the universe of losers. Oh! Oh! How many hearts groan and wail for our holy land! How many young people and young forces are collapsing here under the subjugation of the exile! How many sacrifices have we offered here on the altar of the god known as "the war of bread"! Give us the ability to go to our land, to live there on its soil and enjoy its sun. Why should we all live like a nation of merchants? Are there no more Jewish farmers?! Why must we ask for [legal] status in a foreign country? I don't want America or any other country in the world. I want only to work the land of my forefathers. Just give me the ability!

Forgive me, sir, if my letter contains lots of nonsense in addition to errors. First of all, I am from Russia. How could I know Hebrew if I wanted to speak Hebrew? With whom would I speak? Second, it was not I who wrote this, but the blood of my heart, which longs to be rescued from the subjugation of the exile, which is even tougher than the parting of the Red Sea. When someone is a bit weak,[149] one does not demand of him manners and wisdom.

I trust that you will not ignore my request. Thank you in advance.

With complete respect, [illegible] Rabinovich

P.S. I forgot to tell you that I am still young and have only a wife but no children, and my needs are minimal.

---

148. Jekaterinoslaw, a city in the province of Jekaterinoslaw. According to the census of 1897, there were 121,216 inhabitants, including 36,600 Jews (29.7 percent).

149. The word he uses actually means "blurs," but it is likely that he means "weak" instead.

• 51 •

Central Zionist Archives, L2 I30

Chorzele,[150] Wednesday, Sivan 9
To the Information Bureau of the Palestine Office

Dear Sir!

Please let me know if 1,500 rubles is enough to establish some industrial business in Palestine that will support a family of two. I myself am thinking about the following things: for example, opening a small factory for buttons made of mother of pearl or linen thread, or maybe better—for candy or for umbrellas and parasols. If one cannot support oneself with these occupations there, then please tell me if there is any occupation that one can take up. Please just answer me as soon as possible. I was in Palestine three years ago and worked in the colonies for a year, but I couldn't make it as a laborer.

Respectfully and with blessings of national rebirth,
M. Eisenstadt

My address:
M. Eisenstadt
Chorzele gub. Plock
Russland

150. Chorzschele, a town in Poland, in the province of Plotzk, where in 1908 there were 4,411 inhabitants, including 2,432 Jews (55.1 percent).

• 52 •

Central Zionist Archives, L2 133 III

A. Heitler
Varsovie
Rue Żelazna No 41
Telephone 157–67
Warsaw, January 24, 1914
Dr. Arthur Ruppin
in Jaffa
Palestine

Greatly Esteemed Gentleman,

I am grateful to the Central Zionist Bureau of Berlin for giving me your worthy address, and so I permit myself, owing to the bad times in general, and more narrowly to the boycott in particular, pol[itely] to petition your worthy opinion on whether emigration to Palestine makes any sense for a middle-aged man and wife who have two sons of eight to nine years old and who have put together a small sum amounting to approximately 2,000 rub. cash, along with letters of recommendation from bank-houses and prominent merchants.

Perhaps it would be more prudent to communicate with organizations like the ITO-ICA-Hilfsverein and others by contacting them first by telephone and then by letter.

I await your swift communication. I thank you in advance for your efforts, and I am ready and willing to return the service.

I sign off respectfully yours,
Avrom Heitler

Letters can be written in Russian, German, and Polish.

To Mr. A. Hitler[151]
Żelazna No. 41
In reply to your letter of January 24

Dear Sir,

Since you have explained to us in your letter in which profession you wish to work here, we cannot give you a clear answer. In a commercial enterprise it is difficult to manage with 2,000 rubles especially for a new person who is not familiar with the conditions of the place and the languages that are spoken here. With regard to settlement in the Land of Israel, we herewith send you a printed booklet that contains the detailed information.

Yours truly,

• 53 •

Central Zionist Archives, L2 133 III

Honorable Rabbi, Esteemed and Dear Dr. Ruppin

Since Dr. Epshteyn was here, I told him about my circumstances with the capital that I have. My capital amounts to approximately 1,000–1,200 rubles. My husband is in America. He is a Hebrew teacher. Every month he sends me 100 rubles. But he also has a feeling for Palestine. I know full well that with my capital I will not be able to accomplish anything big, but I would be satisfied with an ordinary life. All I want is to be able to make decent people out of my children. Please—I beg your pardon—write me an answer as soon as possible because I'm on my way. I figure that I might be able to put up retirees or start a small business. Here I ran a dry-goods store.

151. The name Heitler appears on the letterhead of the writer. In the reply he received from the Palestine Office, they addressed it to A. Hitler. At the beginning of the twentieth century this was a Jewish name, which meant in Yiddish "a hatmaker." It may be assumed that after the Holocaust, Jews who bore this family name changed it.

My family consists of sons[,] two [illegible] and [illegible] daughters[,] four. The eldest daughter is fifteen years old, and the eldest son is thirteen. I beg of you, since you are the friend of the Jewish people, please reply to me right away.

From me, your as yet unacquainted
Rivke Lifshits

Address
Bobruisk,[152] Minsk Province
Shmerel Lifshits
Textile Trade

• 54 •

Central Zionist Archives, L2 133 III

In the name of God who has chosen Jerusalem!
Lipsko,[153] province of Radom, Tammuz 2, 5673[154]

Dear wise, perfect, Honorable Rabbi!

On the advice of the agent Mr. Heshe Farbstein, I am writing to you, honorable doctor, with my request. But before I say what I have to say, I will allow myself to relate my life history in brief in order to give you an accurate idea so that you can understand my present situation:

I am now sixty-three years old. From my thirtieth year until my fortieth year, I taught students in the city of Warsaw, or to put it more simply, I was a Lithuanian-style teacher in Warsaw. I was one of the first whose teaching

152. Bobruisk, a town in the province of Minsk. According to the census of 1897, there were about 34,369 inhabitants, including 20,759 Jews (60.4 percent).
153. Lipsko, a small town in Poland in the province of Radom. According to the census of 1908, there were about 2,903 inhabitants, including 1,610 Jews (55.4 percent).
154. July 7, 1913.

and conduct satisfied the hasidim of Warsaw and were also chosen by people from Lithuania to teach their sons. I taught many students, including the most illustrious—the sons of Farstein, the sons of Wilner, Bieler, and Shpilerin, and other distinguished people of Warsaw. My subjects are Bible, a little grammar, and classes for beginners. [The results of] my work were, thank God, evident in my students. I implanted in their hearts love of our faith, our Torah, and our nation, and when I [illegible] my job I earned good wages for what I had done. But as my family absolutely did not want to move from their town to Warsaw, they entreated me when I had a decent sum of money in my hands to leave my holy work and return to my town to help them in the brandy business. At the time this was a common business among our brethren and, before I was familiar with it, I thought it was respectable. I did well in this business, too, according to our town's scale of values, and I worked in it for a long time until a new law went into effect in our land, taking this line of work away from our Jewish brethren.

At first I went back to Warsaw to look for work, leaving my household to eat what was already prepared[155] [illegible] and thinking that I would resume my first occupation. But unfortunately, I did not find it to my liking because times had changed: the melamdim[156] had become full-fledged teachers, the constant teaching and study had become occasional, the schools had become factories where the work was done by [illegible] with rough hands, and I received no recognition for my status. I also tried finding [illegible] in commerce and decided to live in Lodz, but instead of making a profit I lost a considerable sum, almost half of what I had, so I returned disappointed to my home and my small town, where [illegible] small children. All this time my only wish was to settle in our holy ancestral land. Although I was among the first Hovevim[157] and the last Zionists, I could not take action due to many obstacles and for many reasons. Now, in my old age, I am left alone with my wife, as my sons and daughters have moved out. I still have enough left to pay my way and to support us for a while. I have started thinking again about how to go about making the voyage to our holy land. I suggested it to [illegible] Mr. Heshe Farbstein,

155. This probably refers to living on savings.
156. Lower-level teachers for small children.
157. The writer was a member of Hovevei Zion (lovers of Zion). See note 43 in the introduction.

who advised me to ask you, distinguished doctor, saying that you would instruct me and advise me as to what to do. Therefore, it is my honor to ask you, distinguished doctor, to be so good as to give me good advice regarding how and in what manner we can go about settling [there]. Be aware that I am from a small town and my household's needs are very few. We make do with little, and thank God I am still strong enough for physical or intellectual work as befits the time and place. I await your reply.

Respectfully and with the blessings of Zion,
N. H. Kaplan

My address:
H. Kaplan, Lipsko, Suwalk Gub.
(Rus-Pol)

• 55 •

Central Zionist Archives, L2 138

Caucasus-Volzhsk
commercial and industrial
joint-stock company
Kiev office
Telephone N 26–89
Menachem Av 7, 1914[158]

To the great, honorable, and noble Dr. Ruppin

Dear Sir!

Two families want to go to our ancestral land to start a bread bakery in Jaffa or somewhere else, having heard that there is no such business there and

158. July 30, 1914.

that one cannot get a good piece of bread in Jaffa. If the business requires large-scale management, they can take on a partner so as to ensure that there is sufficient money to run the business. The partner is a rich man and has agreed to do this for the sake of the Yishuv,[159] but he nevertheless does want to make a profit on the money that he invests in the business. So I am asking you:

1. Is it true that there is no such business there?
2. Even if there is, can such a business support two families that need 100 rubles a month each?
3. Approximately how much money is needed to run such a business?
4. Is it necessary to bring over expert bakers from Russia, or can they be found there? I should mention, too, that the members of these families cannot do the work themselves. Furthermore, the business is completely foreign to them, but they think that it does not require great expertise and that in [illegible] time they will know how to run the business.

With confidence that you will give us your answer soon for the sake of the Yishuv, I express my thanks in advance.

Respectfully and with the blessings of Zion,
Hillel Spanusky

• 56 •

Central Zionist Archives, L2 138

To the director of the Palestine Office,
the honorable Dr. Ruppin!

---

159. Jewish settlement in Palestine before the establishment of the State of Israel.

Dear Sir!

For some time I have wanted to go to our holy land and settle there, but I did not know where to turn to find out about various financial matters that would affect me. It is essential for me to know these things in order to prepare a secure position in life for myself there. Now that I have your address, I am honored to ask you a few questions. Please, great sir, answer them and do not turn me away empty-handed:

1. Can I establish a factory in our country for whatever oil is in great demand in Palestine or abroad? What kind of oil is this?
2. Can I obtain all the machinery and apparatus necessary for the factory there, and will 6,000 rubles be sufficient for establishing such a factory?
3. Can I hope to earn at least 100 rubles a month?
4. What is the name of the place where I can open such a factory?
5. Let me know the name of the flower or seed from which I can make oil. How much will it cost me by weight and volume before it is processed in the factory, and how much profit will I make on the oil produced from that quantity?
6. What would my monthly expenses be in such a factory?

As I write this letter, I am making a big request: that you answer my questions quickly and send your letter with the enclosed stamp. In the strong hope that you will heed my request and answer my question, I conclude my letter with thanks in advance.

Respectfully and with the blessings of Zion, Israel Nevelstein.

My address:
Russie
Verhnyaya Belozerka (Tavr. Province) Melitopol County
To Israel Nevelstein
Iyar 12, 5674[160]

160. May 8, 1914.

• 57 •

Central Zionist Archives, L2 138

Kovno,[161] May 12, 1914
Dr. A. Rupin [*sic*], Jaffa

I am honored to ask you to tell us what to do with respect to a chicory factory in Jaffa. This is what I have to say:

I have worked here in my chicory factory for fifteen years. My merchandise is very good, and is sold here throughout the area and in faraway towns. I have a seventeen-year-old daughter who has completed five grades in the gymnasium, has learned a lot of Hebrew, and knows how to write it fluently, and a fourteen-year-old son who has thus far studied only Bible and Talmud. In my concern for their future, I found no option other than to send them to America to complete their education and achieve the goal of becoming doctors or lawyers. But they have no desire to go to America; they would prefer, if possible, to establish a chicory factory in Jaffa. I have samples of the chicory that is available in Palestine. There is a merchant from Haifa who sent an acquaintance of his from here as a courier to have me prepare chicory for him and send it to him via Odessa to Haifa and Jaffa. My children are hard-working and quick, nationalists, lovers of the Land of Israel. I have inculcated in them a great love for our ancestral land. They want me to teach them the trade and the work in my factory here. I will establish a small factory in Jaffa with a gas- or oil-powered machine, all the necessary machinery, and I will myself come and spend two months setting up the factory properly and producing good merchandise: I will bring the materials from Russia or some other country—wherever appropriate—and will start processing the chicory in Jaffa. And this is my request of you, since I have heard about you that [illegible] settling Palestine, and because your entire desire is to see the country rebuilt: tell me your opinion of the leaves that I have enclosed here and answer a few questions for me:

161. A town in the province of Kovno. According to the census of 1897, there were about 71,064 inhabitants, including 25,441 Jews (35.8 percent).

1. Will the authorities in Jaffa let Russian Jews establish a factory, and would this require a permit?
2. Are heating fuels such as coal, oil, and wood available in Jaffa?
3. If a permit is needed, how much does it cost and how long will it take to get?
4. How do I pay the customs fee for materials imported from Russia or some other country, especially chicory?

I have already decided that my daughter, may she live long, will go to Palestine this summer to learn the local conditions and find out whether the place is suitable for my intentions. Then I will wait to hear what you have to say.

That is all, so I send you greetings from afar and a blessing in everything you do. May you witness the consolation of Zion and Jerusalem, speedily in our days. Amen.

Faithfully and respectfully, Ts. Schilenski

My address:
Kovno Russland
H. L. Schilenski
Cichorieufabrick

• 58 •

Central Zionist Archives, L2 140

Jakob L. Rosenbaum
Noworadomsk[162]
(by Goldberg on behalf of M. Segal)
March 16, 1914

162. A town in Poland in the province of Petrokov. According to the census of 1908, there were about 17,160 inhabitants, including 7,975 Jews (46.4 percent).

Dear Dr. Ruppin, Jaffa, Palestine

It is my honor to ask you whether there might be a market in our holy land for various kinds of embroidery for women's adornments, for tunics and [other] clothing, and whether a man with a family can earn a living from this work.

I am about thirty-five years old and have a wife and three sons, and I have 1,000 rubles in cash. If I could make a living from this work in Palestine, I would move my business there. Please answer me immediately and clearly, for if you agree, I am ready to go there right after Passover.

Respectfully and with thanks in advance,
Moshe Segal Halevy

April 7, 1914
To Mr. Moshe Segal
Noworadomsk *(Russia)*

In reply to your letter of March 16:
There is no demand here for embroidery for clothes (according to the sample you sent us). But there is demand for mesh fabric to sew dresses for women because of the intense heat here where people dress with light clothing. If you know this kind of work you may gain a livelihood from it. But we are doubtful if the sum of 1,000 rubles would be sufficient for this purpose.

We assume that you know the work (otherwise it is difficult to expect success). It is worth coming here (if you know this kind of fabric work) and try it out. Hopefully you will succeed, and if so you can bring your family. But you should not close down this business (if you have one) in Russia.

Yours truly,

• 59 •

Central Zionist Archives, L2 131 VI

Korbwaren-Industrie
Schussheim, Achselrad, and Fahn
Halicz[163] (Galizien)
Halicz, December 28, 1911

Dear Dr. E. Ruppin, president of the Palestine Office, Jaffa

We hereby permit ourselves to ask you whether merchants can be found in Jaffa, Jerusalem, and the other cities of Palestine to sell all sorts of baskets from our factory. As far as we know, these items are sold from Austria to eastern countries, but we do not know the merchants' names and addresses. Please give us the addresses of merchants who would be willing to enter into a commercial pact with us. Thank you very much in advance!

And now we would like to investigate thoroughly the following question regarding settling the land:

We want to settle in Palestine and run our basket-making business there. But first we have to know the following conditions: (1) Are there wide squares with willows growing by rivers? (2) If not, is there moist land there on the shore of a watercourse that is suitable and fit for planting and growing the willows? Or moist land fit for planting willows even if it is not next to a watercourse or river? It would be best if these were already in place not far from a railroad and near a settlement. Basically, we think such a factory would be appropriate there because wicker furniture—the kind [of material] one thinks of for clothing baskets, small travel baskets (like hampers), bookcases, children's cradles, beds, baskets for letters, flower baskets, and so on—is virtually tailor-made for hot countries, and also due to the high price of wood there.

163. A town in Galicia. According to the census of 1910, there were about 4,987 inhabitants, including 1,232 Jews (24.7 percent).

Two of our partners would be willing to settle in Palestine and run this business there—if possible. A major issue is whether there are wide squares in Palestine with willows, or at least suitable land for planting them, and whether willows will grow in the climate of Palestine as they do in Europe. Please consult an expert on this subject and answer us as soon as possible in great detail.

Thank you very much in advance. Respectfully,
Ruben Pfaun

· 60 ·

Central Zionist Archives, L2 131 VI

Dear Sir:

This is an urgent request. The reason: tickets for the journey. Due to the harsh economic situation in Galicia, I must leave this country. I am the son of poor parents. We earn our living by renting a field, and we live in distress and terrible destitution. I am eighteen years old and very knowledgeable about farming. I very much want to travel to Palestine as a worker. Please, therefore, let me know what the situation is there. Can one find work there? How much are the wages? How much would the journey cost?

Respectfully,
Z. Kurtzbem

• 61 •

Central Zionist Archives, L2 138

Lyakhovtsy,[164] Pesach Sheni, 5674[165]
To the information bureau in Jaffa

Dear Sirs!

A craftsman with a family who is an expert at making nonkosher and kosher laundry soap of all sorts, and who has worked in this craft in his home for many years, is ready to immigrate to Palestine together with his family in order to settle there. But before he moves there, he suggested that I consult with you about whether or not he should take this step. I therefore implore you to answer the following questions as soon as you receive this letter:

1. Is a soap factory a good business that would make its owner a decent profit in Palestine?
2. Is there currently a need for new factories of this sort?
3. Do any of the people who have settled or want to settle in Palestine want to establish a factory of this sort?
4. Will the aforementioned craftsman find work making soap in one of the existing factories as soon as he arrives?
5. What are the monthly wages of such a worker?

Please answer as quickly as possible.

Respectfully and with blessings of national rebirth,
The agent of the Odessa Committee for the Settlement of Palestine
Yisrael Kozovoy

164. Lyakhovtsy, a town in the province of Minsk. According to the census of 1897, there were about 5,016 inhabitants, including 3,846 Jews (76.7 percent).
165. May 10, 1914.

My address:
To Yisrael Kozov
Shtetl Lyakhovtzy
(Vol. Province)

• 62 •

Central Zionist Archives, L2 135 I

Dentist
H. M. Linetskii
Shtetl Rybnitsa, Pod. Province
Stomatology
laboratory
of teeth implantation
on the basis of caoutchouc
and gold
prosthetic bridges
Passover Eve, 5674,[166] Rybnitzy[167]
Labor Bureau
Jaffa

Dear Sir!

It is my honor to ask the distinguished bureau to let me know clearly as soon as possible where and how I can open a laboratory in one of the towns or colonies of Palestine for the aforementioned craft in which I am certified. I want to move to Palestine after the holiday together with my household. I am an expert in making all sorts of false teeth, as attested by my diploma and my extensive experience in all kinds of jobs of this sort.

In addition, please give me information for my brother-in-law, who is an

166. April 10, 1914.

167. Rybnitzy, a town in the province of Podolia. According to the census of 1897, there were about 4,029 inhabitants, including 1,574 Jews (39.0 percent).

outstanding barber and a great artisan, and whose wife knows how to make all sorts of hair braids and wigs for actors.

I have tremendous confidence that all my questions will be answered in great detail. I have attached a ten-[denomination not stated] stamp for your reply.

With the blessings of Zion and complete respect,
Chaim Linetsky

May 3, 1914
To Mr. Chaim Linetsky
Rybnitzy
Podolia District

Dear Sir,

The Labor Department here has forwarded us your letter and here is our answer. Both in Jaffa and in the other cities in the Land of Israel there are technicians of false teeth and we are doubtful if you can find sufficient work for a livelihood.

Yours truly,

• 63 •

Central Zionist Archives, L2 133 III

Jewish Colonization Association
Proskurow Committee
Proskurow,[168] Iyar 4, 5674[169]

168. Proskurow, a town in the province of Podolia. According to the census of 1897, there were about 23,006 inhabitants, including 11,411 Jews (49.6 percent).
169. April 30, 1914.

The honorable Dr. Ruppin
Jaffa

Dear Sir!

Recently people have been coming more and more often to ask our advice about whether to move to Palestine instead of to America. The Jewish press in the exile is agitating strongly for emigration, and we don't know whether to encourage or discourage it. In both places there are, for instance, artisans, tailors who make women's clothing, ironworkers, and carpenters who, according to the information in our possession, can promise them work. We therefore asked Mr. Sheinkin[170] at the information bureau about working conditions, the conditions of the land, living conditions, and wages, but he did not see fit to reply. What is the information bureau's job if not to answer such questions? So now we are being so bold as to ask you to look into and clarify whether the country needs artisans (male and female) and what kind of artisans are needed. What are the wages and living conditions in general this year? With complete confidence that you will answer us, we thank you in advance.

Respectfully and with the blessings of Zion,
[illegible]

• 64 •

Central Zionist Archives, L2 135/1

Pharmaceutical Warehouse
N. S. Greismann, Boyarka
May 4/17, 1914
Committee for the Settlement of Syria and Palestine

170. Menachem Sheinkin (1871–1924), head of the Information Bureau in Jaffa, 1906–14.

Dear Sir!

Here in Russia I earn my living as a pharmacist on the lowest level (pharmaceutical warehouse). I know my work thoroughly but am not certified. My material situation here is not terrible, but I am concerned about the future of my children—a twelve-year-old girl, who is a fourth-year student in the gymnasium, and a two-year-old boy—and everyone knows about our spiritual situation in Russia.

And now, please advise me as to whether I would be able to earn a living for my household in Jaffa or some other town—not necessarily in luxury, but enough that my children will grow up and flourish in our ancestral land. (In particular, please tell me how pharmaceutical work is done there: Does one need certification? What is the certification program?) I can save up a little money. I know Hebrew, although I don't speak it quickly because I am not accustomed to it. In addition to Russian, I know a tiny bit of English, and even less French and German. My wife, my daughter, my son, and I are healthy.

Please be so good as to send me a prospectus about emigration to Syria and Palestine in general. Many people are now asking, but it is impossible to answer them and advise them based solely on the periodicals that are scattered here and there.

I am enclosing a stamp. I await your prompt reply and your good advice.

Respectfully,
N. Greismann

Address:
Kiev Province, Zvenigorod County
Post station Poradovka
To N. Sh. Graismann

·65·

Central Zionist Archives, L3, File 162

Mrs. Rachel Zamaro,

I wish to inform you that I have recently met a friend of mine who told me of his meeting with your brother-in-law Rahamim and that the latter asked him for details about me. My friend answered with the intention of provoking him that I was about to get married. Your brother-in-law threatened him that he was prepared in such a case to bring you to America and to prove to the world that I was a married man and also gave him our photograph as bride and groom which was taken eight years ago to show to my new wife. When I heard this from my friend and saw our picture, I burst out laughing, and such words went in one ear and out the other. I am sure that I cannot love you any more or bring you to America in order to live like a family. Since I do not love you, no one can force me here in America to live with you. The most the American government can do is to oblige me to support my daughter until the age of seventeen or eighteen. I now suggest that you send me the bill of divorce (*get*) from the rabbis in Jerusalem and say that you have divorced me and I am prepared to pay the dues of the *ketuba* [marriage settlement] and also to provide for my daughter till she is eighteen.[171] Consider my proposal carefully and realize what you must do. It is already eight years since we have been apart from each other and you have suffered far more than I have since I am a man and can easily manage anywhere. It is good that you are in another corner of the world because if you were here or your brother-in-law had brought you here, who knows what would happen to you. I very much wanted your brother-in-law

171. From the exchange of letters between Haim Abushdid, his lawyer, the National Desertion Bureau in Manhattan, and the American Joint Distribution Committee, it appears that after the death of his elder brother, Abushdid was forced by tradition to marry his wife, who was fifteen years old at the time. The marriage to the wife of his brother was displeasing to him, and he decided to sail to America and break off contact with her and their child. When he arrived in America, he was exposed to the American way of life, which enchanted him. Far from his family and free of religious restraints, he decided to begin a new life according to the norms and values of the surrounding society.

to bring you here. It would be all the better for him to dance the infernal dance with me. I am sure he would lose tooth and eye by doing so, just as he wanted me to join up with you [illegible] without success. It would be better for you to divorce me and to marry some old man. Think about it and do whatever seems best for you. I used to [live] at a distance of three days from your brother-in-law and am now ten days away. Let us see what he can do to me. I also wrote to your relative Moïse Valero. Consult with him and hurry up as fast as you can with the procedure since the extension I gave you is till the beginning of 1921. One cannot buy love with money [illegible] Take this into account [illegible] before everything else and do all that is necessary.

Signed Haim Abushdid.

Present address:
Mr. Henry Camley
Santa Monica, California

Former address:
Henry Camley
235 St. Figuera Av
Los Angeles

• 66 •

Der yidisher emigrant,[172] *April 15 1912, no. 7, page 15.*
Rovno,[173] *February 18, 1912*

When I left Bremen with the intention of going to America, I decided to describe my journey to you from the beginning until the end, that is to say,

172. Bimonthly newspaper that was devoted entirely to migration issues and was published in St. Petersburg between 1907 and 1914. Baron Gintsburg was the editor of the paper until his death in 1910; from then on the editor was Yanovsky, the general secretary of the information bureau.
173. Rovno, a town in the district of Volhynia. According to the census of 1897, there were 24,563 inhabitants, including 13,780 Jews (56.1 percent).

from the border until New York. Unfortunately, I was not able to realize my plan. As you see, I am not writing from American but from Ravenna, since I did not manage to reach the land of the free—they disqualified me. . . .

I crossed the border not badly, but when I reached Myslowitz, I began to feel how migrants lived. As soon as I arrived there, they pushed me with all the migrants into a large room, the old, the young, children, women, and men all together. The room was full of dirt, more than in the worst "Chates"[174] of my village. Food was an expensive matter, the servants were rude, shouting and insulting the migrants. It was not unusual to feel the harassment of a servant. In exchange for a sailing ticket, I paid whatever they wanted. And immediately they stood over me and demanded that I exchange the little money I still had in Russian currency into American money. But I resisted and said that I did not have any more money, and the man in the office was very angry.

We spent the night in barracks in Myslowitz, some on the floor and some on benches. There was dirt everywhere. And they were not concerned that men were sleeping in the same room as women. In the morning a doctor came and carefully examined our eyes. After this they thrust us like sheep into low dense railway carriages and we set off.

During the entire journey to Bremen they did not let us out. In Bremen they led us to the Warsaw Hotel. I was assigned to sleep in one room with twenty women and young girls. The sheets were dirty and the floors had obviously not been washed for a long time. It was very cold at night and the air was very bad. With regard to food, in the morning they gave us tea sweetened with syrup and a few small rolls with some kind of butter that we never had eaten in Russia. I was told that this was coconut butter. At noon [we received] a small piece of dried meat and potato soup. In the evening it was once again tea with syrup, herring or some other kind of fish, and again rolls with coconut butter. The servants were very rude, only two or three of them treated the migrants as human beings.

In the Myslowitz office they ordered us to exchange our money for American money, and if we did not do so they would not issue the sailing tickets to us. Here I had no choice and I exchanged my money.

174. Chate is some form of dwelling. In the Polish dictionary, *chata* = *chalupa*, which is a shack, hut, or cabin.

I want to add that every morning a doctor arrived at "Stadt Warschau"[175] to examine the migrants, to see if they were healthy. But in fact he does not look at the migrants at all. One day before the ship sailed they sent us to the ship's doctor, and he rejected me. They gave me a red ticket on which my disease was written. I returned to the "Stadt Warschau" and the manager there sent me to the office doctor. The doctor examined my eyes and said it was just an infection and within a week I could recover and travel to America. Since I was not reassured I went to ask the advice of the Jewish Committee. There the secretary looked at my eyes and said that in order to be sure he would send me to a professor to test my eyes. The professor examined me thoroughly and said that I had trachoma scarring, and in America they would definitely not let me enter. I still doubted this, and two days later I went once more to the office doctor. Now he also saw trachoma scarring and told me I would have to return to Russia. There were many other people besides myself who were rejected.

I asked: We allowed doctors in Russia to examine us; at the border a doctor also examined our eyes. Why did the border doctors allow us to continue our journey? We would have returned immediately the way we came, and we could have saved ourselves a lot of expense and trouble.

Rachel K.

175. The Jewish emigrants who arrived at Bremen stayed at the edge of the city in an area known as "Stadt Warschau."

Appendix A

The Extent of Jewish Migration

Table A.1. Jewish Immigration to the United States from the Russian Empire, 1875–98

Year	Number of immigrants	Year	Number of immigrants
1875	1,796	1888	28,881
1876	1,140	1889	25,352
1877	1,426	1890	28,639
1878	719	1891	51,398
1879	988	1892	76,398
1880	4,332	1893	76,373
1875–80	10,401	1894	35,322
1881	5,692	1895	29,179
1882	13,202	1896	26,191
1883	8,731	1897	32,848
1884	11,445	1898	20,372
1885	16,862	1881–98	541,102
1886	21,173	...	...
1887	33,044	1875–98	551,503

Sources: For the data on Jewish immigration in 1875–80, Ira Glazier, ed., *Migration from the Russian Empire* (Baltimore, 1995–98), vols. 1 and 2, xv–xvi; for the data from 1881–98, Samuel Joseph, *Jewish Immigration to the United States from 1881 to 1910* (New York, 1914), 93.

Table A.2. Jewish Immigration to Various Destinations from the Russian Empire, 1899–1914

Year	USA	Canada	Argentina	Australia	South Africa	Palestine[a]	Total
1899	37,415	...	...	...	...	...	...
1900	61,764	2,765	...	100	...	...	...
1901	58,098	1,015	...	119	...	...	...
1902	57,688	2,066	...	156	...	...	...
1903	76,203	3,727	...	130	...	...	...
1904	106,236	7,715	4,000	170	...	...	...
1905	129,910	7,127	7,156	298	...	1,230	...
1906	153,748	6,584	13,518	394	...	3,450	...
1907	149,182	7,712	2,500	394	...	1,750	...
1908	103,387	1,636	5,444	383	...	2,097	...
1909	57,551	3,182	8,557	501	...	2,459	...
1910	84,260	5,146	6,581	749	...	1,979	...
1911	91,223	5,322	6,378	1,041	...	2,326	...
1912	80,595	7,387	13,416	1,200	1,804	2,430	106,832
1913	101,330	11,252	10,860	1,350	872	3,050	128,714
1914	138,051	3,107	3,693	1,492	193	2,180	148,716
Total	1,486,641	75,743	82,103	8,477	20,069[b]	32,951[c]	1,705,984[d]

Sources: For immigration to the United States, Liebman Hersch, "International Migration of the Jews," in *International Migrations,* ed. Imre Ferenczi and Walter Willcox (New York, 1931), 474. For immigration to Canada and Argentina, Jacob Lestschinsky, *Di yidishe vanderung far di letste 25 yor* (Berlin, 1927), 19–20; and Liebman Hersch, "Jewish Migrations during the Last Hundred Years," in *The Jewish People: Past and Present,* vol. 1 (New York, 1946), 413. For immigration to Australia and South Africa, Mark Wischnitzer, *To Dwell in Safety: The Story of Jewish Migration since 1800* (Philadelphia, 1948), 293–94. For immigration to Palestine from the ports of Trieste and Odessa, Gur Alroey, *Immirantim: ha-hagirah ha-Yehudit Le-Erets Yisrael be-reshit ha-me'ah ha-esrim* (Jerusalem, 2004), 235.

[a] Emigration via Odessa.

[b] Including 17,200 in 1900–1911.

[c] Including 10,000 Jews who arrived in 1904–14 after traveling via Trieste.

[d] Total migration for which a breakdown is available by destination country.

Appendix B

Towns

The names of the towns were transliterated into German in the early twentieth century. They are taken from Jacob Segall's *Internationale Konfessionsstatistik,* published by the Bureaus für Statistik der Juden.

Bobruisk, Minsk province
Brest Litowsk, Grodno province
Chabno, Kiev province
Cherkassy, Kiev province
Chorzschele, Plotzk province
Dubossary, Kherson province
Fergana, Uzbekistan
Grodisch, Warsaw province
Halicz, Galicia
Horodenka, Galicia
Ilya, Vilna province
Jekaterinoslaw, Jekaterinoslaw province
Kadyan, Unknown province
Kazulop, Minsk province
Kiev, Kiev province
Kovno, Kovno province
Kretingen, Kovno province
Kutais, Kutais province (beyond the Pale of Settlement)

Libau, Kurland (beyond the Pale of Settlement)
Lipsko, Radom province (Poland)
Ljubischow, Minsk province
Ljublin, Ljublin province (Poland)
Lodz, Petrokov province (Poland)
Minsk, Minsk province
Neswizsch, Minsk province
Noworadomsk, Petrokow province (Poland)
Odessa, Kherson province
Plonsk, Warsaw province
Ponewesch, Kovno province
Proskurow, Podolia province
Radzyn, Ljublin district province
Rovno, Volhynia province
Rozsadon, Galicia
Rybnitzy, Podolia province
Sjedletz, Sjedletz province (Poland)
Stryj, Galicia
Vitebsk, Vitebsk province
Warsaw, Warsaw province (Poland)
Wengrow, Seidlce province (Poland)
Vilna, Vilna province
Wladimir, Volhynia province
Wolozysk Andrashavka, Volhynia province
Zakharino, Mogilev province
Zhovnino, Poltava province

Selected Bibliography

Archives

American Jewish Historical Society, New York (AJHS)
Central Archives for the History of the Jewish People, Jerusalem (CAHJP)
Central Zionist Archives, Jerusalem (CZA)
YIVO Archives, New York

Primary and Secondary Sources

A. A. "Di daytshe kontrol stantsyes." *Der yidisher emigrant,* July 15, 1909, 3.

"Aberatung fun di murshim." *Der yidisher emigrant,* March 2, 1909, 13.

"Agunot." *Der yidisher emigrant,* January 1, 1912, 13.

Alroey, Gur. "Galveston and Palestine: Immigration and Ideology in the Early Twentieth Century." *American Jewish Archives Journal* 56, no. 1–2 (2004): 138–40.

———. *Immigrantim: ha-hagirah ha-Yehudit Le-Erets Yisrael be-reshit ha-me'ah ha-esrim.* Jerusalem, 2004.

———. "The Jewish Emigration from Palestine in the Early Twentieth Century." *Journal of Modern Jewish Studies* 2, no. 2 (2003): 111–31.

———. "Patterns of Jewish Migration from the Russian Empire in the Early Twentieth Century." *Jews in Russia and Eastern Europe* 2, no. 57 (2006): 24–51.

———. *Ha-Mahpekha ha-Sheketah: ha-hagirah ha-Yehudit meha-Imperyah har-Rusit, 1875–1924.* Jerusalem, 2008.

Antin, Mary. *The Promised Land.* New York, 1912.

Aschheim, Steven. *Brothers and Strangers: The East European Jew in German and German Jewish Consciousness.* Wisconsin, 1982.

Avni, Haim. *Mi-bitul ha-inkvizitsya ve-ad "hok ha-shevut": Toledot ha-hagira ha-yehudit le-argentina.* Jerusalem, 1982.

Baily, Samuel L. *Immigrants in the Land of Promise: Italians in Buenos Aires and New York City, 1870 to 1914.* Ithaca, N.Y., 1999.

Baines, Dudley. *Emigration from Europe, 1815–1930.* Cambridge, 1995.

Baker, Mark. "The Voice of the Deserted Jewish Woman, 1867–1870." *Jewish Social Studies* 2 (1995): 98–123.

Baron, Salo Wittmayer. *Steeled by Adversity: Essays and Addresses on American Jewish Life.* Philadelphia, 1971.

Best, Gary Dean. "Jacob H. Schiff's Galveston Movement: An Experiment in Immigration Deflection, 1907–1914." *American Jewish Archives Journal* 30, no. 1 (1978): 43–79.

Bloch, S. "Fun bremen kan argentina." *Der yidisher emigrant,* December 16, 1910, 6.

Cohen, Jocelyn, and Daniel Soyer, eds. *My Future Is in America: Autobiographies.* New York, 2006.

Cohen, Morris Raphael. *A Dreamer's Journey.* Boston, 1949.

Diner, Hasia. "Before the Promised City: Eastern European Jews in America before 1880." In *An Inventory of Promises,* edited by Jeffrey S. Gurock and Marc Lee Raphael, 43–62. New York, 1995.

Dizengoff, Meir. "Me'et ha-va'ad ha-palistinai be-odessa." *Ha-tsofeh* 658 (March 20, 1905): 3.

D. R. "Verbalen." *Der yidisher emigrant,* February 15, 1909, 10–11.

Eliyahu, Ben. "An erneste frage." *Der yidisher emigrant,* March 18, 1909, 2.

Emigrantn un agentn: Nit keyn oysgetrakhte mayses. St. Petersburg, 1912.

Fitzpatrick, David. *Oceans of Consolation: Personal Accounts of Irish Migration to Australia.* Ithaca, N.Y., 1994.

Frankel, Jonathan. "The Crisis of 1881–82 as a Turning Point in Modern Jewish History." In *The Legacy of Jewish Migration: 1881 and Its Impact,* edited by David Berger, 9–22. New York, 1983.

Fridkis, Ari Lloyd. "Desertion in the American Jewish Immigrant Family: The Work of the National Desertion Bureau in Cooperation with the Industrial Removal Office." *American Jewish History* 71 (1981): 285–99.

Friedman, Reena Sigman. "Send My Husband Who Is in New York City: Husband Desertion in the American Jewish Immigrant Community." *Jewish Social Studies* 44, no. 1 (1982): 1–18.

"Fun der preysikh-rusisher grenits." *Der yidisher emigrant,* January 28, 1909, 3.

Gartner, Lloyd. "Notes on the Statistics of Jewish Immigration to England." *Jewish Social Studies* 22, no. 1 (1960): 97–102.

Glazier, Ira, ed. *Migration from the Russian Empire,* 6 vols. Baltimore, 1995–97; Baltimore, 1995–98.

Green, Nancy. *The Pletzel of Paris: Jewish Immigrant Workers in the Bell Epoque.* New York, 1986.

"Halalei ha-emigratsya." *Ha-zeman* 144 (July 17, 1909): 2.

"Ha-nedida ha-yehudit veha-temikha la-nodedim." *Hed ha-zeman* 169 (August 2, 1908): 1.

Harkavy, Alexander. *Etses far emigrantn velkhe forn keyn amerika (fareynigte shtatn).* Minsk, 1905.

Hersch, Liebman. "International Migration of the Jews." In *International Migrations,* edited by Imre Ferenczi and Walter Willcox, 471–520. New York, 1931.

———. "Jewish Migrations during the Last Hundred Years." In *The Jewish People: Past and Present,* vol. 1, 407–30. New York, 1946.

Himer, Kurt. *Die Hamburg-Amerika Linie im sechsten Jahrzehnt ihrer Entwicklung, 1897–1907.* Hamburg, 1907.

Howe, Irving. *World of Our Fathers.* New York, 1977.

Joseph, Samuel. *Jewish Immigration to the United States from 1881 to 1910.* New York, 1914.

Kahan, Arcadius. *Essays in Jewish Social and Economic History.* Chicago, 1986.

Kula, Withold, Nina Assorodobraj-Kula, and Marcin Kula. *Writing Home: Immigrants in Brazil and the Unites States, 1890–1891.* New York, 1986.

Kuznets, Simon. "Immigration of Russian Jews to the United States: Background and Structure." *Perspectives in American History* 9 (1975): 35–126.

Lamar, Cecil. *Albert Ballin: Business and Politics in Imperial Germany, 1888–1918.* Princeton, N.J., 1967.

Lederhendler, Eli. *Jewish Immigrants and American Capitalism, 1880–1920: From Caste to Class.* Cambridge, 2009.

Lestschinsky, Jacob. *Di yidishe vanderung far di letste 25 yor.* Berlin, 1927.

———."Hashkafot kalkaliot." *Ha-olam,* January 12, 1912, 5.

"Le-toledot provokatsya ahat." *Ha-tsefira,* February 12, 1914, 2.

Lifschitz, Ezekiel. "Di erste rusishe yidishe masn imigratsye un di amerikaner yidn." *YIVO bletter* 4–5 (December 1932): 312–29.

Lilienblum, Moshe Leib. "Derekh la-avor golim." In *Ketavim otobiografi'im,* vol. 3, 7–78. Jerusalem, 1970.

Marinbach, Bernard. *Galveston: Ellis Island of the West.* New York, 1983.

Mendelsohn, Ezra. *Class Struggle in the Pale: The Formative Years of the Jewish Workers' Movement in Tsarist Russia.* Cambridge, 1970.

"Mitoch ha-tehum: Rishmei masa." *Ha-zeman* 143 (July 16, 1907): 3.

Nadell, Pamela S. "En Route to the Promised Land." In *We Are Leaving Mother Russia,* edited by Kerry M. Olitzky, 11–24. Cincinnati, 1990.

———. "From Shtetl to Border: East European Jewish Emigrants and the Agents' System, 1868–1914." In *Studies in the American Jewish Experience.* Vol. 2. Edited by Jacob Rader Marcus and Abraham J. Peck, 49–78. Cincinnati, 1984.

———. "The Journey to American by Steam: The Jews of Eastern Europe in Transition." *American Jewish History* 71 (1981): 269–84.

Obolensky, V. V. "Emigration from and Immigration into Russia." In *International Migrations.* Vol. 2. Edited by Walter F. Willcox and Imre Ferenczi, 521–80. New York, 1931.

Perlmann, Joel. "The Local Geographic Origins of Russian-Jewish Immigrants, circa 1900." Available at www.levyinstitute.org/publications/?docid=791.

Rakeffet-Rothkoff, Aaron. "Rabbi Yitshak Spektor of Kovno: Spokesman of Agunot." *Tradition* 29, no. 3 (1995): 5–20.

Rischin, Moses. *The Promised City: New York's Jews, 1870–1914.* New York, 1962.

Rockaway, Robert. *Words of the Uprooted: Jewish Immigration in Early Twentieth-Century America.* New York, 1998.

Rubin, Ruth. *Voices of a People: The Story of Yiddish Folksong.* Philadelphia, 1979.

Rubinow, Isaac M. "Economic Condition of the Jews in Russia." *Bulletin of the Bureau of Labor* 72 (September 1907): 487–583. Reprinted as a book: New York, 1970.

Rubinstein, Ben Zion. *Galitsye un ir bafelkerung.* Warsaw, 1923.

Sarna, Jonathan. "The Myth of No Return: Jewish Return Migration to Eastern Europe." *American Jewish History* 71 (1981): 256–68.

Segall, Jakob. *Veroeffentlichung des Bureaus fuer Statistik der Juden.* Berlin, 1914.

Shilo, M. "Changing Attitudes in the Zionist Movement towards Immigration to Eretz Israel." *Cathedra* 46 (December 1987): 109–22.

Stampfer, Saul. "The Geographic Background of East European Jewish Migration to the United States before World War I." In *Migration across Time and Nation,* edited by Ira Glazier and Luigi de Rosa, 220–30. New York, 1985.

Szajkowski, Zosa. "The Sufferings of Jewish Immigrants to America in Transit through Germany." *Jewish Social Studies* 39 (1977): 105–16.

Taylor, Philip. *The Distant Magnet: European Emigration to the U.S.A.* London, 1971.

Thomas, William I., and Florian Znaniecki. *The Polish Peasant in Europe and America.* Reprint. Urbana, Ill., 1984.

"Vi azoy bakumt men an oyslendishn pas?" *Der yidisher emigrant,* December 24, 1907, 9.

"Virbalen." *Der yidisher emigrant,* February 15, 1909, 11.

Weinberg, Sydney Stahl. *The World of Our Mothers: The Lives of Jewish Immigrant Women.* Chapel Hill, N.C., 1988.

Wertheimer, Jack. *Unwelcome Strangers: East European Jews in Imperial Germany.* New York, 1987.

Wischnitzer, Mark. *To Dwell in Safety: The Story of Jewish Migration since 1800.* Philadelphia, 1948.

Yanovsky, Samuel. *Divrei ha'arakha, zikhronot, ketavim nivharim.* Tel Aviv, 1947.

Yanovsky, S. Y., and A. I. Kastelyansky. *Spravochnaya kniga po voprosam emigratsii.* St. Petersburg, 1913.

Zangwill, Israel. *Land of Refuge.* London, 1907.

Index

Note: Italicized page numbers indicate tables or illustrations.